Yale Studies in English, 183.

Sir Walter Ralegh. Miniature by Nicholas Hilliard. National Portrait Gallery, London.

Sir Walter Ralegh

The Renaissance Man and His Roles

Stephen J. Greenblatt

New Haven and London, Yale University Press

1973

Library of Congress catalog card number: 73-77150
International standard book number: 0-300-01634-4

Designed by John O. C. McCrillis
and set in Baskerville type.
Printed in the United States of America by
The Vail-Ballou Press, Inc., Binghamton, N.Y.

Published in Great Britain, Europe, and Africa by
Yale University Press, Ltd., London.
Distributed in Latin America by Kaiman & Polon,
Inc., New York City; in Australasia and Southeast
Asia by John Wiley & Sons Australasia Pty. Ltd.,
Sydney; in India by UBS Publishers' Distributors Pvt.,
Ltd., Delhi; in Japan by John Weatherhill, Inc., Tokyo.

To Ellen

Contents

Preface

In a life like Sir Walter Ralegh's, an extremely active life marked by intrigue and adventure, we would not expect art to play a major part. Most of his poems were the incidental accomplishments of an Elizabethan courtier: few were published and fewer acknowledged as his own. Apart from *The History of the World,* his writings in prose were almost always hastily composed to meet the needs of a moment, to advertise or to excuse. Ralegh's greatest works, *Ocean to Cynthia* and the *History,* were written during (or perhaps in the former case, shortly after) separate imprisonments, periods of enforced inactivity when, seemingly, he had nothing to do *but* write.

It can be argued, then, that Ralegh was a writer almost by accident. Certainly, when he glanced back at his remarkable career moments before laying his head on the block, he did not think of himself as a man of letters. He had lived, he told the crowd around the scaffold, "a sinful Life, in all sinful Callings, having been a Souldier, a Captain, a Sea-Captain, and a Courtier." [1] I believe, however, that art was of crucial importance in Ralegh's life. In his major writings, which often originated as surrogate actions or histrionic gestures, he struggled with the deepest tensions and conflicts of his being, fundamental problems that he could not resolve through action. Moreover, Ralegh's creative imagination was not confined to literature. In the great crises of his life, under pressures that would have broken a lesser man, he attempted to fashion his own identity as a work of art. His writings often derive much of their meaning and importance from their part in this larger process of creation.

At key moments in Ralegh's career, the boundaries between life and art completely break down, and to understand such moments, the conventional distinction between reality and the imagination must give way to a sense of their interplay. The problem is not at all unique to Ralegh. To name a few

recent examples, Maynard Mack's study of Alexander Pope
at Twickenham, *The Garden and the City* (Toronto, 1969),
describes the transformation of literary conventions into a
life-style; Richard Poirier's *The Performing Self* (New York,
1971) is concerned with the modern breakdown of literary
forms and the shaping of the self in other media; Conor
Cruise O'Brien, in his essays in *Power and Consciousness*
(London, 1969) and in *The United Nations: Sacred Drama*
(London, 1968), describes the often vicious intermingling of
politics and the shapes of art. Closer to the subject of the
present study, Joan Webber's book on self-consciousness in
seventeenth-century prose writers, *The Eloquent "I"* (Madison, 1968), contains valuable reflections on the relationship
of life and art, particularly in the career of the Puritan rev-
olutionary John Lilburne. Recently, Miss Webber has written,

In Renaissance studies, it is impossible to ignore the pervasive effect, in the age, of the belief in an essential interplay between life
and art, but in criticism, knowledge of that belief has primarily
been used as a basis for discussion of rhetorical strategies within
accepted literary works.[2]

In this study, I have tried to broaden the focus of criticism
to include works not usually considered literary and, beyond
these, to include Ralegh's life itself. By so doing, I hope to increase our grasp on works whose underlying rhythms are one
with the motion of idea, feeling, and action in the author's
life. Further, I hope to elucidate one aspect of that life, important not only for Ralegh but for many figures in the Renaissance.

One aspect. This study is not intended as a biography.
Whole areas of interest and importance, such as Ralegh's military service in France and Ireland, his finances, and his parliamentary career, have been excluded. Even in those events
I have chosen to discuss—his two Guiana voyages, treason
trial, and execution—I have been highly selective, focusing
on those elements which illuminate my theme. Moreover, I
need scarcely add what Johnson has put so eloquently:

The main of life is, indeed, composed of small incidents, and petty occurrences; of wishes for objects not remote, and grief for disappointments of no fatal consequence; of insect vexations which sting us and fly away, impertinencies which buzz a while about us, and are heard no more.[3]

Ralegh's letters record their fair share of such vexations and help to bring us down to earth.

In the ensuing pages, I shall frequently use the word "role." I have adopted the term more for its convenience than its precision; indeed its very vagueness is of some value in this context. For I wish to have a single term to designate a variety of related aspects of Ralegh's personality and behavior, ranging from a deliberate and prearranged performance to an all but unconscious fashioning of the self.[4]

Ralegh's role-playing has been noted before, at least in passing. Writing in the 1650s, Francis Osborne remarked that "*his death* was by him managed with so high and religious a resolution, as if a Roman had acted a Christian, or rather a Christian a Roman." [5] More directly to the point, Pierre Lefranc speaks of Ralegh's "théâtralisme" which he finds more Italian than Romantic, by virtue of its cold control and extreme attention to the public.[6] And Philip Edwards, at the end of his book on Ralegh, touches on issues central to my study:

The full expression of his imagination was his whole life. He was fortunate to live in an age when art and life were as closely wedded as they have ever been. Literature and learning and action were all essential parts of his being. . . . His epic was himself, with his poetry and his personal ambition, his explorations into science and into goldfields, his fighting and his meditation.[7]

Among the many biographies of Ralegh, I am most indebted to Edward Edwards's two-volume *Life and Letters;* among recent criticism to Pierre Lefranc's *Sir Walter Ralegh, Ecrivain.* I have profited greatly from Lefranc's painstaking textual scholarship, though I have ventured to disagree with him on the attribution of two poems. In both cases the textual evidence is inconclusive.

Like all students of Ralegh, I owe a great deal to the work of Agnes Latham. In addition, special thanks are due to her and to Walter Oakeshott for kindness to me at an early stage in my project. I am deeply grateful to Martin Price, A. Bartlett Giamatti, Richard Sylvester, and the late Rosalie Colie for advice and encouragement; likewise to Richard Bridgman, Paul Alpers, Jonas Barish, Norman Rabkin, Alex Zwerdling, Stephen Orgel, and Murray Cohen, who read and criticized part or all of my manuscript. Leopold Damrosch read the whole with extraordinary care and made many valuable suggestions. As my thesis adviser and friend, Alvin B. Kernan gave his untiring guidance and support to an earlier version of this book. This earlier version received the John Addison Porter Prize at Yale University.

Research funds from the University of California helped to make possible the completion of the manuscript.

My deepest indebtedness is to my wife.

Abbreviations

Discoverie   Sir Walter Ralegh, *The Discoverie of the Large, Rich, and Bewtiful Empyre of Guiana* . . . (London, 1596). Edited by V. T. Harlow. London, 1928.

Harlow   V. T. Harlow. *Ralegh's Last Voyage.* London, 1932.

H.W.   Sir Walter Ralegh. *The History of the World.* London, 1614. Citations are to book, chapter, section, part (where indicated in the text), and page. The 1614 edition is paged 1 to 651 for Books I–II and 1 to 776 for Books III–V.

Letters   Edward Edwards. *The Life of Sir Walter Ralegh . . . Together with His Letters.* London, 1868. Volume 2.

Poems   *The Poems of Sir Walter Ralegh.* Edited by A. M. C. Latham. London, 1951.

1 Ralegh's Final Performance

Sir Henry Yelverton, the king's attorney general, was no friend to Sir Walter Ralegh. Yelverton owed his office to the influence of the Howards, the great and powerful Catholic family, secret pensioners of the king of Spain and long-time virulent enemies of Ralegh. And yet, in the attorney's solemn address before the King's Bench at Westminster on October 28, 1618, expressing His Majesty's pleasure that Ralegh should die, there is a strange note of pity, of awe even, in the face of Ralegh's destiny: "He hath been a star at which the world hath gazed; but stars may fall nay they must fall when they trouble the sphere wherein they abide." [1] These words catch the sense, felt even in his own day, that Ralegh's life had a very special quality, something almost mythic, something usually found only in the creations of art, which set it apart from the lives of other men. Ralegh himself did everything in his power to encourage such a feeling, for he was an actor, and at the great public moments of his career he performed unforgettably.

Certainly King James had cause to remember the treason trial at Winchester fifteen years before, when Ralegh's courage and eloquence had transformed a populace ready at the start literally to tear him to pieces into a crowd of admirers shocked at the harshness of the verdict. "Never was a man so hated and so popular in so short a time," recorded one contemporary witness, and a Scotsman, commissioned by the king to report on the trial, said that "whereas, when he saw Sir Walter Ralegh first, he was so led with the common hatred that he would have gone a hundred miles to see him hanged, he would, ere they parted, have gone a thousand to save his life." [2]

Now, in 1618, James was determined not to repeat the mistake. A special commission recommended to the king that Ralegh "be called before the whole body of your Council of State, and your principal Judges, in your Council-Chamber; and that some of the nobility and gentlemen of quality be admitted to be present to hear the whole proceeding." [3] But the king knew better: "[W]e think it not fit, because it would make him too popular, as was found by experiment at the arraignment at Winchester, where by his wit he turned the hatred of men into compassion for him." [4] Instead, on October 22, Ralegh was brought before a small body of examiners behind closed doors. The conclusion was never in doubt: Ralegh was pronounced guilty. A few days later, he was brought before the King's Bench for sentencing.[5] The prisoner was reminded that fifteen years before he had been convicted of treason and sentenced to die and that since then he had been "as a dead man in the law." Now His Majesty's justice, "stirred up" by "new offences," required the execution of that former judgment. The actual cause of the king's anger was the disastrous failure of Ralegh's expedition to Guiana in search of gold. But this was not specified, and the lord chief justice, Sir Henry Montagu, quickly interrupted the prisoner when he began to speak of the "fatal" voyage, telling him that such discussion was irrelevant. Ralegh then turned to the earlier judgment, the conviction of 1603, for which he was to be executed: "As concerning that judgment which is so long past, and which I think here are some could witness, nay His Majesty was of opinion, that I had hard measure therein. . . ." But again the chief justice interrupted: "Sir Walter Ralegh you must remember yourself; you had an honourable trial, and so were justly convicted; and it were wisdom in you now to submit yourself and to confess your offence did justly draw upon you that judgment which was then pronounced against you." Praising Ralegh for expressions of faith in *The History of the World* and counseling him to face death like a valiant captain and a good Christian, Montagu concluded with the words "Execution is granted."

Ralegh was an old man, racked by malarial fever and exhausted by the terrible events of the past months: the failure of the Guiana expedition, the death of his eldest son Wat, the loss of all he owned and the consequent ruin of his family. He had been betrayed by those he trusted, and his attempt to escape to France had been foiled. He was imprisoned once again in the Tower where he had spent nearly thirteen bitter years. Now the final hearing was over and the sentence delivered without the permission of a word of defense or self-justification. He was given no choice but to submit quietly and accept his fate. Yet Ralegh did not submit, not completely. In his final words to the chief justice, there is a barely suppressed note of defiance in the very declaration of loyalty to the king:

My Lord, I desire thus much favour; that I may not be cut-off suddenly, for I have something to do in discharge of my conscience, and something to satisfy His Majesty in, something to satisfy the world in, and I desire I may be heard at the day of my death. And here I take God to be my judge, before whom I shall shortly appear, I was never disloyal to His Majesty; which I will justify where I shall not fear the face of any king on earth. And so I beseech you all to pray for me. [Harlow, p. 304]

This urgent will to be heard is one of the essential elements of Ralegh's character, asserting itself again and again throughout his life, often to the detriment of his career. As his remarks suggest, he had three rather distinct audiences: himself, his sovereign, and "the world." He was determined to address them all, however much they were in conflict with one another. In the course of his life, he wrote countless letters, pamphlets, and memoranda; he composed commendatory verses, popular lyrics, verse petitions, formal epitaphs, satires, translations, and intense, passionate love poetry; he wrote a travel book that was to become a classic and a million-word universal history that went through more editions than almost any other book of its age. He spoke out frequently in the Commons, often defending unpopular positions, and delivered his opinions to the queen's councilors and later to Prince Henry, the eldest son of King James. When words would not serve, he used other means—rich jewels and gorgeous clothing, a certain facial expression that infuriated his enemies, violent, histrionic gestures of anguish and despair. And when, upon his return from the disastrous Guiana voyage, it seemed that he would be given no chance to make himself heard, he went to fantastic lengths to buy time to write. On June 27, 1618, one of Ralegh's servants came to Sir Lewis Stukeley, who was conducting the prisoner from Plymouth to London, with word that Ralegh "was out of his wits, and that he was naked in his shirt upon all fours, scratching and biting the rushes upon the planks." [6] When Stukeley ran to see, Ralegh "began to draw up his legs and arms all on a heap, as it had been in a fit of convulsions and contractions of his sinews" and proceeded to vomit violently. Soon afterwards terrible boils appeared all over his body so that his guards would not approach him for fear of leprosy, and the doctors who were called in said that the prisoner could not be moved. All of this was a desperate ruse: the apparent disease was brought on by ointments and emetics given to Ralegh by a French physician named Manourie. Ralegh needed time to write, and this was the only way to get it. During the four-day "recuperation," he composed his "*Appologie* for the ill successe of his enterprise to *Guiana.*" When Manourie later betrayed him and confessed everything, Ralegh justified his pretense by the example of David: "The Prophet David did make himself a Fool, and did suffer Spittle to fall upon his Beard to escape the hands of his Enemies, and it was not imputed to him as sin." [7]

The *Appologie,* however, did nothing to help Ralegh's case. Its proud assertion of England's imperial claim on Guiana and its open challenge to Spain must have seemed to King James more a confession of guilt than a defense. James's stance after the enterprise failed was that of an injured party who had no idea of any hostile intentions against the king of Spain and his dominions. Had he not forced Ralegh to swear before setting sail not to harm or offend a single Spaniard? It is probable that James knew all along that the expedition was a serious provocation and might lead to bloodshed, but, in view of his grave financial troubles of 1616, he was willing to take considerable risks for the vast amount of almost pure gold that Ralegh promised was there practically for the taking. Or, alternatively, it may be that, lulled with dreams of treasure, James had never permitted himself to face up seriously to the possible consequences of the voyage. Now that the expedition had failed to find any mine and had instead senselessly fought with the Spanish and destroyed their town of S. Thomé, James found it expedient in a highly embarrassing and volatile situation to condemn the entire enterprise, forgetting all he had implicitly sanctioned by allowing the ships to set sail. In his almost desperate eagerness to be rid of the problem and to placate the Spanish government, James solemnly promised Gondomar, the Spanish ambassador, that Ralegh would be handed over to the king of Spain for execution in Madrid. Many members of the Privy Council vehemently objected to such total capitulation to England's traditional enemy, but James was adamant. Only Philip III's prudent refusal of the offer prevented that shameful end.

Given these grim circumstances, it is difficult to see what Ralegh could have written to assuage the king's anger. Still, Ralegh chose the worst possible defense in the light of James's clearly expressed position toward Spain in Guiana.[8] Ralegh's stance in the *Appologie*—open hostility to Spain, insistence upon the English claim to Guiana, assertion of the justice of the destruction of S. Thomé—is the result of his complete commitment to an ideology and, still more, commitment to a role from which he would not and could not disengage himself.

Ralegh's whole life was caught up in a struggle against Spain. From his earliest days in the West Country, his family was actively engaged in financing and actually carrying out piracies against Spanish ships. As a young captain, he led his men in a massacre of Spanish troops (and some women and children as well) who had surrendered their fort at Smerwick to the English. As a courtier, Ralegh readily embraced the anti-Spanish policy of the queen, wishing only that it were more militant and aggressive. In 1588, he was in charge of the protection of Cornwall and Devon against what seemed an imminent Spanish invasion, and in later years he played a lead-

ing part in the famous occupation of Cadiz and the abortive
Islands Voyage. But, unlike the queen, Ralegh was not content with clever diplomacy, piracy, and the occasional spectacular raid. He dreamed of a far grander enterprise, of a challenge to the entire Spanish empire in the New World. He
sought, in effect, not only to take the lead from Spain in
America but to strike a crippling blow at all Spanish power
and influence. In his view the Spanish king's vast power,
which had dominated Europe for decades, rested entirely
upon his American possessions:

[T]hese abilities rise not from the trades of sackes, and Civil [Se-
ville] Orenges, nor from ought else that either Spaine, Portugal, or
any of his other provinces produce: It is his Indian Golde that indaungereth and disturbeth all the nations of Europe, it purchaseth
intelligence, creepeth into Councels, and setteth bound loyalty at
libertie, in the greatest Monarchies of Europe. [*Discoverie*, p. 9]

And Ralegh saw himself as the heroic destroyer of that great
power and the founder of his nation's future greatness. The
immediate goal of the Guiana expedition of 1616 was the fabulous gold mine, but Ralegh's vision was not merely of a gold
mine but of a golden world, a vast empire, rich in all things
and loyal to the English crown. It is this vision which is behind everything he wrote about Guiana and which led him,
even when fighting for his life in the *Appologie*, to carry on
the propaganda campaign for the New World:

[B]esides the excellent ayre, pleasantnes, heilthfullnes, and riches, it
hath plentie of Corne, fruits, fishes, fowles, wilde and tame, Beeves,
horse, sheepe, hogges, deere, conies, hares, tortoises, amadylles [ar-
madilloes], nanaes [bananas], oyles, hony, wax, pottatoes, sugar-
canes, Medicaments, Balsum, simples, gumes, and what not.[9]

This inventory was of no interest to King James, who had determined not to war with Spain in the New World and
certainly not over Guiana. But then Ralegh did not address
the king alone. His words were directed to the literate public
whom he had exhorted to empire twenty-two years before in
The Discoverie of Guiana, to the readers of Hakluyt and Pur-

chas and the other New World propagandists. Moreover, Ralegh's deepest commitment was neither to the king nor to this public, but to himself. Regardless of the consequences, Ralegh had to maintain his vision of himself as the discoverer of a golden world. This role was part of his very identity; he could not put it on or off like his feigned sickness on the road to London.

The reason this identity is properly called a *role*, with its suggestions of theatricality and artifice, will become clear by turning once again to the last scenes of Ralegh's life. On the day of Ralegh's appearance at the King's Bench, James issued a warrant releasing the prisoner from the earlier judgment to be hanged, drawn, and quartered. The king's pleasure was "to have the head only of the said Sir Walter Ralegh cut-off." [10] Ralegh asked for a delay of a few days but was refused, and it was determined to carry out the execution on the following morning, October 29, 1618. That was the day of the Lord Mayor's Pageant, which would be sure to draw a large crowd to the east end of London and thus, it was hoped, deprive the actor of an audience. Ralegh was taken from Westminster Hall to be lodged at the adjacent gatehouse, and a scaffold was hastily erected in the Old Palace Yard nearby. It appears that from the moment when he perceived that there was no further hope, he became almost totally self-possessed and seemed even to savor what lay before him. Encountering an old acquaintance during the brief transit from the Hall to the gatehouse, Ralegh asked him to come the next morning, adding, "I know not what shift you will make, but I am sure to have a place." [11] The friends who came to the prison that evening to bid him farewell were struck by his calmness, even mirth. A kinsman, Charles Thynne, was disturbed and advised him, "Sir, take heed, you goe not too muche upon the brave hande; for your enemies will take Exceptions at that." Ralegh replied with a consciousness of the role he had determined to play: "Give me leave to be mery for this is the last merriment that Ever I shall have in this worlde: but when I come to the sad parte, thou shalte see, I will looke on it like a man." [12] Dr.

Tounson, the dean of Westminster, was also disquieted by
Ralegh's mood, though for different reasons:

When I begann to incourage him against the feare of death, he
seemed to make so light of itt that I wondred att him; and when I
told him, that the deare servants of God, in better causes than his,
had shrunke backe and trembled a little, he denyed not, but yet
gave God thanks, he never feared death; and much lesse then, for it
was but an opinion and imagination; and the manner of death
though to others might seeme greevous, yet he had rather dye so
then of a burning fever: with much more to that purpose, with such
confidence and cheerefulnesse, that I was fain to divert my speach
another way, and wished him not to flatter himselfe; for this extraordinary boldnesse, I was afrayd, came from some false ground.
If it sprong from the assurance he had of the love and favour of
God, of the hope of his Salvation by Christ, and his own innocency, as he pleaded, I sayd he was an happy man; but if it were
out of an humour of vain glory or carelessnesse or contempt of
death, or senselessnesse of his own estate, he were much to be lamented, &c. For I told him, that Heathen Men had sett as little by
their lives as he could doe, and seemed to dye as bravely.[13]

Poor Tounson! If only Ralegh "had shrunke backe and trembled a little," the dean would have comforted him with the
balm of Christian hope, but as it turned out the prisoner did
not stand in need of comfort. It is utterly characteristic of Ralegh that observers were in doubt whether his courage in the
face of death was Christian or pagan, whether he was inspired
by piety or vainglory.

Dr. Tounson at least was eventually satisfied that the condemned was a good Christian, but on the morning of the execution he was again troubled by Ralegh's behavior. After taking his last Communion, Ralegh "was very cheerfull and
merry, and hoped to perswade the world, that he dyed an innocent man, as he sayd." Tounson thereupon rebuked Ralegh
with the classic words of a man who must reconcile morality
with his service to the state: "I told him, that he should do
well to advise what he sayd; men in these dayes did not dye in
that sort innocent, and his pleading innocency was an oblique

taxing of the Justice of the Realm upon him." Ralegh replied politely that he acknowledged the "Justice" of the legal technicality whereby he was to be executed on the basis of the conviction of 1603, but asked Dr. Tounson to give him leave "to stand upon his innocency in the fact." Tounson, of course, was perfectly correct: Ralegh's behavior was indeed a calm and dignified rebuke to King James and the entire judicial system. Ralegh was not going to emulate Essex—no last-minute repentance, no praise of the sovereign's divine justice, no impassioned appeals to Christ for forgiveness and mercy.[14] Instead, Ralegh acted as if he were innocent of the charges for which he was condemned to die and curiously beyond the power of the king who had condemned him. Ralegh's serene control of himself was more than a simple rebuke; it was a rejection of the king's sovereignty over him, foreshadowed in his words to the commission that he would shortly be "where I shall not fear the face of any king on earth."

This tacit rejection of the king's power is echoed in the epitaph upon himself which, it is said, Ralegh inscribed in the flyleaf of his Bible and left at the gatehouse at Westminster:

> Even such is tyme which takes in trust
> Our yowth, our Joyes, and all we have,
> And payes us butt with age and dust:
> Who in the darke and silent grave
> When we have wandred all our wayes
> Shutts up the storye of our dayes.
> And from which earth and grave and dust
> The Lord shall rayse me up I trust.
>
> [*Poems*, p. 72]

It is Time the Destroyer, not the judgment of the king, that is executing Ralegh, and death is not punishment for failure in Guiana, but the universal human tragedy. The poem arises directly from Ralegh's situation—one manuscript goes so far as to claim that it was written "but twoe howers before his death"[15]—and yet the king, the gold mine, the empire, and even the axe have all dropped away, leaving time, the poet, and God. Behind the accidents of history, the poet discerns a universal, inevitable pattern of defeat, common to kings and prisoners alike.

The theme of the triumph of time is, of course, a familiar commonplace in both Renaissance and medieval literature, but the brief epitaph merits close attention, as its meaning, origin, and occasion all reveal a great deal about Ralegh. "Trust" in legal terminology is the confidence reposed in a person in whom legal ownership of property is vested to hold or use for the benefit of another, but in man's transaction with time that confidence is cruelly betrayed—and yet such is the inevitable course for which there is no redress. The poet accepts, as he must, the "payment" of age and dust as the inescapable lot of all men, and at the same time he bitterly resents it. The notion of an arrangement which is legal and yet unjust may perhaps reflect Ralegh's remark to the dean of Westminster that he both acknowledged the legality of his execution and insisted upon his innocence in fact. But, if so, Ralegh sees in his fate a symbol of the condition of all men, at once innocent and condemned to die.

In the second part of the poem the mood shifts slightly from the sense of inevitable betrayal to anguish at the finality of the transaction. The anguish is restrained and quiet, but it is unmistakably felt in the phrase "the darke and silent grave" and the emphatic and terrible "Shutts up the storye of our dayes." The latter image suggests both that time closes a man's life as one closes a book and that time buries a man's history in an obscure grave. Nothing will remain behind of all the wanderings—not even the memory. The closing lines seem to turn in an entirely different direction, contrasting trust in the Lord to the trust that was abused by time. But the last words, "I trust," modify this faith, even as they express it. They shift the emphasis at the last moment from God to the poet, and in the slight pause that inevitably precedes them—

> The Lord shall rayse me up   I trust

lurks a wry doubt if even this promise will be kept in a world so unjust.

With its dramatic associations—the once glittering favorite of Queen Elizabeth cast down, the failure of the desperate gamble in Guiana, the long night in the gatehouse awaiting morning and the scaffold—Ralegh's epitaph was assured of a wide circulation, almost invariably with a note specifying the date and circumstances of its composition. But these verses which appeared so rooted in their tragic occasion were originally composed, except for the first three words and the final couplet, decades earlier as the final stanza of another poem:

> Nature that washt her hands in milke
>   And had forgott to dry them,
> In stead of earth tooke snow and silke
>   At Loves request to trye them,
> If she a mistresse could compose
> To please Loves fancy out of those.
>
> Her eyes he would should be of light,
>   A Violett breath, and Lipps of Jelly,
> Her haire not blacke, nor over bright,
>   And of the softest downe her Belly,
> And for her inside hee'ld have it
> Only of wantonnesse and witt.
>
> At Loves entreaty, such a one
>   Nature made, but with her beauty
> She hath framed a heart of stone,
>   So as Love by ill destinie
> Must dye for her whom nature gave him
> Because her darling would not save him.
>
> But Time which nature doth despise,
>   And rudely gives her love the lye,
> Makes hope a foole, and sorrow wise,
>   His hands doth neither wash, nor dry,
> But being made of steele and rust,
> Turnes snow, and silke, and milke to dust.
>
> The Light, the Belly, lipps and breath,
>   He dimms, discolours, and destroyes,
> With those he feedes, but fills not death,
>   Which sometimes were the foode of Joyes;
> Yea Time doth dull each lively witt,
> And dryes all wantonnes with it.

> Oh cruell Time which takes in trust
>   Our youth, our Joyes and all we have,
> And payes us but with age and dust,
>   Who in the darke and silent grave
> When we have wandred all our wayes
> Shutts up the story of our dayes.

[*Poems*, pp. 21–22] [16]

It is difficult to date this poem, but the resemblance of the artificial mistress to Spenser's False Florimell suggests that Ralegh wrote it between the summer of 1589 when he met Spenser in Ireland and 1592/93, the probable date of his masterpiece, *Ocean to Cynthia*.[17] Whatever the precise date, "Nature that washt her hands in milke" displays the central concern of Ralegh's poetry: the brooding analysis of the sources of human failure. Characteristically, the terms are simple and abstract—Nature, Love, and Time—but the relationships between them are elusive. Nature is a generous friend who fulfills Love's fancies, but that fulfillment is the fashioning of a wholly unnatural mistress whose coldness kills Love. Nature failed to give the beautiful creature a human heart, but the uneasy artificiality of the diction in the early stanzas—violet breath, lips of jelly, etc.—suggests that Love's request was itself misguided, that joy is better sought in creatures of earth than of snow and silk. That suggestion, however, is undermined in the remainder of the poem by Time, the mortal enemy of Nature and Love alike, who turns everything to dust. The motifs cut across each other, unresolved even by the powerful ending.

When, on the eve of his execution, Ralegh recalled the final stanza, lifted it from its original context, and changed it slightly, he created in effect a new poem, a somber meditation on death. Even if one isolates the final stanza of the original, the transformation is profound. As Ralegh's bibliographer, T. N. Brushfield, observes, the additional couplet "throws a halo of religious feeling" over lines that were "essentially Pagan, and might have been recited at a Pompeian banquet or at a Medicean supper." [18] Just as striking, perhaps, is the distance that separates "Oh cruell Time" from the final "Even such is tyme." The former is the outcry of a man who perceives that his joys are only transitory and is compelled to protest this outrage. The world weariness, resignation, and bitterness that weigh upon the latter version reflect the harsh experience of more than two decades, the gap between the favorite of the 1590s and the ruined old man of 1618.

Again and again in his career as poet and historian, Ralegh returned to earlier works, adding, revising, recalling words and phrases. The poem, "A Farewell to false Love," for example, began in 1584 as a reply to Sir Thomas Heneage's "Most welcome love, thou mortall foe to lies." By 1588 Ralegh had added a fourth stanza, and after 1592 he returned to it again to add a fifth and concluding stanza. In *Ocean to Cynthia,* he quoted a line from an earlier piece, "Farewell to the Court," as a premonition of the disaster that had now befallen him. Twenty-five years later, in 1618, Ralegh stitched together fragments of *Ocean to Cynthia* and apparently considered presenting them as a "Petition" to Queen Anne. Pierre Lefranc has seen in this habit of repetition and self-quotation an indication that Ralegh's poetic vein was relatively thin, that he practiced a kind of creative economy, preferring to deepen and extend what he had written rather than to embark on new works.[19] But surely there is more than poetic economy in these repetitions and reworkings. They suggest that Ralegh was constantly reflecting upon his past, turning in upon himself, analyzing his experience in terms of the larger patterns that were seen to be at work in it over the years. As in *Ocean to Cynthia* he recalls a line he had written years before, only now perceiving its full significance and truth, so in "Even such is tyme" he brings together the past and the present. He relates his feelings on the eve of death, the ruins of his career stretching out behind him, to observations made years before in a very different human and poetic context. The epitaph, like much of Ralegh's poetry, carries with it hidden memories and a continuing secret dialogue within the self, a dialogue spanning Ralegh's entire life. In the poetry of this most theatrical of men, with his eye ever on his audience and directed toward a particular goal, there is a strong current of private meaning, self-reference, and self-expression.

Thus the simple terms "joyes" and "dust" in the epitaph acquire special resonance from their recurrent use in Ralegh's writings over the years.[20] They recall not only the original poem, "Nature that washt her hands in milke," but *Ocean to Cynthia*, with its "Joyes under dust that never live agayne," and *The History of the World*, with the far-stretched greatness of man covered over with the dust of time. Indeed, in the course of Ralegh's works, joys come to suggest not only the human response to pleasure but all of the great aspirations of the men of the Renaissance: the dream of vast empires and inexhaustible riches, unlimited knowledge of the universe and control of its forces, fame that never fades, love that never dies, a world created anew in the image of man's desires, and man free to remake himself. All that negates human dignity and achievement is signified by dust, that stubborn matter which resists the shaping power of man, the substance to which both empires and individuals decay at last, the end of love and life.

Beyond the powerful realization of a truism, the political overtones, and the private resonances, the epitaph has yet another meaning: its contribution to the role Ralegh was acting out in his last hours. This was the poem's primary significance for Ralegh's contemporaries. John Chamberlain, writing to his friend Dudley Carleton, November 7, 1618, encloses "halfe a dosen verses he [Ralegh] made the night before his death, to take his farewell of poetrie wherein he had ben a pidler even from his youth," and Thomas Lorkin writes to Sir Thomas Puckering that "the night before his execution [Ralegh] made his own Epicedium, or funeral song, which I have here sent you."[21] These observers saw the poem as part of the behavior befitting a gentleman on the eve of his execution, a graceful and dignified mode of leave-taking. For Englishmen of this age, a man's comportment at the point of death was of the utmost interest and importance. Everything was eagerly noted, from grandiloquent speeches to the slightest indications of dread or repentance, and the whole was judged in terms which seem as much aesthetic as moral. Malcolm's famous account of the execution of the Thane of Cawdor captures the sense of connoisseurship, the appreciation of a "good death":

> Nothing in his life
> Became him like the leaving of it; he died
> As one that had been studied.in his death
> To throw away the dearest thing he ow'd,
> As 'twere a careless trifle.
>
> [*Macbeth*, I, iv, 7–11]

"Studied in his death"—a "good death" was no accident of blind courage; it was the result of discipline, intelligence, timing, and careful preparation. The truly memorable death scenes of the age, on the scaffold, at home, or even on the battlefield—Sir Thomas More, Mary Queen of Scots, Sir Philip Sidney, John Donne, Ralegh, Charles I—were precisely that: *scenes,* presided over by actor-playwrights who had brilliantly conceived and thoroughly mastered their roles. Ralegh's epitaph upon himself, his memorable witticisms, his final speech to the crowd were all carefully weighed elements of such a role. His was an unforgettable performance. But then, as the epitaph suggests, Ralegh had in a sense been preparing for his last scenes for a very long time.

This feeling of preparation and control, this deliberate transformation of a dreadful trial into a triumphant act of will inevitably—and perhaps intentionally—recall the imprisonment and execution of Thomas More. Ralegh's strange blend of serenity and irony, the poem composed in prison, the sense of having passed beyond the merely temporal power of an unjust king, even the cheerful last words to the executioner, all reflect the high tragedy of More's end. As More at his death symbolized that adherence to the Old Faith which was being ruthlessly destroyed by a harsh new order, so too Ralegh embodied a whole age which was passing beneath the axe. But

the comparison reveals how much was lost in the years between 1535 and 1618. Thomas More the humanist had allowed his mind free play over an imaginary country, a radically new society that tested and criticized actuality. Ralegh
was no humanist, and he voyaged for gold, for glory, and for
power. Even at the height of his worldly success, More was
deeply attracted by monasticism: beneath the robes of his high
office, he secretly wore a hair shirt. For Ralegh, the contemplative life had no appeal. Instead of More's rich humanity
and deep faith in God, instead of the love and forgiveness that
radiated from him at the close of his life, there is Ralegh's
cold brilliance, a heroism more pagan than Christian, the subtle last stab at his enemies. More, like Ralegh, was a consummate actor, a man who knew how, in William Roper's phrase,
to "make a part of his own." [22] But strip away More's role and
you are left with his unshakable faith in Christ; strip away
Ralegh's role and you look into the abyss. Ralegh's last scenes
were not so much an imitation as a demonic parody of More's.

On the morning of his execution, according to an eyewitness, Ralegh was "very cheerfull . . . eate his breakfast hertily,
and tooke tobacco; and made no more of his death, than [it]
had bene to take a journey; and left a great impression in the
minds of those that beheld him." [23] He dressed himself richly
for the occasion, but not ostentatiously as he had done in his
days of royal favor. On account of the fever he had contracted
on the Guiana voyage and had never completely shaken, he
wore under his hat a wrought nightcap. Seeing a bald-headed
old man in the crowd that thronged about him on the way to
the scaffold, Ralegh asked him whether he wanted anything.
"Nothing," replied the old man, "but to see [you], and to pray
God to have mercy upon [your] soul." "I thank thee, good
friend," answered Ralegh, "and I am sorry I have no better
thing to return thee for thy good will; but take this night-cap
. . . for thou hast more need of it now than I." [24] The allu-
sion to Sir Philip Sidney's famous "Thy necessity is yet greater
than mine" would not have been wasted on an audience that
treasured such scenes.

Ralegh ascended the scaffold with a smiling face and greeted his acquaintances and the important personages in the crowd. Then, after an officer had called for silence, the condemned began to speak, anxious that no one think him afraid of death: "I desire to be borne withal, because this is the Third day of my Feaver: And if I shew any weakness, I beseech you to attribute it to my Malady, for this is the Hour I look for it" (Harlow, p. 306). After a pause, he looked up at a window where the earl of Arundel, Viscount Doncaster, and other men of rank were seated and continued in a louder voice: "I thank God of his Infinite Goodness, that he hath sent me to Die in the sight of so Honourable an Assembly, and not in Darkness." But again he paused, afraid that the honorable assembly sitting at the window, the audience he cared most about, could not hear him and that his words would be wasted on the groundlings at the foot of the scaffold. "I will strain my self, for I would willingly have your Honours hear me," he shouted. But the lords put him out of his difficulty by coming down from the balcony and mounting the scaffold. Ralegh then began again, repeating his opening remarks: "As I said, I thank God heartily, that he hath brought me into the Light to Die, and hath not suffered me to Die in the dark Prison of the Tower, where I have suffered a great deal of Adversity, and a long Sickness; and I thank God that my feaver hath not taken me at this time, as I pray'd God it might not." He proceeded, with the aid of a "Note of Remembrance," to answer the main points of suspicion against him—intrigues with the French, disloyalty to the king, questionable intentions in the Guiana voyage, the sham illness and attempted escape upon his return, arrogant mocking at the execution of his rival the earl of Essex almost nineteen years before—omitting to mention only the conviction of 1603 on the basis of which he was about to be executed. He spoke with all the fervor and conviction at his command, frequently calling upon God to witness the truth of his words and to punish him eternally if he lied. He was especially ardent, it appears, in his denial of a French commission:

But this I say, for a Man to call God to Witness to a Falshood at
any time is a grievous sin, and what shall he hope for at the Tribunal Day of Judgment? But to call God to Witness to a falshood
at the time of Death, is far more grievous and impious, and there is
no hope for such an one. And what should I expect that am now
going to render an Account of my Faith? I do therefore call the
Lord to Witness, as I hope to be saved, and as I hope to see Him
in his Kingdom, which I hope will be within this quarter of this
Hour; I never had any Commision from the King of France, nor
any Treaty with the French Agent, nor with any from the French
King; neither knew I that there was an Agent, or what he was, till I
met him in my Gallery at my Lodging unlooked for. If I speak not
true, O Lord, let me never come into thy Kingdom. [Harlow, p.
307]

These vehement protestations of innocence would be quite
convincing were it not for considerable evidence proving that
Ralegh did in fact have important secret dealings with the
French before he embarked for Guiana. The details might
never have been known had it not been for Ralegh's singular
want of judgment in choosing his confidants. His career is
strewn with betrayals, and to the list which includes Sir Lewis
Stukeley and the physician Manourie must be added the two
emissaries, Faige and Belle, to whom Ralegh entrusted his
delicate negotiations with the French government in 1617. Instead of carrying out their instructions upon arriving in
France, they embarked inexplicably on a trading voyage in
the Mediterranean. Their ship was captured by pirates, and
the two were separated. Faige eventually arrived in Genoa and
was soon after cast into debtor's prison; nothing further is
known about him. Belle made his way to Rome, where he
confessed his dealings with Ralegh to a Jesuit; he was then
sent to Madrid, at his own request according to the official
documents, to repeat the story. He produced as evidence a letter in Ralegh's own hand to De Buisseaux, a member of the
Council of State of France, and other documents relating, it
appears, to an attempt to bring the French into the Guiana
enterprise. These documents were eventually sent on to the

state archives at Simancas where they were discovered by S. R. Gardiner in the nineteenth century.

Ralegh's letter asks the assistance of De Buisseaux "pour obtenir le brevet qui m'est promis." Of course, this letter was never delivered, and Ralegh never received the commission promised him, but the evidence still provides a startling contrast to the impassioned declaration of innocence Ralegh made on the scaffold. Gardiner observes that this declaration is "a marvel of ingenuity": "Not a word of it is untrue, but the general impression is completely false." [25] Ralegh was determined to die an innocent man in the eyes of the world.

The same artfulness, the product no doubt of considerable forethought, is evident in his other remarks. He nobly forgives Sir Lewis Stukeley and prays God to do the same, but he feels "bound in Charity" to expose Stukeley's treachery before the world "that all Men may take good heed of him." He swears that he wept when the earl of Essex was beheaded but omits to mention his letter to Robert Cecil urging him, in effect, to be merciless and to press for the execution of their dangerous enemy.[26] Only when Ralegh avows that he never had "in all my Life, a thought of ill of his Majesty," does he appear to lie outright, though, of course, there is no proof against him but common sense.

Throughout his final declaration Ralegh manipulated the facts of his life in order to present the desired last image of himself, just as the writer of a history play manipulates the chronicler's facts to accord with his conception of the characters. Not only the speech but the entire scene was a splendid piece of rhetoric, daringly seized and turned against the king who had commanded the execution. Its success as a rhetorical act may be judged by the response it elicited from its audience: on the following day Sir Edward Harwood wrote to Sir Dudley Carleton that Ralegh's "Christian and truthful" conduct on the scaffold "made all believe that he was neither guilty of former treasons nor of unjustly injuring the King of Spain." And years later Sir John Eliot, who had been present as a follower of Buckingham, the king's favorite, recalled, "Such was

his unmoved courage and placid temper that, while it changed
the affection of the enemies who had come to witness it, and
turned their joy to sorrow, it filled all men else with emotion
and admiration." [27]

At the close of his speech, which had lasted, according to
one observer, three quarters of an hour, Ralegh looked back
upon his life and took his leave:

And now I intreat you all to join with me in Prayer, that the Great
God of Heaven, whom I have grievously offended, being a Man full
of Vanity, and have lived a sinful Life, in all sinful Callings, having
been a Souldier, a Captain, a Sea-Captain, and a Courtier, which
are all places of Wickedness and Vice; that God (I say) would for-
give me, and that he would receive me into everlasting Life. So I
take my leave of you all, making my Peace with God. [Harlow, p.
310]

With that, the sheriffs ordered the scaffold cleared of spectators, and Ralegh gave some clothes and money away to those
near him and said farewell to his friends, remarking, "I have a
long Journey to go, and therefore will take my leave." The
Spanish agent informed his king that "Ralegh's spirit never
faltered, nor did his countenance change," and Lorkin wrote
to Puckering that "he seemed as free from all manner of apprehension, as if he had been come hither rather to be a spectator than a sufferer; nay, the beholders seemed much more
sensible than did he." As soon as the preparations were completed, Ralegh turned to the executioner and asked to see the
axe. When the man held back, he repeated, "I pray thee let me
see it, Dost thou think that I am afraid of it?" He ran his
finger along the edge and then, smiling, said to the sheriff,
"This is a sharp Medicine, but it is a Physitian for all Diseases." Then after entreating the people to pray for him and
forgiving the executioner, he knelt down and laid his head
upon the block. Someone suggested that he ought to face the
east, and Ralegh replied, "What matter how the head lie, so
the heart be right." Here again at the penultimate moment,
Ralegh was recalling and reworking something he had written

years before. In *The History of the World,* discussing the custom of praying toward the east, Ralegh had asserted that "the serving of God is every where in the world, the matter is not great which way wee turne our faces, so our hearts stand right" (i, i, 3, p. 36). In fact, having uttered his splendid line, Ralegh did move to face the east, but the remark was made and had left its impression.

The role was practically played out. Refusing the executioner's offer of a blindfold, Ralegh told the man to strike when he lifted his hand. After a brief pause, he gave the signal. The executioner did not move. In a last magnificent assertion of courage and the will to control his destiny, Ralegh shouted, "What dost thou fear? Strike, man!" [28] In two blows the head was severed, and the performance was over.

2 Ralegh and the Dramatic Sense of Life

What is our life? A play of passion

At his execution, as at other crucial moments of his life, Ralegh displayed the talents of a great actor. Again and again we see him performing a brilliant part in what he called "this stage-play world" (*H.W.*, ii, ii, 2, p. 27), reciting his splendid lines, twisting facts for dramatic effect, passionately justifying his actions, and transforming personal crises into the universal struggle of *virtù* and *fortuna*. Emotions are exaggerated, alternatives are sharpened, moods are dramatized. Ralegh's letters, like his actions, reveal a man for whom self-dramatization was a primary response to crisis:

I only desire thatt I may be stayd no on[e] houre from all the extremetye that ether lawe or presedent can avowe. And, if that be to[o] litle, would God it weare withall concluded that I might feed the lions, as I go by, to save labor. [*Letters*, p. 54]

I am sure, if I weare a Turke I could not be worss dealt withall then I am by them, who have dun nothinge for Her Majesties sake butt rackt mee yeven asunder. [*Letters*, p. 97]

[A]nd yeven so, only gasing [gazing] for a wynde to carrye mee to my destiny, I humblie take my leve. [*Letters*, p. 107]

[Y]our Majesty havinge left mee, I am left all alone in the worlde, and am sorry that ever I was att all. [*Letters*, p. 259]

Name, bloud, gentillety or estate, I have none; no, not so mich as a beeing; no, not so mich as *vita plantae*. I have only a penetent sowle, in a body of iron, which moveth towards the loadstone of Death. [*Letters*, p. 296]

For my own tyme, good my Lord, consider that it cannot be calde a life, but only misery drawn out and spoone into a long thride, without all hope of other end then Death shall provide for mee; who, without the healp of kings or frinds, will deliver mee out of prison. [*Letters*, p. 313] [1]

22

The letters display an intense histrionic sensibility constantly striving for a moving presentation of the self. Even at their most personal and emotional, there is little that seems to reach back into the tangled inner world of the suffering individual: the reader is asked to pity and to admire, but not to inquire too deeply. Ralegh's letters are miniature stages on which to perform, spaces to be filled with grand—usually tragic—gestures. There are moments of inadvertent comedy and self-parody: "So I leve to trouble yow at this time, being become like a fish cast on dry land, gasping for breath, with lame leggs and lamer loonges" (*Letters*, p. 51). But at their best, the self-dramatizations have none of this clumsy and anxious grop-ing after effect. Rather, they take simple words and images and infuse them with unexpected power. Perhaps the finest of such moments occurs in what Ralegh thought would be his farewell to his wife, the letter he wrote on the eve of his ex-pected execution in 1603:

I cannot wright much. God knowes howe hardlie I stole this tyme, when all sleep; and it is tyme to separate my thoughts from the world. Begg my dead body, which living was denyed you; and ei-ther lay itt att Sherborne if the land continue, or in Exiter church, by my father and mother. I can wright noe more. Tyme and Death call me awaye. [*Letters*, p. 287][2]

The final words seem to place us for a moment at the close of a morality play where the hero, severed from the world and all of its concerns, is at last literally called away by Time and Death.

At times, Ralegh succumbs to the dangers of the histrionic sensibility: self-indulgence, self-pity, posturing. For example, when the aging queen discovered his secret marriage and im-prisoned him in the Tower, Ralegh sent an account of his sor-rows to Robert Cecil in the hope that Cecil would show it to the queen. The excuse for this effusion is the "bills for the Gards' coats, which are to be made now for the Prograsse":

My heart was never broken till this day, that I hear the Queen goes away so far of[f],—whom I have followed so many years with so

great love and desire, in so many journeys, and am now left behind
her, in a dark prison all alone. While she was yet nire at hand, that
I might hear of her once in two or three dayes, my sorrows were the
less: but even now my heart is cast into the depth of all misery. I
that was wont to behold her riding like *Alexander,* hunting like
Diana, walking like *Venus,* the gentle wind blowing her fair hair
about her pure cheeks, like a nymph; sometime siting in the shade
like a Goddess; sometime singing like an angell; sometime playing
like *Orpheus.* Behold the sorrow of this world! Once amiss, hath be-
reaved me of all. O Glory, that only shineth in misfortune, what is
becum of thy assurance? All wounds have skares, but that of fanta-
sie; all affections their relenting, but that of womankind. Who is
the judge of friendship, but adversity? or when is grace witnessed,
but in offences? There were no divinety, but by reason of compassion; for revenges are brutish and mortall. All those times past,—
the loves, the sythes, the sorrows, the desires, can they not way
down one frail misfortune? Cannot one dropp of gall be hidden in
so great heaps of sweetness? I may then conclude, *Spes et fortuna,
valete.* She is gone, in whom I trusted, and of me hath not one
thought of mercy, nor any respect of that that was. Do with me
now, therefore, what you list. I am more weary of life then they are
desirous I should perish; which if it had been for her, as it is by
her, I had been too happily born. [*Letters,* pp. 51–52]

The anguish is genuine enough, for the imprisonment of 1592
had shaken Ralegh to the core, but the voice is false. The letter unintentionally calls attention to exactly what it should
conceal: the distance between role and reality, the passionate
lover and the calculating courtier, the elusive nymph and the
spinsterish queen. As a failure of the histrionic sensibility, it
evokes those epithets—"exhibitionist," "stagey," "melodra-
matic," "theatrical," etc.—which embody the age-old prejudice
against the theater.[3] The problem, however, is not theatricalism itself, but the clumsiness of these particular gestures and
the inappropriateness of this particular stage. In Ralegh's poetry of the period, the same emotions receive more convincing
expression:

> My boddy in the walls captived
> Feels not the wounds of spigh*t*ful envy,

Butt my thralde mind, of liberty deprived,
Fast fettered in her auntient memory,
Douth nought beholde butt sorrowes diinge face;
Such prison earst was so delightfull
As it desirde no other dwellinge place,
Butt tymes effects, and destinies dispightfull
Have changed both my keeper and my fare,
Loves fire, and bewties light I then had store,
Butt now close keipt, as captives wounted are,
That food, that heat, that light I finde no more,
  Dyspaire bolts up my dores, and I alone
  Speake to dead walls, butt thos heare not my mone.[4]

The feelings here are those expressed in the letter, but the uneasiness, the confusion, and the falseness have fallen away. In the letter, Ralegh had tried to use the language and cadence of lyric poetry and had sounded forced and insincere. Now, in lyric poetry itself, he found a coherent and effective dramatic role. The courtly lovers of scores of poems from the time of Wyatt and Surrey had expressed exactly the tangle of emotions, the love, despair, and resentment, which Ralegh was trying to convey.

This correspondence between life and art was not accidental. In his relationship with the middle-aged queen, Ralegh had cast himself in the part of a passionate lover pursuing a remote and beautiful lady. That fantasy was all but shattered by the queen's discovery of the secret marriage. Imprisoned in the Tower, Ralegh attempted to recreate the poetic illusion, now as the faithful lover cruelly mistreated by his mistress. In his sonnet, role and reality, the literary type and the actual situation, spill over into each other. The woman in whose "auntient memory" the poet is imprisoned has actually put him in prison. The poem enables Ralegh to reenter the realm from which his disgrace had driven him, that zone at the boundary of fiction and truth in which he chose to exist.[5]

Ralegh's adoption of the conventional *persona* of a rejected lover in "My boddy in the walls captived" corresponds to the

self-dramatization in his letters and the role-playing in actual
scenes of his life. He seems to have had what I should like to
call a "dramatic sense of life": a histrionic life-style and, with
this, a consciousness of the universe and of the self shaped in
theatrical terms. It is not surprising that for Ralegh, as for so
many of his contemporaries, the theater was a central metaphor for man's life: [6]

> What is our life? a play of passion,
> Our mirth the musicke of division,
> Our mothers wombes the tyring houses be,
> Where we are drest for this short Comedy,
> Heaven the Judicious sharpe spectator is,
> That sits and markes still who doth act amisse,
> Our graves that hide us from the searching Sun,
> Are like drawne curtaynes when the play is done,
> Thus march we playing to our latest rest,
> Onely we dye in earnest, that's no Jest.
>
>   [*Poems*, pp. 51–52] [7]

Ralegh's epigram, probably written during his thirteen-year
imprisonment in the Tower, weaves back and forth between a
sense of the triviality of life and a feeling of anxiety in the face
of death and God's judgment. Man's actions have no more dignity or permanence than the hollow gestures of an actor, yet
they will be judged severely by a searching critic. We might
note that Plotinus had used the play metaphor to make death
seem less dreadful:

It comes to no more than the murder of one of the personages in a
play; the actor alters his make-up and enters in a new role. The
actor, of course, was not really killed; but if dying is but changing a
body as the actor changes a costume, or even an exit from the body
like the exit of an actor from the boards when he has no more to
say or do—though he will still return to act on another occasion—
what is there so very dreadful in this transformation of living
beings one into another? [8]

For Ralegh, life is a brief, uneasy comedy, while death is the
only reality. He confronts this somber thought with a kind of

jauntiness and courage, but beneath the wit of the epigram there lurks the bitterness of Macbeth's image of man as a poor player who struts and frets his hour upon the stage and then is heard no more.

Ralegh uses the play metaphor again and again in his works, almost always with undertones of disillusionment. Birth is merely the player's entrance onto the tawdry stage; rank and title are but a false show of power like a player's costume; man's vaunted freedom is no more than the illusory spontaneity of an actor, reciting the lines assigned to him. Like Shakespeare, Ralegh sees Richard III as the epitome of the actor in history:

To *Edward* the fourth succeeded *Richard* the Third, the greatest Maister in mischeife of all that fore-went him: who although, for the necessity of his Tragedie, hee had more parts to play, and more to performe in his owne person, then all the rest; yet hee so well fitted every affection that playd with him, as if each of them had but acted his owne interest. [*H. W.*, Preface, sig. A4ᵛ]

Two distinct notions of "playing" are at work here in the figure of Richard. On the one hand, there is the subtle and treacherous Richard, playing a great variety of roles that both mask and further his villainy. The evil king so cunningly manipulates the fears and ambitions of men like Hastings and Buckingham ("so well fitted every affection") that they become mere instruments of his own designs, extensions of his own will to power ("as if each of them had but acted his owne interest"). But set against this kind of playing is the notion of Richard and his accomplices as unwitting actors in a tragedy. All of Richard's schemes were ultimately "for the necessity of his Tragedie"; Richard used those "that playd with him." He could dissemble brilliantly, but he never understood that he was an actor in a play not of his own making, and appropriately his fate was to become "a spectacle":

And what successe had *Richard* himselfe after all these mischefes and Murders, policies, and counter-policies to Christian religion: and after such time, as with a most mercilesse hand hee had pressed

out the breath of his Nephews and Naturall Lords; other than the
prosperity of so short a life, as it tooke end, ere himselfe could well
looke over and discerne it? the great outcrie of innocent bloud, ob-
tayning at Gods hands the effusion of his; who became a spectacle
of shame and dishonor, both to his friends and enem[ie]s. [*H. W.,*
Pref., sig. Bl^r]

The whole course of English (and European) history as Ralegh presents it in the Preface to *The History of the World*
shows this pattern of the false presumption of men and the
"secret and unsearchable judgment" of God (*H.W.,* Pref., sig.
A3^v). Those who have the most confidence in their power to
shape their destiny are always brought the lowest:

Oh by what plots, by what forswearings, betrayings, oppressions, imprisonments, tortures, poysonings, and under what reasons of State,
and politique subteltie, have these forenamed Kings, both strangers,
and of our owne Nation, pulled the vengeance of God upon themselves, upon theirs and upon their prudent ministers! [*H.W.,* Pref.,
sig. C2^r]

There are a very few wise men who strive to make themselves
the willing instruments of God's plan, and thereby attain a
measure of happiness, but they too come to dust in the end.
The proper attitude toward this "stage-play world," Ralegh
suggests, is a bitter resignation to the vicissitudes of fortune
and a harsh contempt for man's pretensions to greatness:

For seeing God, who is the Author of all our tragedies, hath written
out for us, and appointed us all the parts we are to play: and hath
not, in their distribution, beene partiall to the most mighty Princes
of the world; That gave unto *Darius* the part of the greatest Emperour, and the part of the most miserable begger, a begger begging
water of an Enemie, to quench the great drought of death; That appointed *Bajazet* to play the *Grand Signior* of the *Turkes* in the
morning, and in the same day the *footstoole* of *Tamerlane* . . . :
why should other men, who are but [as] the least wormes, complaine of wrongs? Certainly there is no other account to be made of
this ridiculous world, than to resolve, That the change of fortune on
the great Theater, is but as the change of garments on the lesse. For
when on the one and the other, every man weares but his owne
skin; the Players are all alike. . . . For seeing Death, in the end of

the Play, takes from all whatsoever Fortune or Force takes from any one: it were a foolish madnes in the shipwracke of worldly things, where all sinks but the Sorrow, to save it. [*H.W.*, Pref., sigs. DI^v – D2^r] [9]

Two rather different attitudes are mingled in this pessimistic vision of the world as stage. One evokes the tragic figures of history, men who had experienced what Marlowe's Tamburlaine calls the "sweet fruition of an earthly crown" only to lose everything; the other likens such stupendous changes of fortune to an actor's change of costume. One looks to God, "the author of all our tragedies," who shows us by the spectacle of the misfortune of mighty princes the insignificance of our own troubles; the other looks to Death, the great leveler, who shows us the miserable quality of all mortal beings in the shipwreck of worldly things. One sees life as a tragedy; the other as a bitter comedy. Finally, one sees man as a tragic hero; the other as a miserable player tricked out, like Shakespeare's great rebel York in *3 Henry VI*, with a paper crown.

This ambivalent vision of life and the play metaphor by which it is expressed are rooted in medieval thought. John of Salisbury, the learned and influential bishop of Chartres, entitles a chapter of the *Policraticus* (1159), "De mundana comedia, vel tragedia." Comedy or tragedy—it does not really matter which term is used provided we agree that all the world's a stage:

[T]he end of all things is tragic, or if the name of comedy be preferred I offer no objection, provided that we are agreed that, as Petronius remarks, almost all the world is playing a part. . . . It is surprising how nearly coextensive with the world is the stage on which this endless, marvelous, incomparable tragedy, or if you will comedy, can be played; its area is in fact that of the whole world.[10]

Like Ralegh, John of Salisbury points to sudden and violent changes of fortune in the lives of the great to show that all the men and women are merely players:

The different periods of time take on the character of shifts of scene. The individuals become subordinate to the acts as the play of mocking fortune unfolds itself in them; for what else can it be that

invests at one moment some unknown upstart with wide flung
power and raises him to a throne and again hurls another born to
the purple from his imperial height down into chains, dooms him
to captivity, and casts him forth into extreme misery? Or, and this
is his usual fate, stains the blades of ignoble men or even vile slaves
with the blood not merely of rulers but of princes.[11]

But the bishop of Chartres finds consolation for the human
condition in contemplation of a merciful and loving God and
in trust that Paradise awaits the just man beyond the grave.[12]
For Ralegh, there is no such consolation; his God is stern, the
heavens are "high, far-off, and unsearchable" (*H.W.*, Pref., sig.
C2ʳ), and death is an undiscovered country from whose bourn
no traveler returns.

Deep pessimism, linked with the dramatic sense of life, is
central to *The History of the World* and to much of Ralegh's
poetry as well. The play metaphor was a conventional vehicle
for such pessimism. It had been used for centuries to suggest
the limitations of man's life on earth, its transience, its unreality, its lack of freedom, the instability of its greatness. Yet, paradoxically, the actual effects of the dramatic sense in Ralegh's
life seem bound up with an intense optimism about the possi-
bilities of human achievement and a belief in man's power to
control his destiny. In the final scenes of his life, for example,
Ralegh's role-playing (when it was not simply, like the feigned
illness, a device to gain time) was an assertion of human dignity. At a moment when circumstances conspired to reduce
him to total impotence, his theatrical self-possession acted out
the integrity and even the freedom of the individual. And, of
course, this is only the extreme example. At those other moments of his life when we most sense the histrionic sensibility,
as in the assault on Cadiz, the 1603 treason trial, and the two
voyages to Guiana, Ralegh's theatrical heroism similarly affirmed the power of the human will over fortune.

The dramatic sense of life as self-affirmation and the vision
of life as no more real than a play may both be traced ultimately to the writings of the Stoics. Seneca, for example, following Epictetus, at once exposes the vanity of human
greatness—

None of those whom you behold clad in purple is happy, any more than one of those actors upon whom the play bestows a sceptre and a cloak while on the stage; they strut their hour before a crowded house, with swelling port and buskined foot; but when once they make their exit the foot-gear is removed and they return to their proper stature—

and asserts the necessity of performing well in whatever part you have been assigned—

It is with life as it is with a play—it matters not how long the action is spun out, but how good the acting is.[13]

In Ralegh's life and art, however, one finds not the realization of a single tradition but a struggle between opposing forces. On the one hand, the play metaphor as an image of life's limitations reaches back to medieval theologians like John of Salisbury, to Fathers of the Church like St. John Chrysostom and St. Augustine, and to a diverse array of classical authors. Behind all of these is most probably the Book of Job with its dark picture of human fortunes manipulated and marked by God.[14] Ralegh's self-assertive theatricality, on the other hand, has its intellectual origins in those Renaissance writers who saw in man's mimetic ability a token of his power to transform nature and fashion his own identity. The belief in this power, which goes far beyond anything conceived by the Stoics, had a profound effect upon Ralegh, and I should like to consider three of its leading spokesmen: Vives, Castiglione, and Machiavelli.

The Spanish humanist Juan Luis Vives made acting the central symbol of man's nature in his *Fable about Man* (1518). Almighty Jupiter, the fable goes, created the world as a great theater in celebration of Juno's birthday. As in Ralegh's epigram, heaven is the judicious spectator, but, acording to Vives, the gods do not sit and mark "who doth act amiss." Instead, they are delighted with all that they see, especially with the master actor, man, whose range and flexibility are astonishing:

He would change himself so as to appear under the mask of a plant, acting a simple life without any power of sensation. Soon after, he withdrew and returned to the stage as a moral satirist,

brought into the shapes of a thousand wild beasts. . . . After doing
this, he was out of sight for a short time; then the curtain was
drawn back and he returned as man, prudent, just, faithful, human,
kindly, and friendly, who went about the cities with the others, held
the authority and obeyed in turn, cared for the public interest and
welfare, and was finally in every way a political and social being.[15]

Even this feat of humanity does not exhaust the talents of
"that great player": to the amazement of the gods, he next appears on stage as one of them. Finally, "he had transcended
the characters of the lower gods and was piercing into that inaccessible light surrounded by darkness where Jupiter dwells,
of kings and gods the king" (p. 390). By the unanimous decree
of the gods, man is given divine honors and elevated to the
heavens.

Vives' fable is based on Pico della Mirandola's famous *Oration on the Dignity of Man* (1486). The *Oration* opens with a
reference to "this stage of the world" and, more important, affirms the absolute freedom of man to play any part in the entire universe. God tells Adam, in Pico's fable of creation:

We have made thee neither of heaven nor of earth, neither mortal
nor immortal, so that with freedom of choice and with honor, as
though the maker and molder of thyself, thou mayest fashion thyself in whatever shape thou shalt prefer. Thou shalt have the
power, out of thy soul's judgment, to be reborn into the higher
forms, which are divine.[16]

As man in Vives' fable could pierce into that "inaccessible
light surrounded by the darkness where Jupiter dwells," so for
Pico, if man "happy in the lot of no created thing . . . with-
draws into the center of his own unity, his spirit, made one
with God, in the solitary darkness of God, who is set above all
things, shall surpass them all" (p. 225). But at this very point
of similarity, there is a telling divergence between Pico and
Vives. With breathtaking optimism, Pico asserts that man, in
an ecstasy of divine love, may actually merge completely with
God: "And at last, roused by ineffable love as by a sting, like
burning Seraphim rapt from ourselves, full of divine power we

shall no longer be ourselves, but shall become He Himself Who made us" (p. 234). In Vives' *Fable* the resemblance between God and man is striking, but complete union is denied, though the gods themselves must look twice to assure themselves of the difference:

[T]hey glanced repeatedly at Jupiter's stall wondering whether he himself was sitting there or whether he had appeared masked to play a part. Seeing him there, they gazed back again at man and then at Jupiter. With such skill and propriety did he play Jupiter's part that, up and down, from Jupiter's stall to the stage, they kept glancing, lest they be misled by a likeness or the accurate mime of an actor. Among the other players there were some who swore that this was no man but Jupiter himself, and they underwent severe punishment for their error. [p. 390] [17]

Vives' play metaphor alters the conception of man derived from the *Oration*, modifying the fervor of Pico's affirmations, introducing an Erasmian note of man's limitations and an increased emphasis upon life on earth.

Man's protean flexibility is splendid and admirable, but there is something vaguely disturbing about it. The gods admire man's acting, but then they ask Jupiter to stop the show, take man from the stage into heaven, and remove his mask (*persona*):

The whole man lay bare, showing the immortal gods his nature akin to theirs, this nature which, covered with mask and body, had made of him an animal so diverse, so desultory, so changing like a polypus and a chameleon, as they had seen him on stage. . . . When the gods saw man and embraced their brother, they deemed it unworthy of him to appear on the stage and practice the disreputable art of the theater [*ludicramque . . . artem infamam*]. [pp. 390–91]

Although, in the end, man is allowed to put on once again his "stage costume" for the feast of the gods, man's mimetic genius remains problematical. Is it the essence of man's greatness or only the means of achieving a higher existence in which miming is superfluous and even disreputable?

There is a submerged tension in Vives' *Fable* between an ardent appreciation of man's powers—the beauty and perfection of his body, the inventiveness of his mind, above all his supreme acting ability—and a desire to pass beyond the merely human. For Pico, contemplation of the divine enabled man to transcend his mortal state and achieve a mystical oneness with God, but the image of acting, which is central to Vives' conception, is not easily reconcilable to the ideal of the contemplative life. The thought of Pico and Vives is very close, but the play metaphor in the *Fable* still points up a significant shift of emphasis in the humanist conception of man, a movement away from the transcendent and toward the problems and powers of man on earth. The implications of this shift are most fully realized in a work almost exactly contemporary with Vives' *Fable,* Castiglione's *Book of the Courtier.*[18]

In its own subtle and beautiful way, *The Courtier* is also a fable about man as actor. The figure of the ideal courtier described by the gentlemen and ladies of the court of Urbino is a role for a consummate performer, an actor who can transform the ugly and ragged conflicts of reality into a harmonious work of art. The key to this transformation for Castiglione is the imitation of worthy models: "Therefore, whoever would be a good pupil must not only do things well, but must always make every effort to resemble and, if that is possible, to transform himself into his master" (p. 42). But where are masters worthy of such emulation to be found? According to Count Ludovico da Canossa, one of the chief participants in the conversation, the courtier has no single model from whom he can acquire all the grace needed for perfection, but "even as in green meadows the bee flits about among the grasses robbing the flowers, so our Courtier must steal this grace from those who seem to him to have it, taking from each the part that seems most worthy of praise" (pp. 42–43). The goal of Castiglione's book is, in a sense, to provide a single master by "forming in words a perfect Courtier, setting forth all the conditions and particular qualities that are required of anyone who deserves this name" (p. 25).

The courtier's supreme attribute is grace, a term which here has an aesthetic rather than theological meaning.[19] For Castiglione's conversationalists, grace is that mysterious quality which renders a man's speech, his actions, the movements of his body not merely impressive or accomplished but appealing, touching, beautiful. Though a few men have it "from the stars," most actually learn to have it by the mastery of certain techniques, the most important of which is *sprezzatura* or "disgracing" as the sixteenth-century translator Hoby wittily rendered it. *Sprezzatura* is a technique for the manipulation of appearance, a device for masking all the tedious conning of lines and secret rehearsals that underlie successful performances.[20]

Potentially, this self-fashioning could be a mode of escapism, a flight into a rarefied, insulated aestheticism. But Castiglione is deeply committed to the world, so deeply indeed that Pietro Bembo's famous discourse on love in Book IV seems slightly at odds with the major concerns of the assembled lords and ladies. The conversation of these smooth, carefully controlled selves is shaped far less by transcendental longings than by political pressures, by the need to discover a viable relation between the cultivated individual and the source of power in the state.[21] How is the sensitive and imaginative man to behave in the court of an absolute prince where there is no direct channel for his ambition? How can he serve his prince without becoming merely servile? And, above all, how can the absolute prince, liberated from the restraints of law and even popular opinion, be prevented from doing evil and directed toward good?

The solution to these interlocking problems lies in the deft manipulation of appearances: the courtier must artfully fashion himself to win the favor and mind of the prince, so that he may then speak the truth effectively and without risk. The element of feigning is made perfectly explicit:

In this way the Courtier will be able to lead his prince by the austere path of virtue, adorning it with shady fronds and strewing it with pretty flowers to lessen the tedium of the toilsome journey for one whose strength is slight; and now with music, now with arms and horses, now with verses, now with discourse of love, and with all those means whereof these gentlemen have spoken, to keep his mind continually occupied in worthy pleasures, yet always impressing upon him also some virtuous habit along with these enticements, as I have said, beguiling him with salutary deception; like shrewd doctors who often spread the edge of the cup with some sweet cordial when they wish to give a bitter-tasting medicine to sick and over-delicate children. [p. 294]

Art and the courtier's life-style are almost fused here, for this conception of the courtier's function is closely linked with Renaissance rhetoric and poetics. The *topos* of the bitter medicine made sweet appears again and again in the sixteenth century to justify fictions and eloquence. The poet, writes Sidney, "cometh to you with words set in a delightful proportion" and "with a tale which holdeth children from play, and old men from the chimney corner."

And pretending no more, doth intend the winning of the mind from wickedness to virtue; even as the child is often brought to take most wholesome things by hiding them in such other as have a pleasant taste.[22]

Even the profoundest truths and the most sanctified moral imperatives, it is claimed, are unpalatable and hence ineffectual without what Lucretius calls "the pleasant honey of poetry." [23] The philosopher can only discuss the nature of the good and formulate abstract moral precepts, but the poet, armed with the magical power of fables and figured speech, can fire the blood and move the will of his audience. Castiglione transforms these literary principles into political principles: the courtier's career is a kind of moral poetry, making the cold truths of reason and virtue agreeable to the prince.

Set against the harsh realities of court life, such a vision of politics seems highly idealized, but it is worth noting how negative certain aspects of Castiglione's vision are. The courtier can only achieve his ends indirectly through "salutary deceptions"; the prince is an overgrown, dangerous child who must

be lured to the good with baubles; virtue can never seem sufficiently attractive by itself but must be tricked out in a pretty
costume.

If moral virtue does not of its own accord assume a pleasing
and effective shape, neither does the human individual. Castiglione's political reflections ultimately involve the still more
basic problem of the powers and limitations of the self. The
courtier's part is not inherited, ready-made, nor does it have
divine sanction; it is the product of a unique historical moment, a new set of social and intellectual conditions, and is an
act of human imagination and will. The ideal figure is fashioned not out of the sentences of venerable authorities, but in
the course of a living conversation, with all its crosscurrents
and its interplay of vivid personalities. Underlying the work is
the sense, expressed so brilliantly by Pico and Vives, that men
have the power to shape their own existence, to fashion their
own roles. We seem to glimpse that birth of the individual
which, along with the conception of the state as a work of art,
Burckhardt placed at the heart of the civilization of the Renaissance in Italy:

Man [in the Middle Ages] was conscious of himself only as member
of a race, people, party, family, or corporation—only through some
general category. In Italy this veil first melted into air; an *objective*
treatment and consideration of the State and of all the things of
this world became possible. The *subjective* side at the same time asserted itself with corresponding emphasis; man became a spiritual
individual, and recognized himself as such.[24]

A reading of *The Courtier* from this point of view would find
in its techniques of self-presentation those resources which enabled the men of the age to give, in Burckhardt's words, "the
fullest and freest play to their individuality" (1:168).

Yet finally *The Courtier* will not fit into such a picture of
the Renaissance. Inherited models may indeed have broken
down, but the major thrust of the work is to limit the self, to
mark the boundaries of acceptable behavior, to fashion a role
that the individual can assume only through discipline, re-

straint, and a partial suppression of the personality. The courtier must transform the most volatile forces of his being—love, aggression, and raw physical energy—into the controlled and exquisite gesture, the harmonious surface. Castiglione offers not a paradigm of man's freedom, but a model for the formation of an artificial identity; his courtier is an actor completely wedded to his role. That this fashioning of the self as a work of art does not appear to constrain and imprison the individual is due to the courtier's mastery of techniques to conceal art and create the illusion of spontaneity.[25]

The energies and pressures which gave rise to the need for new models are carefully hidden from view in *The Courtier,* though they may be felt subtly shaping the work. But they glow with remorseless intensity in another work of the same period, Machiavelli's *The Prince,* which, as its title suggests, may be seen as a mocking and demonic counterpart to Castiglione's graceful book.

It may at first seem rather willful and perverse to link two such strikingly different works. *The Courtier* is self-consciously idealizing, portraying a court suffused with grace and beauty, and fashioning the perfect courtier whose end is to lead his prince on the narrow path of virtue. *The Prince* explicitly rejects such idealizing, laying its claim to authority on precisely the opposite quality:

[M]y intention being to write something of use to those who understand, it appears to me more proper to go to the real truth of the matter than to its imagination; and many have imagined republics and principalities which have never been seen or known to exist in reality; for how we live is so far removed from how we ought to live, that he who abandons what is done for what ought to be done, will rather learn to bring about his own ruin than his preservation.[26]

But, despite the sharp opposition between the two works, there are correspondences, particularly in the notion of the fashioning and presentation of the self.

Just as Castiglione "formed in words" a perfect courtier, so Machiavelli gradually builds up the image of the perfect prince, the man who knows how to use the lion and the fox. Of course, Machiavelli understands even better than Castiglione that his ideal figure can never be; in fact, he does not even allow himself the luxury of a fully realized fiction. Instead, there are numerous historical examples throughout *The Prince*, nearly all of which carry with them overtones of ultimate defeat. Nevertheless, taken all together, these examples and the more general precepts do present a vague but impressive composite portrait—necessarily vague, for the key to this figure is his total adaptability to circumstances and his total control of himself.

For one brief moment at the end of the work, in a conditional sentence that belies the assertion, Machiavelli offers a glimpse of the ideal type and the ultimate goal toward which *The Prince* has been moving: "if one could change one's nature with time and circumstance, fortune would never change" (p. 93). Buried deep within Machiavelli's coldly realistic book is the myth of Proteus.[27] The man who could alter not just his mode of action but his entire nature as the situation required would transcend mutability; indeed he would transcend his state of man and become a god. For all Machiavelli's tough worldliness and cynicism, the core of his vision strongly recalls Vives' *Fable about Man*, where the gods hail man the actor as "multiform Proteus, the son of the Ocean," and raise him to divine status. Despite its profound pessimism, *The Prince* is rooted as deeply as *The Courtier* in the humanist vision of man freed from any single, fixed nature and able to assume any role. Of course, Machiavelli denies the possibility of so complete a flexibility and demonstrates the way men are inevitably trapped in their selves, often as a result of the very success of an earlier adaptation. Nevertheless he persists heroically in his vision, knowing full well that it is ultimately doomed to failure, and presents in *The Prince* a model of the protean self to which a prince can at least aspire if not attain.

As Castiglione conceived the courtier's self as artificially constructed by means of imitation and the astute manipulation of appearances, so too Machiavelli's prince must deliberately fashion his own identity, masking his personal inclinations and character traits where necessary, imitating carefully chosen historical models, pretending to qualities and values he does not possess. Like the courtier, the prince moves in a world of appearances, surfaces, "salutary deceptions," where it is more important to seem than to be. But Machiavelli goes far beyond Castiglione in reducing all traditional values to the status of mere means by which a role may be successfully played. Mercy and ruthlessness, generosity and avarice, fidelity and treachery have no value in themselves and become positively dangerous if the prince commits himself, regardless of the circumstances, to any one of them. The moment that flexibility is lost, the prince himself is lost. The verb *usare* and its derivatives echo and re-echo throughout *The Prince*, along with words like *parere, colorire, farsi, fondarsi, volgersi*. They advance the conception of the perfect prince as the maker of himself, a being of astonishing flexibility because he lacks a fixed nature or a commitment to anything. Ideally, he is the man without any assured quality but that of wariness.

The prince, like the courtier, is all surface; he is the actor completely fused with his role, and that role is whatever assures his success at the moment. Machiavelli does not and cannot offer a picture of the "real" self beneath the artificial and manipulated one. Beneath the mask there is nothing but a chaos of infinite desire. This is made terribly clear, not in *The Prince,* where it suffices to say that men are *tristi* ("wretches"), but in the *Discourses:*

> [W]hen men are no longer obliged to fight from necessity, they fight from ambition, which passion is so powerful in the hearts of men that it never leaves them, no matter to what height they may rise. The reason of this is that nature has created men so that they desire everything, but are unable to attain it; desire being thus always greater than the faculty of acquiring, discontent with what they have and dissatisfaction with themselves result from it. [p. 208]

Man's exhilarating freedom trumpeted by Pico has in Machiavelli become a nightmare of unlimited, insatiable desire.

In the *Oration on the Dignity of Man* freedom is not disquieting because there is a clear hierarchy of existence, a chain of being extending from vegetable and beast to God. Though man no longer has a fixed place in the universe, his life has meaning and value in relation to his place on the grand scale. But, as Thomas Greene has observed, for Machiavelli, man's movement on this chain of being "is very limited, and such as it is, leads downward to the brute rather than upward to the angel." [28] One must qualify, however, Greene's conclusion that *The Prince* lacks "a belief in fashioning and in metaphysical freedom." For Machiavelli, man is free insofar as he is able to adapt himself to changing circumstances, and he can adapt insofar as he can fashion his identity. The entire book is devoted to an exposition of the "methods and rules" (p. 56) which govern self-fashioning. If he is pessimistic about the ultimate success of the prince, he nonetheless writes his book so that "our free will may not be altogether extinguished" (p. 91). For both Castiglione and Machiavelli, the natural man must be superseded by the artificial, but for Castiglione the fashioning of the self is an escape from freedom, while for Machiavelli it is the only way to preserve a vestige of freedom in the face of fortune.

Ralegh knew Pico's *Oration* and the works of Machiavelli extremely well and most likely had read Vives' *Fable* and Castiglione's *Courtier,* but this knowledge is not essential to the kind of relation which I wish to suggest between Ralegh and these writers. His life did not neatly illustrate their ideas but reflected and expressed the forces that brought their works into being. Through this quality of reflection, his career takes on a special, almost paradigmatic significance, for it points beyond itself to issues of greater scope and magnitude than a single life can encompass. Ralegh's behavior in his last hours, for example, presents a remarkable spectacle of cool heroism, but it would remain only an interesting historical anecdote were it not for the deep resonances that it sounds, resonances brought out by a reading of works like *The Courtier* and *The Prince.* His response to the pressure of his impending execution as a

traitor was the careful and deliberate creation of a dramatic
role for himself. In so doing, he asserted a fundamental
human dignity and strength in the face of annihilation. While
there was still hope for his life, Ralegh was willing to submit
to humiliation—pleading, feigned illness, attempted escapes
—but once his fate became perfectly clear, he adjusted to circumstances in such a way as to make them the setting for a
triumphant self-justification. The key to this adjustment was
the interaction of art and life, the fashioning of the self as a
work of art.

The epitaph upon himself, the witty remarks on his own
doom, the speech on the scaffold, with its clever distortions
and its resounding phrases repeated for the benefit of the audience, the self-conscious display of indifference to death, the
command to the executioner, all bespeak the self-control, the
brilliant manipulation of appearances advocated by both Castiglione and Machiavelli. Ralegh's use of the last stanza of
"Nature that washt her hands in milke" and of the line from
The History of the World to convey the impression of a splendid presence of mind and detachment in the face of death is a
kind of *sprezzatura,* art which conceals art. As with Castiglione's courtier, *sprezzatura* masks the pressures and con-
straints under which the individual labors, transforming all
thoughts and anxieties into a perfectly articulated, flawless
role.

There were some who felt that Ralegh's performance, artful,
polished, and yet seemingly so natural, masked not only anxiety and the dread of death, but also treachery and guilt. So
thought Sir Lewis Stukeley, who guarded him on the journey
from Plymouth to London and who informed the king of Ralegh's plans for escape to France. Stukeley had a special reason
for his view of the matter: in his speech on the scaffold, Ralegh had rather sourly forgiven his "Kinsman and Keeper"
while in the same breath warning the world of his treacherous
nature. After the execution, Stukeley was branded with the
name of Sir Judas and treated as a pariah. He attempted to
clear his name in a short pamphlet addressed to King James,

in which he gave his interpretation of Ralegh's behavior on the scaffold:

[A]n Angel of darkenesse, did put on him the shape of an Angel of light at his departure, to performe two Parts most cunningly; First, to poison the hearts of discontented people; Secondly, to blemish me in my good name, a poore instrument of the just desires of the State, with false imputations. . . . All men have long knowen, that this mans whole life was a meere sophistication, and such was his death, in which he borrowed some tincture of holinesse, which he was thought not to love in his life, therewith to cover his hatred of others in his death.[29]

Beyond his personal resentment, Stukeley's remarks indicate that, like Dr. Tounson and other "poor instruments" of the Crown, he resented Ralegh's profession of innocence and refusal to speak the customary phrases of repentance. Any display of dignity was, as Tounson put it, "an oblique taxing of the state." Moreover, there is in Stukeley's accusation that Ralegh's "whole life was a meere sophistication" an echo of the age-old fear of the actor as by nature a dangerous hypocrite, a liar who violates his God-given identity.[30]

All the accounts of Ralegh's last hours suggest, however, that behind his performance were motives other than slander and sedition. His seventeenth-century editor, Humphrey Moseley, gets closer to the spirit of the final scenes in his introductory note to a group of Ralegh's essays:

It cannot be accounted either arrogancy or ostentation in *Augustus Caesar* who dying, desired of his friends that stood about his Bed, That when he expired they would give him a *Plaudite,* as if he were conscient to himselfe he had plaid his part well upon the Stage. Nor will it offend any I am sure to say, That this most worthy *Heroe* truly deserved the *Plaudites* and *Encomiums* of the *Amphitheaters* of the whole Universe.[31]

Ralegh wished to create out of the final ruins of his career an image of man at his most heroic, self-possessed, and independent. The self is fashioned as a work of art not to serve as a mask for something else but to stand on its own and affirm

its integrity and wholeness. For Castiglione, the art of the self
is intended to serve the moral improvement of the ruler, but
Ralegh has moved toward Machiavelli. Ralegh's performance,
using the scaffold as a stage for self-justification rather than for
confession or repentance, was a heroic assertion of *virtù*
against the power of *fortuna*.

For Ralegh, as for Machiavelli, *virtù* was associated with
man's flexibility, with his capacity to adapt himself to the circumstances generated by fortune, with his ability, in short, to
fashion himself. Both recognized that the ultimate weapon of
fortuna was death.[32] Ralegh not only faced imminent death,
but he stood as one whom the courts had ruled "civilly dead"
for the past fifteen years. To have had any self-control at such
a moment was an achievement, but to have performed as he
did was the supreme triumph of *virtù*. If the end was inevitable, he at least made that end seem an expression of his own
will. If this sounds like a romantic version of his death, it is
because Ralegh, and not his romantic biographers, fashioned
it that way.

Behind Ralegh's dramatic sense of life, I have suggested,
were two contradictory traditions, one that likened life to a
play to express the emptiness and unreality of man's earthbound existence, the other that saw in playing an image of
man's power to fashion the self. A major source of the fascination and complexity of Ralegh's career is that neither of these
deeply antagonistic views of human nature and destiny could
gain a decisive ascendancy; indeed, they needed and fed upon
one another. At one moment Ralegh writes of the vanity of
mortal endeavors in this stage-play world, at the next he is
sailing to Guiana to discover El Dorado and found an empire;
at one moment he likens man to a player to suggest the hollowness of human existence, at the next he deliberately plays a
part to affirm human dignity. And in several extraordinary instances during his long career—in *Ocean to Cynthia,* in *The
History of the World,* and in the final scenes of his life—both
traditions seem inseparably bound up in the same words and
actions.

To understand the complex relation between these two traditions and, still more, to grasp their simultaneous expression,
we must consider another manifestation of the dramatic sense
of life in late sixteenth- and early seventeeth-century England,
the theater itself. Elizabethan public theaters like the Globe
were, by a symbolism inherent in their very structure, models
of the world. As scholars have observed, they represented em-
blematically the hierarchical order of the universe, as conceived by late-medieval thought.[33] Still more significant, I suggest, is their *ambivalence* as emblems. They may imply that
life is no more real than a play, that "the great globe itself"
will dissolve like their own wood and plaster and leave not a
rack behind. But they may also point to the immense, godlike
power of human creativity which can range through all the elements and fashion wonderful images of the universe. For certain optimistic humanists, the capacity to create a mirror of
nature, a model of the world, is almost equivalent to the Creation itself. Thus Marsilio Ficino shows boundless admiration
for the model-making power displayed in Archimedes' spheres
of brass:

Since man has observed the order of the heavens, when they move,
whither they proceed and with what measures, and what they produce, who could deny that man possesses as it were almost the same
genius as the Author of the heavens? And who could deny that man
could somehow also make the heavens, could he only obtain the
instruments and the heavenly material, since even now he makes
them, though of a different material, but still with a very similar
order? [34]

Ficino relates this creative genius in man to his power of self-
transformation. Like Pico and Vives, whom he strongly influenced, he celebrates the soul as a kind of supreme actor capa-
ble of playing all parts: "Does not the soul try to become
everything just as God is everything?"

The implied connection between such models—emblems of
man's power to understand and control his world—and the
theater was often made explicit in the Renaissance. According
to Thomas Heywood, for example, in the "little compass" of

Caesar's theater "were comprehended the perfect modell of the firmament, the whole frame of the heavens, with all grounds of Astronomicall conjecture." [35] Likewise, an imaginary stage described in the "English Wagner Book" of 1594 manages to squeeze within its limits practically the whole universe: the firmament above, "often spotted with golden teares which men callen Stars," "the whole Imperiall Army of the faire heavenly inhabitaunts," the king's high throne, a splendid castle, a battlefield, even a hell-mouth.[36]

The theater then is a vivid and powerful model of heaven, earth, and hell, including all the creatures who inhabit these regions, a model more admirable and complex even than Archimedes' spheres. It may retain its ageold suggestions of human emptiness, it may represent a static, closed world-order, but at the same time it may be both symbol and proof of those qualities which make man "a great miracle, a living creature worthy of reverence and adoration." [37]

The dramatists of the age—and, as we might expect, Shakespeare above all—made full use of the ambivalence of the theater and of the dramatic sense of life. In Hamlet's famous description of his melancholy state, for example, the play metaphor evokes precisely those contradictory poles of belief which we have seen at work in Ralegh:

I have of late—but wherefore I know not—lost all my mirth, forgone all custom of exercises; and indeed, it goes so heavily with my disposition that this goodly frame, the earth, seems to me a sterile promontory; this most excellent canopy, the air, look you, this brave o'er hanging firmament, this majestical roof fretted with golden fire—why, it appeareth no other thing to me than a foul and pestilent congregation of vapors. What a piece of work is a m: n! how noble in reason! how infinite in faculties! in form and m)ving how express and admirable! in action how like an angel! in apprehension how like a god! the beauty of the world, the paragon of animals! And yet to me what is this quintessence of dust? [ii, ii, 307–22]

The terms Hamlet uses for the world are also technical terms for the various parts of the theater.[38] "Goodly frame," "most excellent canopy," "majestical roof"—the theater is the symbol for all that is splendid and reassuring in the universe, just as the power of acting helps to define the greatness of man. But at the same time the theater darkly suggests the illusory quality of life, the element of artifice and feigning, the final insubstantiality of an existence which ends in dust.

We get even closer to Ralegh's special kind of theatricalism in *Othello,* so close indeed that it is worth pausing to examine the way the idea of man as actor is explored in the play. Iago is the epitome of the actor as hypocrite and dissembler. As he tells Roderigo, he is one of those

> Who, trimm'd in forms and visages of duty,
> Keep yet their hearts attending on themselves;
> And, throwing but shows of service on their lords,
> Do well thrive by them, and when they have lin'd
>   their coats,
> Do themselves homage. . . .
> . . . .
> Heaven is my judge, not I for love and duty,
> But seeming so, for my peculiar end;
> For when my outward action doth demonstrate
> The native act and figure of my heart
> In compliment extern, 'tis not long after
> But I will wear my heart upon my sleeve
> For daws to peck at. I am not what I am.
>   [i, i, 50–54, 59–65]

"Forms," "visages," "shows," "seeming," "outward," "extern" —this is the language of the man who has adopted a role in order to hide his true identity. But in Iago's final phrase Shakespeare contrives to suggest a disturbing meaning that somehow goes beyond the contrast of role and reality. We expect Iago to say "I am not what I seem," asserting at least a hidden identity, but his actual words imply a sinister and terrifying emptiness, an absence of being that is outside the pale of human logic and experience. They are a cosmic negation, a mockery of God's words to Moses at the burning bush: "I AM THAT I AM" (Exodus 3 : 14).

"Acting" in the Iago sense leads to a terrible, almost un-
thinkable annihilation of being. Each time Iago lowers his
voice to speak in soliloquy or in confidence to Roderigo, we
expect the mask to be stripped away for a moment and the
true face, however hideous, to show forth. But always we are
disappointed. One mask is removed to reveal what is patently
only another mask beneath it. At the end, when the deception
has been exposed and the role can no longer be played, Iago
ceases to have any human identity at all—he becomes a creature without words, voluntarily abjuring that which distin-
guishes man from beasts:

> Demand me nothing. What you know, you know.
> From this time forth I never will speak word.
>
> [v, ii, 303–04]

Set against Iago, of course, is Desdemona, who is, by total
contrast, all being, the embodiment of pure love and beauty.
There is in Desdemona no hint of the theatrical, of self-dramatization. Instead, she is characterized by a wonderful, simple
frankness:

> That I did love the Moor to live with him,
> My downright violence, and storm of fortunes,
> May trumpet to the world.
>
> [I, iii, 249–51]

This simplicity is not only an assertion of all that Iago seeks
to negate, but, in its absence of theatricality, a contrast to
Othello's romantic self-dramatization:

> *Othello.* It gives me wonder great as my content
>   To see you here before me. O my soul's joy!
>   If after every tempest come such calms,
>   May the winds blow till they have waken'd death!
>   And let the labouring bark climb hills of seas
>   Olympus-high, and duck again as low
>   As hell's from heaven! If it were now to die,
>   'Twere now to be most happy; for I fear
>   My soul hath her content so absolute

> That not another comfort like to this
> Succeeds in unknown fate.

> *Desdemona.*   The heavens forbid
> But that our loves and comforts should increase
> Even as our days do grow!

> [ii, i, 185–97]

Othello stands between Iago and Desdemona; he is neither a hypocrite nor a man of radical simplicity, but an actor in the more complex and subtle sense of which we have spoken. He is an alien who, by his valor and energy, has carved out a role in a hostile world, and he has a powerful sense of the identity he has fashioned. His is by no means the self-consciousness of a Hamlet—of all Shakespeare's tragic heroes, Othello is the least aware of the complexities of his own character—but rather a feeling for his role and a mastery of self-manifestation. Almost his first words recall his services to the Signiory which have earned for him his place in Venice. When Iago counsels him to hide from Desdemona's angry father, Othello replies with a full and serene awareness of himself and the part he must play:

> Not I. I must be found.
> My parts, my title, and my perfect soul
> Shall manifest me rightly.

> [i, ii, 30–32]

The sense of role becomes even clearer when Othello grandly prevents a fight between his followers and those of Brabantio:

> Were it my cue to fight, I should have known it
> Without a prompter.

> [i, ii, 83–84]

And we hear the Othello voice, rich with a sense of its own dignity, in his acceptance of the commission to fight the Turks:

> The tyrant Custom, most grave senators,
> Hath made the flinty and steel couch of war
> My thrice-driven bed of down. I do agnize

A natural and prompt alacrity
I find in hardness; and do undertake
These present wars against the Ottomites.

[I, iii, 230–35]

Here is that phenomenon we have had occasion to note in
Ralegh: the full commitment of the self to a role which is yet
recognizable as a role.

But Iago does not believe in this kind of "acting" any more
than he credits or understands Desdemona's pure being. For
him Othello is only an "erring barbarian" with a thin veneer
of civilization, and Desdemona is a "supersubtle Venetian."
He sets out to destroy Othello's role, his identity, by convincing him that Desdemona is a dissembler, just such a hypocriti-
cal actor as Iago is in reality. Othello's identity cannot sustain
the blow. Stripped of the role to which he was so utterly committed, he disintegrates into a chaos of mad passions. It is
only when Desdemona lies dead and Iago's plots have been exposed, when Othello has been made to realize what he has
done and to acknowledge the horror and the folly of it, that
the role can be reestablished, and then only in the moment of
self-destruction:

I have done the state some service, and they know't.

[v, ii, 339]

These words recall Othello's opening lines:

Let him do his spite.
My services which I have done the signiory
Shall outtongue his complaints.

[I, ii, 17–19]

But, of course, everything has changed. He can recover his heroic identity, the greatness of heart by which he had forged a
place for himself in Venice, only by the single grand, histrionic act left to him: he kills himself as he had once killed the
hated Turk.

As in *Othello,* so in many of his plays Shakespeare explores
what happens when a man's identity, fashioned by himself or

by society, or most commonly by both together, is stripped away, discarded, or rendered useless. He was fascinated, it appears, by characters—Richard II, Brutus, Lear, Coriolanus, Othello, Timon—who seem to have a deep sense of self as role-player and who, consequently, suffer most terribly when these roles—king, noble Roman, hero, patron—are shattered. The pressures that led Castiglione and Machiavelli to create the ideal courtier and the perfect prince as models of the artificial self are profoundly felt in Shakespeare's plays. But where the former sought in their works to teach men to relieve those pressures by fashioning the self as a work of art, Shakespeare constantly looks face to face at unaccommodated man, stripped of all his roles.

If man's greatness and dignity are deeply allied to his power to commit himself to a role and thereby transform his own nature, the villainy of Iago, the dissembler, the man totally without commitment, is the ultimate villainy. As they were intrigued by those who were wedded to their roles, Shakespeare and his contemporaries were also fascinated, frightened, and repelled by the cold players, the clever manipulators of the self as mask and the world as stage prop. In their fundamental hollowness, in the disintegration and annihilation of the self which inevitably results from their hypocrisy, these characters are the negation of the optimistic vision of man as actor. Iago's terrible refusal to speak, Richard III's nightmare vision of his murderous self-hatred, the Jew of Malta's inability to free himself from the habit of dissembling and treachery even when he has triumphed over all his enemies, Flamineo's death "in a mist"—these are images of human emptiness which reflect the darkest aspect of the dramatic sense of life.

At work in the Elizabethan and Jacobean theater was the same dialectic that manifested itself so powerfully in Ralegh's life and writings. Indeed, the theater of the age, like *The Courtier* and *The Prince*, most probably contributed indirectly to the development of his dramatic sensibility. But there was a more direct contemporary source. At the very heart of

Ralegh's society, at the symbolic center of England and quite literally at the center of power and glory, there was a figure who perfectly embodied the idea of the individual as an actor totally and irreversibly committed to a role: Elizabeth I. The English court was truly, in Ralegh's phrase, "the great theater," with the queen as playwright, director, and leading performer. Both by temperament and intellect she understood, as no one before or since, the latent drama in kingship and exploited it to the fullest. "We princes," she told a deputation of Lords and Commons in 1586, "are set on stages in the sight and view of all the world duly observed." [39]

The queen's power was linked in a quite technical sense with the assumption of a fictional role: her reign witnessed the first major elaboration of the mystical legal fiction of "the King's Two Bodies." When she ascended the throne, according to the crown lawyers, her very being was altered; in her mortal "Body natural" was incarnated the immortal and infallible "Body politic." Her body of flesh would age and die, but the body politic, as Plowden wrote, "is not subject to Passions as the other is, nor to Death, for as to this Body the King never dies." Her visible being was a hieroglyphic of the timeless corporate being with its absolute perfection, just as, in Coke's phrase, "a king's crown was a hieroglyphic of the laws." [40] She was a living emblem of the immutable within Time, a fiction of permanence.

Even without this elaborate doctrine, of course, kingship always involves fictions, theatricalism, and even mystification. The notion of "the King's Two Bodies" may, however, have heightened Elizabeth's conscious sense of her identity as at least in part a *persona ficta* and of her world as a theater. She believed deeply—virtually to the point of religious conviction [41]—in display, ceremony, and decorum, the whole theatrical apparatus of royal power. Her gorgeous clothes, the complex code of manners and the calculated descents into familiarity, the poetic tributes she received and the poetry she herself wrote, the portaits and medals she allowed to circulate like religious icons or the images of the Roman emperors, the nicknames she imposed upon her courtiers—all were pro-

foundly theatrical and all contributed to the fashioning of
what was perhaps the single greatest dramatic creation of the
period: the queen herself.

This was the fashioning of the self as a work of art on the
grandest scale, and, as Machiavelli understood, the primary reward was quite simply survival. For, when she assumed the
throne in 1558, Elizabeth's position was by no means secure.
Not only was her title in itself subject to question, but her sex
was a profound hindrance, especially because England had
just undergone an exceedingly unhappy period of female rule.
With consummate skill she managed to turn this dangerous
obstacle into a triumphant advantage—and one key to her
success was the brilliant employment of all that was most "artificial" in kingship.

In the official progresses and pageants, everything was calculated to enhance her metamorphosis into an almost magical
being, a creature of infinite beauty, wisdom, and power.[42] But
even her ordinary public appearances could be wonderfully
impressive. Bishop Goodman recalled in later years having
seen the queen emerge from council on a December evening
in 1588:

This wrought such an impression upon us, *for shows and pageants are ever best seen by torchlight*, that all the way long we did
nothing but talk of what an admirable queen she was, and how we
would adventure our lives to do her service.[43]

Goodman was anything but a cynic; yet, in recollection at
least, he could see the royal appearance as a performance calculated to arouse precisely the emotions that he felt. And a
performance it was. The queen's words to the crowd on that
occasion—"You may well have a greater prince, but you shall
never have a more loving prince"—were repeated with variations throughout her reign. They were part of a stock of such
phrases upon which she was able to draw when need arose.
Her famous "Golden Speech" of 1601 was little more than a
particularly felicitous combination of these refrains—there is
scarcely a phrase in it that she had not used again and again.

The whole public character was formed very early, then

played and replayed with few changes for the next forty years.
Already in her formal procession through the City on the day
before her coronation, the keynotes were sounded. "If a man
should say well," wrote one observer, "he could not better
tearme the citie of London that time, than a stage wherein
was shewed the wonderfull spectacle, of a noble hearted princesse toward her most loving people, & the peoples exceding
comfort in beholding so worthy a soveraign." Where her sister
Mary had been silent and aloof at her accession, Elizabeth be-
stowed her gratitude and affection on all. "I wil be as good
unto you," she assured her well-wishers, "as ever quene was to
her people. . . . And perswade your selves, that for the safetie
and quietnes of you all, I will not spare, if nede be to spend
my blood." [44]

Mutual love and royal self-sacrifice—in her first address to
Parliament some weeks later, she reiterated these themes and
added a third, perhaps the most important of all: "And in the
end, this shall be for me sufficient, that a marble stone shall
declare that a Queen, having reigned such a time, lived and
died a virgin" (Neale, 1 : 49). The secular cult of the virgin
was born, and it was not long before the young Elizabeth was
portraying herself, and being portrayed, as a Virgin Mother.
"And so I assure you all," she told Commons in 1563, "that,
though after my death you may have many stepdames, yet
shall you never have a more naturall mother than I mean to
be unto you all" (Neale, 1 : 109). In poetry, the cult of the English Virgin was still more intense and explicit:

> When others sing *Venite exultemus!*
> Stand by, and turn to *Noli emulari!*
> For *Quare fremuerunt,* use *Oremus!*
> *Vivat ELIZA!* for an *Ave MARI!*
> And teach those Swains that live about thy cell,
> To sing Amen, when thou dost pray so well! [45]

Through the years, courtiers, poets, ballad-makers, and artists,
provided many other cult images: in Ralegh's partial list,
"Cynthia, Phoebe, Flora,/Diana and Aurora," to which we

may add Astraea, Zabeta, Deborah, Laura, Oriana, and, of course, Gloriana.[46]

The artificial world which had this supreme actress at its center was Ralegh's world during his years of happiness, fortune, and influence. The self-dramatizing that was the essence of the court deeply influenced his life, coloring not only his relations with the queen but his entire personality. His theatricalism in the crucial scenes of his life, his sense of himself as an actor in a living theater, his capacity truly to believe in the role he played though it was in many of its elements an evident fabrication, his self-manifestation in poetry and prose are all profoundly related to the example and effect of the remarkable woman on the throne of England.

Ralegh must have been deeply sensitive and responsive, in a way surpassing mere calculation, to the personality of the queen. For from the autumn of 1582 when he came to the court until his crisis and imprisonment (arising from the queen's discovery of his secret marriage) in the summer of 1592, he held on to the slippery position of favorite in a dangerous, envious, and constantly shifting court. Essex had the backing of his powerful and distinguished family as well as a body of supporters who came more and more to resemble a constituency or even a kingdom within the kingdom. But while Ralegh's vigorous West-country kinsmen helped him get an introduction to the court, he was alone for most of his career. There were temporary alliances—the most notable with Robert Cecil who later contrived to turn King James against him—but no true friends in high places, and, far from having any popular support, he was described (in May 1587) as "the best hated man of the world, in Court, city, and country." [47] It is difficult to fix precisely the source of this hatred—his descent from gentry and not nobility, the extremely profitable monopolies he received at the queen's hand, the simple fact of the queen's favor. Perhaps the best explanation is Aubrey's: "he was damnably proud." [48] Ralegh's extraordinary haughtiness is noted by a wide range of contemporary commentators, from the nameless political correspondent of Lord Burghley—

his pride is intolerable, without regard for any, as the world knows

to Ralegh's virulent enemy, Lord Henry Howard—

Rawlie, that in pride exceedeth all men alive. . . . the greatest Lucifer that hath lived in our age

to Ralegh's uneasy ally, the Earl of Northumberland—

I know him insolent, extremely heated, a man that desires to seem to be able to sway all men's courses

to the balladmaker—

> Ralegh doth time bestride:
> He sits 'twixt wind and tide:
> Yet uphill he cannot ride,
> For all his bloody pride.[49]

The very qualities which won for him his place as a royal favorite—his "brilliance," his desire to master others, the gorgeous clothes he wore, his forwardness, in short, his life-style —inspired passionate resentment, fear, and hatred both in the court and in the world at large. And though Elizabeth herself was fascinated and attracted by him and made him Captain of the Guard so that he would be near her at all times, she too appears to have thought him in some way dangerous or unstable. Of her favorites over the years, only Ralegh was never appointed to the Privy Council. Apart from the tragic folly of her infatuation for Essex, the queen preferred more stable and prosaic men for her councillors.

Without a power-base of any kind, then, Ralegh was totally dependent upon the queen. All his powers of intellect and imagination, all his immense energies—and he could, we are assured by Robert Cecil, "toil terribly" [50]—were focused upon this relationship. Spenser's portrayal of the intense, almost hysterical anguish of Timias when he is abandoned in anger by Belphoebe need not be a poetic exaggeration—the queen's favor was everything to Ralegh. More than anyone of stature in the court, Ralegh was committed in his whole being to that strange, artificial, dangerous, and dreamlike world presided over by Gloriana, the world of adulation so intense that it still has power to shock us.[51]

3 Ralegh's Court Poetry

My soul the stage of fancy's tragedy

Most of Ralegh's poems were intimately linked with his place in the court and, in particular, with his "fantastic courtship" of the queen.[1] As it was considered slightly improper for a gentleman to appear in print, he chose to publish very little.[2] Quite apart from the social stigma, the general public was an undesirable audience, for things that could be safely said in the poems of a favorite to the queen were liable to be grossly misunderstood by readers unfamiliar with the language of the court. Consequently, though his reputation as a poet was widespread, Ralegh's verses circulated in manuscript and were probably known firsthand by only a select few. Yet it is misleading to conclude, as Agnes Latham does, that Ralegh's poetry "was no part of his public character, but something essentially intimate and private."[3] Public and private are perplexing terms here, for Ralegh's relationship with the queen, the subject and occasion for most of his poems, was his chief occupation and career for many years. This career was a constant, demanding theatrical performance, the kind of performance we do not usually associate with the "intimate and private." Like his letters, Ralegh's poetry displays the power of self-dramatization, not a rich and complex inner life. The poetry was both an outgrowth of that power and an important means of creating the finished product: the marvelous image he presented to the court and especially to the queen. Of course, his poems may have had private echoes and hidden meanings—as we have already seen in the epitaph "Even such is tyme"—but such meanings were always embedded in public utterances. His poems then cannot be read as confessions, moments when the favorite put down his mask and spoke out in his own true voice. It is unlikely that there was such a "true voice," for, like the queen, Ralegh was an actor who was thoroughly committed to the role he had fashioned for himself.

In the elaborate and subtle performance that Ralegh and the queen played together, poetry had an important function from the start. Thomas Fuller, who was the first to relate in print the famous story about the cloak laid in the mud for the queen to walk on, adds that Captain Ralegh later inscribed on a window which Elizabeth was sure to pass:

> Fain would I climb, yet fear I to fall;

under which Elizabeth wrote:

> If thy heart fails thee, climb not at all.[4]

Whether or not these stories are in themselves true, they undoubtedly reflect two means of Ralegh's swift rise to favor: the perfect theatrical gesture and the display of courtly wit in poetry.

The kind of poetic dialogue Fuller describes always sounded a bit far-fetched until the recent discovery of an authentic poetic exchange between Ralegh and the queen.[5] Ralegh mourns the loss of his mistress' love in the grand language of poetic despair: he is dead to all joys, he only lives to woe, he searches the heaven and the earth for his lost love. There is something vast and heroic in his sorrow. His love has not simply left him for another; she has been conquered by Fortune, the blind goddess who rules on earth and has no regard for man's virtue. But Ralegh himself is defiantly superior to that great power: "though fortune conquer thee;/no fortune base nor frayle shall alter mee." To this the queen replies: "Ah silly pugge wert thou so sore afraid,/mourne not (my Wat) nor be thou so dismaid." The drop in tone is sharp and immediate. From heroic love and despair, we descend to reassuring but demeaning pleasantries; from the address to "my soules heaven above . . . my worldes joy," we shift to the easy, almost proprietary familiarity of "silly pugge . . . my Wat." The queen assures Ralegh of her good will and encourages him to be confident, but her poem is, on the whole, rather careful and restrained. The central concern is less her regard for Ralegh than her own mastery of Fortune: "never thinke fortune can beare the sway,/if vertue watche & will her not obay." The queen can and must be sovereign over all things, even Fortune. As for Ralegh's protestations of despair, the queen treats them with a light, gentle mockery:

> Dead to all joyes & living unto woe,
> Slaine quite by her that nere gave wiseman blowe
> Revive again & live without all drede.

Elizabeth manages both to play the game of poetic love and to remain aloof from it, to indulge herself without commitment and to participate without danger. Ralegh, however, must assert his total involvement.

In *The Queen and the Poet,* Walter Oakeshott attempts to link each of Ralegh's poems to a particular moment in his career at court. Oakeshott argues that the poems "were written for special occasions, the occasion most often being to please, or pacify, the Queen," [6] and he succeeds in exploding the notion that poetry for Ralegh was merely a pleasant pastime. Unfortunately, both the chronology of the poetry and the history of Ralegh's relationship with the queen are riddled with uncertainties. Moreover, even if the poems could be dated with perfect accuracy and linked precisely with the vicissitudes of Ralegh's career as favorite, a great part of their significance would lie beyond their immediate utility on a particular occasion. For though each poem may have been written to serve the needs of his career, the mark of Ralegh's best poetry is its transcendence of the local and immediate, its capacity to fuse intense personal feeling with a larger vision, its power to transform the self.

Ralegh's self-fashioning is paradoxical: it bends art to the service of life—advancing his career, justifying his actions, enhancing his reputation—and it transforms life into art, leading ever further from the career toward symbolic characterization and transcendent meaning. It exists in time and in spite of time; it addresses a specific historical audience and yet turns inward, cryptically mirroring the self; it reflects the world and

creates its own world. Ralegh's career generated constant pressure to create images of the self, but, conversely, there were
moments when his whole experience of life seemed caught up
in symbolic meanings that had their own generative power.[7]
Thus Ralegh's polished performance at his execution was intended at once to create a heroic image of himself, countering
the charges against him, and to transform the local and particular crisis in his life into the universal struggle of the individual against Time and Death. Similarly, he contrived, largely
through his poetry to the queen, both to fashion a self-enhanc-
ing courtly identity and to transform his troubled personal relations with Elizabeth into a powerful symbolic nexus of love,
time, and mortality.

Consideration of Ralegh's court poetry in recent years has
been dominated by the suggestion that Ralegh was the author
of a vast lost poem portraying himself as the Shepherd of the
Ocean and the queen as Cynthia. This notion was engendered
chiefly by the discovery in the last century of a manuscript in
Ralegh's own hand, preserved in the Cecil archives at Hatfield
House, containing what appear by their titles to be fragments
of a far larger poem: "The 21th: and last booke of the Ocean
to Scinthia" and "The end of the 22 Boock, entreatinge of
Sorrow." [8] The latter breaks off in mid-phrase after some
twenty lines, but the former—though it too shows signs of
incompleteness—is a substantial work over 500 lines long.

Further evidence that Ralegh had planned and at least partially written a great poem to the queen has been seen in
Spenser's tributes to the poetry of his friend and patron.[9] The
two had met in Ireland during the summer of 1589 when Ralegh had left the court in some slight disfavor. Spenser recalls
this meeting in *Colin Clouts Come Home Againe,* describing
a visit from the "Shepheard of the Ocean" whose song

> was all a lamentable lay,
> Of great unkindnesse, and of usage hard,
> Of *Cynthia,* the Ladie of the Sea,
> Which from her presence faultlesse him debard.

> And ever and anon with singulf [s] rife,
> He cryed out, to make his undersong
> Ah my loves queene, and goddesse of my life,
> Who shall me pittie, when thou doest me wrong?
>   [164–71] [10]

It is unlikely that this lament was identical with the poems to
Cynthia in the Hatfield House manuscript, which have no
"undersong" and which probably date from the much more serious disgrace in 1592.[11] But perhaps Spenser heard earlier
portions of the *Ocean to Cynthia* which were subsequently lost
or destroyed. It would be to these too that he refers in *The
Faerie Queene,* praising

> that sweet verse, with Nectar sprinckeled,
> In which a gracious servaunt pictured
> His *Cynthia,* his heavens fairest light.
>
>   [*F. Q.,* iii, Proem, iv]

Likewise, in a dedicatory sonnet to Ralegh, Spenser compares
his own "unsavory" verses to "the streames, that like a golden
showre/Flow from thy fruitfull head, of thy loves praise":

> Yet till that thou thy Poeme wilt make knowne
> Let thy faire Cinthias praises bee thus rudely
>   showne.

Finally, in the famous letter to Ralegh in which he expounds
"his whole intention" in *The Faerie Queene,* Spenser points to
a specific parallel between his great epic and Ralegh's "excellent conceipt":

In that Faery Queene I mean glory in my generall intention, but in
my particular I conceive the most excellent and glorious person of
our soveraine the Queene, and her kingdome in Faery land. And
yet in some places els, I doe otherwise shadow her. For considering
she beareth two persons, the one of a most royall Queene or Empresse, the other of a most vertuous and beautifull Lady, this latter
part in some places I doe expresse in Belphoebe, fashioning her
name according to your owne excellent conceipt of Cynthia,
(Phoebe and Cynthia being both names of Diana).

As if to confirm this parallel, Ralegh twice refers to "Belphoebe" in the 21st Book of *Ocean to Cynthia:*

> Bellphebes course is now observde no more,
> That faire resemblance weareth out of date.

[271–72]

> A Queen shee was to mee, no more Belphebe,
> A Lion then, no more a milke white Dove.

[327–28]

The conceit of Belpheobe, like a once powerful metaphor that
has become a cliché, "weareth out of date." Elizabeth has
changed from mistress to sovereign, breaking the bonds of
love.

It is tempting then to credit Ralegh with a lost poetic masterpiece, like the fabled "second volume" of *The History of
the World* which his seventeenth-century admirers imagined
he had thrown into the fire in despair. But that great poem
may well be as chimerical as the completion of the *History.*
Regarded soberly, Spenser's praises are little more than expressions of gratitude to the powerful patron who had introduced
him to the court and helped to incline the queen in favor of
his poem with two commendatory sonnets. They flatteringly
hint at more, but Spenser's tributes actually tell us only that
Ralegh addressed the queen as Cynthia in some of his poems
and that these poems involved both praise and complaint.

As for those tantalizing fragments, the 21st and 22nd Books
of the *Ocean to Cynthia,* the 21st Book is 522 lines long—this
would suggest, assuming books of equal length, a complete
poem of almost 12,000 lines! It is difficult to imagine Ralegh
even having the time to write so much, let alone the inclina-
tion or inventiveness. Ralegh may simply have used the grandiose titles to create the aura of an immensely long poem, suggesting to the queen—and to himself, perhaps—an almost
boundless suffering immortalized in verse.[12] He need not have
had the slightest intention of continuing the poem, for what
really mattered was the vague impression of epic scope and
grandeur. This picture of Ralegh, the illusionist, accords with

the Ralegh we have seen in his letters and at his execution—
the self-dramatizer, the manipulator of appearances.

While the possibility of a lost great work cannot be ruled
out entirely, and while there were almost certainly some small
losses, there is little likelihood that Ralegh ever wrote the vast
poem implied by those titles. Far more plausible is Agnes Latham's suggestion that "*Cynthia* was a cumulative poem written over a period of years, and that the 'lamentable lay' which
Spenser heard, and which was provoked by the events of 1589,
was no more than the latest installment." [13] This basic theory
is followed by Philip Edwards, Walter Oakeshott and, most recently, Pierre Lefranc to whom the four poems in the Hatfield
House manuscript and another autograph poem unearthed
recently [14] suggest not a single, unified account of the relations
between Ralegh and the queen but a cycle of heterogeneous
pieces written at different moments of his career.[15]

Lefranc includes in this cycle a group of Ralegh's poems
published anonymously in *The Phoenix Nest* (1593). Arrested
in 1592 upon the queen's discovery of his secret marriage, Ralegh released, according to Lefranc, a number of poems intended for the cycle.[16] He took great precautions to keep defi-
nite proof of his authorship from the general public, but the
queen and perhaps a few others would have understood that
the release of these poems constituted an intentional indiscre-
tion and a warning. The silent agreement between Ralegh
and the queen regarding the secrecy of the cycle had been broken, and a threat was thereby implied that the rest of these
private poems might someday be aired before the public.[17]

Such a theory may be attractive in the light of Ralegh's dar-
ing and his power to manipulate men and appearances, but it
is highly implausible, for he would not have been foolish
enough to imagine that he could frighten the queen in this
way. Elizabeth could not be threatened by verses or by anything else. Those who published things offensive to her
quickly learned to repent of their folly, like John Stubbs and
his publisher who both lost their right hands for opposing in
print the Alençon marriage scheme. Ralegh may have intended

certain of the poems in *The Phoenix Nest* as complaints of a rejected favorite, he may have intended them to move the queen's compassion or even remorse, but he could hardly have meant them as threats.

Lefranc's idea of a threat arises in part from his notion of the secrecy of the supposed cycle. He imagines that the very "conceit" of the queen as Cynthia was the intimate possession of Ralegh and Elizabeth, and that consequently, even the allusions in Spenser were the result of "private indiscretions." [18] There does not appear to be any evidence for this theory apart from the fact that the unfinished poems in the Hatfield House manuscript were never published and apparently never circulated during Ralegh's lifetime. This in itself is hardly enough to warrant the notion of a great secret enterprise, planned and partially executed over a number of years, zealously kept from the eyes of all but the chosen few. There is no reason to believe that some poems were written independently and later "attached" to the cycle, as Lefranc would have it,[19] or that Ralegh released to the general public poems which were originally written for the cycle, or indeed that Ralegh ever thought of his poems as part of a cycle. In fact, the only value of the term "cycle" here is to emphasize the powerful shaping imagination that lay behind this body of diverse poems, the imagination that seized upon a troubled relationship and transformed it into a work of art with its own set of meanings and coherences. The poems were evidently written for specific occasions, but they are all caught up in the overarching self-fashioning of Ralegh's life.

At the center of the poems to Elizabeth is the shifting image of the lady—the queen, Cynthia, the mistress—and the changing voice of the poet—chanting the praises of a goddess, crying out against the coldness of his beloved and the misery of age, bewailing his isolation and loneliness, attempting to understand how the same love could be both the emblem of eternity and the embodiment of mutability. In his best poems, Ralegh does not present a complete unit of feeling or thought, a fixed image, a single tone, but attempts, rather, to render in

verse the very process of shifting from one unit to another and
his own futile efforts to stabilize the image and the voice. In
the minor poems printed in *The Phoenix Nest*, however, the
poles of belief and emotion are each given concise, individual
expression.

At one extreme is the queen as goddess and the poet as worshiper:

> Praisd be Dianas faire and harmles light,
> Praisd be the dewes, wherwith she moists the ground;
> Praisd be hir beames, the glorie of the night,
> Praisd be hir powre, by which all powres abound.
>
> Praisd be hir Nimphs, with whom she decks the woods,
> Praisd be hir knights, in whom true honor lives,
> Praisd be that force, by which she moves the floods,
> Let that Diana shine, which all these gives.
>
> In heaven Queene she is among the spheares,
> In ay she Mistres like makes all things pure,
> Eternitie in hir oft chaunge she beares,
> She beautie is, by hir the faire endure.
>
> Time weares hir not, she doth his chariot guide,
> Mortalitie belowe hir orbe is plaste,
> By hir the vertue of the starrs downe slide,
> In hir is vertues perfect image cast.
>
> A knowledge pure it is hir worth to kno,
> With Circes let them dwell that thinke not so.
>
> [*Poems*, pp. 10–11]

Elizabeth is transformed almost completely beyond human
personality, appearing as an image of static, timeless perfection to the mortal who speaks, or rather chants, her praises.
This is not simply a tactful love poem which aims at praising
the "real" person of the queen figured forth as Diana; it does
not establish a coherent set of simple equivalences, like a code,
where each attribute of Diana stands for a praiseworthy quality of the queen. There are such equivalences—Diana's
nymphs and knights and perhaps "hir powre, by which all
powres abound"—but these are intertwined with attributes
which have no simple correspondences—Diana's "faire and

harmles light," "the dewes, wherwith she moists the ground,"
"hir beames, the glorie of the night." The presence of the latter indicates that the poet does not encourage us to look
through his image to the substantial reality behind it—the
reality of the aging Elizabeth—but to know and pay tribute
to the qualities that inhere in the figure of Diana into whom
the queen has been transformed: perfect beauty and virtue, supreme power, and, above all, the mastery of time and mutability. Ralegh's Diana is above the realm of flux, deceptive appearance, sinister transformation, the realm evoked by the
reference to Circe. And she is also above mere human relationships; it is enough simply to have the pure knowledge of her
worth. Insofar as the poem celebrates Elizabeth at all, it celebrates her in her role, the ideal of perfection to which she was
wedded at the moment of her consecration. "In hir is vertues
perfect image cast"—the sculpture metaphor suggests that the
praise is for the wonderful work of art into which the queen
has been transformed.

The poem which pays tribute to this transformation is itself
highly artificial. The anaphora in the first seven lines, the
overall absence of syntactical tension or complexity, the perfect containment of the verse within the shell of its own metri-
cal pattern create the mythic time suited to the ritual of praise
for Diana's static, self-contained virtue. The work seems to reflect the strong Elizabethan sense of the interrelation of poetry
and music, the delight in formal patterns of sound and
feeling. Elsewhere in Ralegh's poetry, there is emphasis on the
divided and tormented self. In "Praisd be Dianas faire and
harmles light," however, the poet is not a fully realized character but an anonymous voice. These verses do not address the
reader as an individual moral agent, but speak for a whole
community, banishing all who disagree:

> A knowledge pure it is hir worth to kno,
> With Circes let them dwell that thinke not so.

Poetry such as this, with its emphasis on fluency rather than
complex syntax, on generalized patterns of feeling rather than

on individual sensibility, affirms man's place in a harmonious, orderly universe where isolation and uniqueness are impossible. The sense of a reassuring correspondence between the order of the cosmos and the order of man is nicely caught in Ralegh's carefully patterned lines, with their play on the meanings of "virtue":

> By hir the vertue of the starrs downe slide,
> In hir is vertues perfect image cast.

"The vertue of the starrs" (i.e., astrological influence) works upon the world of man through the mediation of the sphere of the goddess Diana who is the perfect image of moral virtue. This correspondence accords very well with the notion of the queen's "two persons" which Spenser expressed in his letter to Ralegh: "a most royall Queene or Empresse" by whom, as God's anointed representative on earth, the divine will is expressed on earth, and "a most vertuous and beautifull Lady."

"Praisd be Dianas faire and harmles light" presents the queen as goddess. Elsewhere in *The Phoenix Nest* Ralegh portrays her as the beautiful and gracious lady of innumerable Renaissance love lyrics:

> Those eies which set my fancie on a fire,
> Those crisped haires, which hold my hart in chains,
> Those daintie hands, which conquer'd my desire,
> That wit, which of my thoughts doth hold the rains.
>
> Those eies for cleernes doe the starrs surpas,
> Those haires obscure the brightnes of the Sunne,
> Those hands more white, than ever Ivorie was,
> That wit even to the skies hath glorie woon.
>
> O eies that pearce our harts without remorse,
> O haires of right that weares a roiall crowne,
> O hands that conquer more than Caesars force,
> O wit that turns huge kingdoms upside downe.
>
> Then Love be Judge, what hart may thee withstand:
> Such eies, such haire, such wit, and such a hand.
>
> [*Poems*, p. 78]

Obviously, such flattering verses must have pleased the aging queen and enabled Ralegh to sustain the elaborate fiction of courtship. They also enabled him to display the graceful wit and facility expected of the accomplished gentleman. Castiglione, for example, had advised that the courtier be practiced "in writing verse and prose, especially in our own vernacular; for, besides the personal satisfaction he will take in this, in this way he will never want for pleasant entertainment with the ladies, who are usually fond of such things." [20]

But this kind of poem (of which Ralegh undoubtedly wrote many) had, I believe, a function beyond flattery, self-display, and light entertainment. Like "Praisd be Dianas faire and harmles light," such verses provided—primarily for Ralegh himself—a deep reassurance. Anonymous, superficial, static, and utterly conventional, they evoke a world of shared values, a world in which the individual is almost indistinguishable from the society at large. Even when they speak of the "defeat" of the lover whose heart is held in chains, they bear witness to a public, comprehensible world:

> Sought by the world, and hath the world disdain'd
> Is she, my hart, for whom thou doost endure,
> Unto whose grace, sith Kings have not obtaind,
> Sweete is thy choise, though losse of life be sowre:
>   Yet to the man, whose youth such pains must prove,
>   No better end, than that which comes by Love.
>
> [*Poems*, p. 79]

The familiar rhythms and banal diction underscore the consoling sense of community.

There is no stamp of a single, unique consciousness on these passionless love poems. "Those eies which set my fancie on a fire," for example, is ascribed to Ralegh only because it appears at the heart of the so-called "Ralegh group" in *The Phoenix Nest;* it might otherwise be attributed to virtually any contributor to that anthology or to any other in the period. Only one poem in the group, "Farewell to the Court," creates the sense of an individual:

Like truthles dreames, so are my joyes expired.
And past returne, are all my dandled daies:
My love misled, and fancie quite retired,
Of all which past, the sorow onely staies.

My lost delights now cleane from sight of land,
Have left me all alone in unknowne waies:
My minde to woe, my life in fortunes hand,
Of all which past, the sorow onely staies.

As in a countrey strange without companion,
I onely waile the wrong of deaths delaies,
Whose sweete spring spent, whose sommer well nie don,
Of all which past, the sorow onely staies.

Whom care forewarnes, ere age and winter colde,
To haste me hence, to find my fortunes folde.

[*Poems*, p. 12]

This lyric seems to have occupied a special place in Ralegh's
consciousness. In *Ocean to Cynthia*, he recalls it as a premonition of his present suffering:

Twelve yeares intire I wasted in this warr,
Twelve yeares of my most happy younger dayes,
Butt I in them, and they now wasted ar,
Of all which past the sorrow only stayes.
So wrate I once, and my mishapp fortolde.

[120–24] [21]

"Farewell to the Court" would seem then to refer to an earlier
and less serious disgrace in Ralegh's career than the disaster of
1592, probably to the mysterious trouble in the summer of
1589 which led to his brief exile from the court. Indeed, Lefranc suggests that the shores which have disappeared behind
the horizon are those of England and the "countrey strange" is
Ireland.[22] But the landscape is more psychological than lit-
eral: it is not the coasts of England but "My lost delights" that
are "now cleane from sight of land," and if Ireland was the origin for the "countrey strange," it has been transformed by the
poet's imagination into a metaphor expressing his sense of isolation and of the distance that separates him from the joys of

his past. Cut off from the timelessness of the goddess and the shared time of the community, the voice of the poet conveys a feeling of personal time, a sense of the past and of the ongoing process of aging, which sets it apart from Ralegh's other poems in *The Phoenix Nest.*

"Praisd be Dianas faire and harmles light" and "Farewell to the Court" represent opposite poles in Ralegh's imaginative transformation of his relationship with the queen: the one with its virtually anonymous speaker, its tone of ritual adoration, its sense of timelessness, and, of course, its transcendent goddess, and the other with its personal voice, its tone of sorrow and regret, its deep rootedness in time, and its almost total absorption in the poet's emotions. As Ralegh matured poetically, he did not move from one pole to the other, from an impersonal, hieratic style and subject matter to an intensely individual and resonant verse, but rather discovered ways of bringing them together. One splendid reconciliation of this kind is the famous Walsingham ballad (*Poems,* pp. 22–23).

C. S. Lewis remarked sourly of this poem that "it has no unity of style at all." [23] This is true enough, but it is precisely in the mingling and manipulation of diverse styles that Ralegh achieves his effects. The opening:

> As you came from the holy land
> Of Walsinghame
> Mett you not with my true love
> By the way as you came?

is very much in the manner of the old ballad upon which Ralegh's poem is based, the ballad which perhaps began:

> As I went to Walsingham
> To the shrine with speede.[24]

Likewise, the fifth and sixth lines:

> How shall I know your trew love
> That have mett many one

strongly resemble the version Ophelia sings in her distraction:

> How should I your true-love know
> From another one?
>
> [*Hamlet*, IV, v, 23–24]

But in the third stanza, Ralegh begins to move away from the diction and imagery of the popular ballad (Ophelia's "By his cockle hat and staff/And his sandal shoon") toward the style and thematic concerns of his own sophisticated court poetry. The mistress with her divine form and angelic face recalls the beautiful lady of "Those eies which set my fancie on a fire" and, still more, the goddess, set above time and mutability, of "Praisd be Dianas faire and harmles light." It is because of these associations—timeless perfection, divine grace, heavenly beauty—that the fifth stanza is so poignant and powerful:

> She hath lefte me here all alone,
> All allone as unknowne,
> Who somtymes did me lead with her selfe,
> And me lovde as her owne.

Breaking through both the simple accents of the ballad and the ritual adoration of the court poem is the personal note of suffering and anguish, the voice of "Farewell to the Court":

> My lost delights now cleane from sight of land,
> Have left me all alone in unknowne waies.

The voice of despair and loneliness expresses above all a sense of time, of aging:

> I have lovde her all my youth,
> Butt now ould, as you see,
> Love lykes not the fallyng frute
> From the wythered tree.

Of course, as the image suggests, growing old is natural and inevitable, and yet there is a lingering sense of betrayal and disillusionment, not only in the fickleness of love but in the triumph of time. The image describes not a process of maturation and ripening, but a death—the tree itself is withered.

Up to this point, the seventh stanza, the dialogue form has

been merely a convenience, a conventional device of the ballad to move the poem along:

> How shall I know your trew love
>
> Such an one did I meet, good Sir
>
> Whats the cause that she leaves you alone.

Tension has existed not between the two speakers, the abandoned lover and the pilgrim, but between the conventional form and content with its basic anonymity and the personal voice of suffering in the fifth and seventh stanzas. But in the concluding stanzas the dialogue form is realized and made to carry the full weight of the argument. In response to the lover's bitter sense of age and betrayal, the pilgrim criticizes love as a "careless chylld," both careless of the pain he causes others and free from the care, the suffering of love:

> Know that love is a careless chylld
>   And forgets promyse paste,
> He is blynd, he is deaff when he lyste
>   And in faythe never faste.
>
> His desyre is a dureless contente
>   And a trustless joye
> He is wonn with a world of despayre
>   And is lost with a toye.

By subtle modulations of rhythm, sound, and alliteration, Ralegh manages to convey the uneasiness and instability of passion and the deflating, trivializing fickleness of childish love.

The suffering individual, however, is not satisfied with this view of love. He identifies the "chyldysh desyres / And conceytes" with the love of womankind, and then, looking inward, he perceives a love which is above time and mutability:

> Butt true Love is a durable fyre
>   In the mynde ever burnynge;
> Never sycke, never ould, never dead,
>   From itt selfe never turnynge.

Once again, part of the power of these intense lines is derived from the sharp contrast with the style of the preceding stanzas.

There is an effect of surprise, a sudden rush of energy as the haunting, personal note breaks through the anonymous moralizing that has gone before.

The contrast of styles is linked with the opposition of two kinds of love, symbolized by a blind and faithless child (who is also sometimes deaf, according to Ralegh) and by "a durable fyre/In the mynde ever burnynge." The child is, of course, the blind Cupid of Renaissance mythology, and the opposition is related to a major theme in the iconology of the period. To the modern reader, the blindness of Cupid alludes only to the irrationality of amorous choices, but for the mythographers and artists of the Renaissance it had darker associations. According to Erwin Panofsky, "Blind Cupid started his career in rather terrifying company: he belonged to Night, Synagogue, Infidelity, Death and Fortune. . . ." [25] The figure represented a love that was *morally* blind, an illicit sensuality that was a slave to time and tainted by death. By Ralegh's day, these overtones of evil had been largely dissipated by the frequent use of the figure in different contexts, many of them trivial or neutral. Yet the overtones remained as a potential, to be evoked, as Panofsky observes, "wherever a lower, purely sensual and profane form of love was deliberately contrasted with a higher, more spiritual and sacred one, whether marital, or 'Platonic,' or Christian" (p. 126). Just such a contrast is made in the Walsingham poem, though it is tempered by the simplicity of the ballad framework and by a certain minimal tact. The contrast—between a faithless love that abandons the aging lover and seeks after novelty and a true love that never changes—is a version of the rivalry between "Amor profano" and "Amor sacro." The former love is confined by the body and hence by time—"Love lykes not the fallyng frute/From the wythered tree"—while the latter is a fire which forever burns in the mind. That fire is related ultimately to "the most holy fire of true divine love" [26] of which Bembo speaks so ecstatically in *The Courtier* as the fulfillment of all the strivings of man's soul. This is the very heart of the Neoplatonic system of Ficino and Pico, the *amor divinus*

which "possesses itself of the highest faculty in man, i.e. the
Mind or intellect, and impels it to contemplate the intelligible
splendour of divine beauty" (Panofsky, p. 142). In Ralegh's
poetry, however, the essential content of that system—the religious vision—has disappeared. What remains is the fire which
burns in the mind, the love which leads beyond the self, beyond time, beyond mortality, and this love is focused not
upon God but upon the queen. Yet though his royal mistress
is invested with all the titles of divinity, though she is as fair
as the heavens and possesses a divine form and an angelic face,
still she is human and subject to weakness and inconstancy.
The divine love of the poet is betrayed by the very symbol of
perfection, constancy, and hope, and the result of this betrayal is intense anguish. This anguish is felt in "Farewell to
the Court," in the sonnet "My boddy in the walls captived,"
which I have discussed earlier, and in the Walsingham ballad.
But it receives its ultimate expression in Ralegh's masterpiece,
"The 21th: and last booke of the Ocean to Scinthia."

From an obscure, powerless gentleman of slender means, a
young soldier who had come to the court with neither extraordinary qualifications nor influential friends, Ralegh had risen
by the mid-1580s to a place, as he himself put it, "to be beleved not inferrior to any man, to plesure or displesure the
greatest; and my oppinion is so receved and beleved as I can
anger the best of them" (*Letters*, p. 42). He had all those
things which made the favorites of the queen so virulently
hated by the people—lucrative monopolies, large royal grants
of land and money, an influential and highly conspicuous
place in the court. In 1587 he was named Captain of the
Queen's Guard, a position requiring his constant attendance
upon his royal mistress.[27] This proximity was of enormous importance to him, for although he became involved in many
projects, including privateering and the Virginia Company, although he served as Member of Parliament for Devon, patron-
ized poets, historians, and scientists, his career always remained dependent upon the queen's favor.

Relying on this personal relationship, Ralegh made little or no attempt to align himself with a strong party. His contempt for the "rascal multitude" was notorious, and his relations with the great nobles, who considered him an upstart, were always strained. Newsletters, court circulars, polemical pamphlets, ballads, all were full of stories of his intolerable pride and insolence. There was wild talk about the extravagance of his dress—jewels in his shoes worth 6,600 gold pieces, a suit adorned with £60,000 worth of precious gems. And indeed the magnificence of his clothing is borne out by portraits of this period such as the lovely miniature by Nicholas Hilliard, depicting Ralegh in a jewel-studded cap and a collar edged with beautiful lace (see frontispiece). Likewise, in a painting dated 1588, Ralegh wears a large pearl earring and is resplendently dressed in an embroidered doublet and fur-collared cloak virtually covered with pearls. In the upper lefthand corner of the painting, above his motto "Amore et Virtute," there is a small crescent moon, a symbol of Cynthia or Diana.[28] As this symbol suggests, the splendid adornments were not only arrogant displays of wealth, they were signs of Ralegh's favor and part of the elaborate, slightly exotic image with which he captivated his royal mistress.

In the spring and summer of 1592 Ralegh was at the summit of his career. In May, the queen remitted to him a debt of £5,000, and in June she gave him the beautiful Sherborne estate which she had wrested for that purpose from the Bishop and Chapter of Salisbury. Even more important, perhaps, for a man who desired to hold sway over others, that spring Ralegh was given his first naval command—an expedition against the Spanish fleet. But all during that period of unmatched honor and prosperity, there were dark rumors circulating. On March 10, 1592, Ralegh wrote to Cecil,

I mean not to cume away, as they say I will, for feare of a marriage, and I know not what. If any such thing weare, I would have imparted it unto yoursealf before any man livinge; and, therefore, I pray believe it not, and I beseich yow to suppress, what you can, any such mallicious report. For I protest before God, ther is none, on the face of the yearth, that I would be fastned unto. [*Letters*, p. 46]

We may indeed believe that at that moment there was no one on earth that Ralegh would willingly have been fastened to, but, as we saw in his speech on the scaffold, Ralegh's protestations to God were not to be trusted. There *was* a marriage, to Elizabeth Throckmorton, one of the queen's maids of honor.[29] Even if the "love" between the aging queen and her favorite had been tacitly understood by both to be an elaborate game (which is not at all clear), there was nonetheless a terrible betrayal involved. After a rather mysterious delay during which there may have been unsuccessful efforts to patch things up,[30] Ralegh and his wife were imprisoned in the Tower.

It was in this crisis, in the shock and frustration and anguish of imprisonment that *Ocean to Cynthia* was born. Probably, confession and apologies were called for, but Ralegh turned instead to the abandoned lover's gestures of despair: theatricalism was always closer to his nature than contrition. Verses were only one such gesture. In addition to histrionic letters (like the one to Robert Cecil that I quoted earlier— "My heart was never broken till this day"), he actually staged at least one dramatic scene for the queen's benefit. The incident, touched off by a glimpse of the royal barge on the Thames, evidently occurred when Ralegh was being held in custody, and it was reported to Robert Cecil by Sir Arthur Gorges, Ralegh's kinsman:

I cannot chuse but advertyse you of a straunge Trgedye that this day had lyke to have fallen owte betweene the Captayne of the Guarde, and the Lyuetennaunt of the Ordenaunce; If I had not by great chaunce cummen att the very instant to have turned it into a Commedye. For uppon the report of hyr Majesties beinge att Sir George Caryes; Sir W. Rawly having gazed and syghed a longe tyme att hys study wyndow; from whence he myght discerne the Barges and boates aboute the blackfryars stayers; soodaynly he brake owte into a greate distemper, and sware that hys Enymyes hadd of purpose brought hyr Majestie thethar, to breake hys gaule in sounder [i.e. to break his spirit completely] with Tantalus Torment; that when shee wentt a way he myght see hys deathe before hys Eyes; with many such lyke conceyts. And as a mann transported with passion; he sware to Sir George Carew that he wolde disguyse hymeselfe; and gett into a payer of Oares to Ease hys mynde butt with a syght of the Queene; or els he protested his harte wolde breake. But the trusty Jaylor . . . flatly refused to permitt hyme. But in conclusion uppon this disspute they fell flatt owt to colloryq outragius wordes; with stryving and struggling att the doores, . . . and in the fury of the conflyct, the Jaylor he had hys newe perwygg torne of hys crowne. And yet heare the battle ended not, for att laste they had gotten owte theyr daggers; which when I sawe I played the styckler betwene theme, and so purchased such a rapp on the knockles, that I wysht bothe theyr pates broken; and so with much a doo, they stayed theyr brawle to see my bloodyed fyngers. . . . As yet I cannot reconcyle them by any perswasions. . . . good Sir lett nobody knowe thearof. for I feare Sir W. Rawly; wyll shortely growe to be Orlando furioso; If the bryght Angelyca persever agaynst hyme a lyttle longer.[31]

The language of the letter nicely captures the self-consciously "literary" quality of Ralegh Furioso. Gorges provides the key to the performance in a postscript to Cecil: ". . . I could wyshe hyr Majestie knewe."

Ocean to Cynthia is, on one level, only another such performance, in which Ralegh presents himself as a distracted lover cruelly abandoned by his mistress. Indeed, a reasonably accurate summary of the poem can be lifted directly from Gorges' letter: "when she went away he might see his death before his eyes, with many such like conceits." The actual circumstances of his disgrace were, of course, an impediment to this role, but Ralegh's tactic is simply to dismiss his feelings toward his wife as a regrettable but passing error, while ardently proclaiming his everlasting love for the queen:

> But thow my weery sowle and hevy thought
> Made by her love a burden to my beinge,
> Dust know my error never was forthought
> Or ever could proceed from sence of Lovinge.
> Of other cause if then it had proceedinge
> I leve th'excuse syth Judgment hath bynn geven;

The lymes devided, sundred and a bleedinge
Cannot cumplayne the sentence was unyevunn.

[336–43] [32]

"Her love," that is, Ralegh's love for the queen,[33] weighs heavily upon his mind and soul in his disgrace. His "error" was only a superficial affair, not really affecting him at all except as it brought about the anger of the queen. Indeed that passing fancy, that "frayle effect of mortall livinge" (445), was so insignificant in itself that the queen's reaction, as the brutal image of quartering suggests, was harsh, hasty, and unjust. The offender is transformed into the pitiable victim. In lines which echo the eighth, ninth, and tenth stanzas of the Walsingham ballad, Ralegh boldly turns the tables upon the queen:

Such is of weemens love the carefull charge,
Helde, and mayntaynde with multetude of woes,
Of longe arections such the suddayne fall.
Onn houre deverts, onn instant overthrowes
For which our lives, for which our fortunes thrale.

[228–32]

This approach is maintained as well in Ralegh's letters of this period—the pathetic appeal that is at the same time a reproach:

There were no divinety, but by reason of compassion; for revenges are brutish and mortall. All those times past,—the loves, the sythes, the sorrows, the desires, can they not way down one frail misfortune? [Letters, p. 52]

and the sense of exaggerated, unjust punishment:

I only desire thatt I may be stayd no on [e] houre from all the extremetye that ether lawe or presedent can avowe. And, if that bee to [o] litle, would God it weare withall concluded that I might feed the lions, as I go by, to save labor. For the torment of the mind cannot be greater. . . . [Letters, p. 54] [34]

Ralegh carries the criticism of the queen's fickleness and her tyranny so far in Ocean to Cynthia that the basic assumption

that he wrote the poem to mollify the queen and excuse himself is called into question. As with the *"Appologie* for the ill
successe of his enterprise to *Guiana,"* what begins as an expression of contrition becomes something quite different as he
composes it. The manuscript of *Ocean to Cynthia* is in Ralegh's best hand, "comparable with that in which he addressed
King James after his disgrace in 1603" (*Poems*, p. 123), but it
is clearly unfinished and was apparently abandoned. It would
seem that at some point—possibly as late as the very draft we
possess—Ralegh realized that what he had written could only
enrage the queen still further. This uneasy realization seems to
be the meaning of that difficult little poem, "If Synthia be a
Queene, a princes, and supreame," which accompanies the 21st
and 22nd Books in the Hatfield House manuscript. If Elizabeth no longer loves him, if she is a queen and not Belphoebe,
then the verses he has written must not be shown to her
("Keipe thes amonge the rest, or say it was a dreame"). For
without the predisposition to like them for his sake, she will
only loathe them and disdain him the more. And neither her
disdain nor his despair has any need to be augmented—he has
experienced an excess of both.[35]

Ocean to Cynthia then was probably never shown to the
queen. Addressed, despite its title, not to Cynthia but to the
poet himself, it probes the hidden frustration and resentment
of a man who, as Elizabeth's "silly pug," had played the rapt
worshiper for over ten years. There is no warrant, however,
to dismiss the expressions of love in *Ocean to Cynthia* as mere
cynical flattery. Ralegh's courtship of the queen was for those
years the chief focus of all his intellectual and emotional energies, the central core from which his far-ranging activities
derived their meaning. His secret marriage emphasizes the
quality of acting in that courtship, but it does not prove Ralegh a mere hypocrite; there is ample evidence of his power to
believe in his own fictions, to commit himself to the role he
played. Moreover, commitment to the role of the queen's lover
was reinforced by Elizabeth's extraordinary personal qualities,
by the very practice of idealization over many years in a court

where everyone professed himself a worshiper, and by the whole national cult of Eliza, which was constantly reiterated in pageants and festivals, formal ceremonies and popular ballads, royal progresses and religious services.

Most important, Ralegh's courtship of the queen helped to shape his entire imaginative world and to determine his sense of himself. When he was at the height of his favor, there was an imaginative synthesis of private and public, for Elizabeth was at once mistress and ruler, and Ralegh was both lover and subject. In the role which he played with such conviction, his most intense personal feelings were bound up with his service to the state, his life as a citizen. The world of his imagination was a Golden Age world in which the subjective, individual will and the objective, civic will were one. Ralegh did not need to have a full sense of individuality, for his mistress was the symbol of the nation, the anointed minister of God's will. The absence of full self-consciousness is reflected in the highly generalized voice of early poems like "Praisd be Dianas faire and harmles light" and "Those eies which set my fancie on a fire," the voice that merges so easily with hundreds of others just like it. His poetic imagination participates in the shared emotional life of the entire nation rather than seeking forms which individualize and discriminate.

With Elizabeth's displeasure and Ralegh's disgrace, the synthesis of the individual and the community begins to disintegrate. The community breaks into rival factions, vying for the queen's favor:

> The tokens hunge onn brest, and kyndly worne
> Ar now elcewhere disposde, or helde for toyes;
> And thos which then our Jelosye removed,
> And others for our sakes then valued deere.
> The one forgot, the rest ar deere beloved,
> When all of ours douth strange or vilde apeere.
>
> [263–68]

And the queen herself is now an ambiguous figure, shifting from an abstract symbol of perfection, "Th'Idea remayninge of thos golden ages" (348), to a fickle and cruel woman. This am-

biguity casts shadows upon the past, even, paradoxically, as
the past is being idealized:

> Such force her angellike aparance had
> To master distance, tyme, or crueltye,
> Such art to greve, and after to make gladd,
> Such feare in love, such love in majestye.
> My weery lymes, her memory imbalmed,
> My darkest wayes her eyes make cleare as day.
> What stormes so great but Cinthias beames apeased?
> What rage so feirce that love could not allay?
> Twelve yeares intire I wasted in this warr,
> Twelve yeares of my most happy younger dayes,
> Butt I in them, and they now wasted ar,
> Of all which past the sorrow only stayes.
> So wrate I once, and my mishapp fortolde.
>
> [112–24]

Ralegh's verse manages to retain the significance of both sides
of the exploding image, to convey a complex attitude that
stops short of corrosive sarcasm, even in a moment of sardonic
perception like "Such art to greve, and after to make gladd."
The ageless goddess, the principle of harmony, purity, and
love, is glimpsed for a moment in a vision of the past and
then gives way abruptly to the personal anguish of "Twelve
yeares intire I wasted in this warr." All of the latent tensions
in Cynthia's love, her "art to greve" as well as to gladden, are
suddenly crystallized in the single word "warr": the long courtship is now seen as a destructive and futile struggle. The
poet's memory, pictured a few lines above as a healing force,
bitterly re-evaluates the past. His imagination, which had once
kept his beloved continually present—"Farr off or nire, in
waking or in dreames" (110)—now dwells upon its own pre-
monitions of grief:

> Of all which past the sorrow only stayes.
> So wrate I once, and my mishapp fortolde.

Resentment and adoration continue to struggle and alter-
nate throughout *Ocean to Cynthia,* but underlying both is the

poet's loneliness: the loneliness of disfavor and imprisonment
and, beyond these, the loneliness of the individual who has
come to a full awareness of himself for the first time. With the
breakdown of the synthesis of the objective and subjective
will, the individual is thrown back upon himself, without the
support of the community, nation, or any of those complex
means that man has developed to escape from isolation. His
new self-awareness is above all a sense of time and mortality
against which he is defenseless. Cynthia's love had sheltered
him, for she was above time—"Time weares hir not, she doth
his chariot guide"—but now he is an isolated, mortal individual on the threshold of oblivion:

> But as a boddy violently slayne
> Retayneath warmth although the spirrit be gonn,
> And by a poure in nature moves agayne
> Till it be layd below the fatall stone;
> Or as the yearth yeven in cold winter dayes
> Left for a tyme by her life gevinge soonn,
> Douth by the poure remayninge of his rayes
> Produce sume green, though not as it hath dunn;
> Or as a wheele forst by the fallinge streame,
> Although the course be turnde sume other way
> Douth for a tyme go rounde uppon the beame
> Till wantinge strenght to move, it stands att stay;
> So my forsaken hart, my withered mind,
> Widdow of all the joyes it once possest,
> My hopes cleane out of sight, with forced wind
> To kyngdomes strange, to lands farr off addrest.
> Alone, forsaken, frindless onn the shore
> With many wounds, with deaths cold pangs inebrased,
> Writes in the dust as onn that could no more
> Whom love, and tyme, and fortune had defaced,
> Of things so great, so longe, so manefolde
> With meanes so weake, the sowle yeven then departing
> The weale, the wo, the passages of olde
> And worlds of thoughts discribde by onn last sythinge:
> As if when after Phebus is dessended
> And leves a light mich like the past dayes dawninge,
> And every toyle and labor wholy ended

Each livinge creature draweth to his restinge
Wee should beginn by such a partinge light
To write the story of all ages past
And end the same before th'aprochinge night.

[73–103]

At the heart of this rich and suggestive passage is the anguish
of radical isolation: "Alone, forsaken, frindless onn the shore."
The "shore" refers both to the land of exile, exile from all
hopes and joys and from the lady who was their source, and to
the kingdom of death. The poet's bitter loneliness arises not
simply from his disgrace but from a new and tragic awareness
of mortality, a sense of isolation from any transcendent force
or any movement toward the renewal of life.

The tragic sense darkens everything, from the memories of
Cynthia, to the sterile, empty landscape, to the very act of
writing. Indeed, poetry itself—the circumstances of its composition, the nature of its forms and images, its stylistic level—is
one of the crucial symbols of the poet's tragic condition. If
Cynthia's love was his very life and that love has ended, then
his writing can be only the twitching of a corpse, his creative
energy no more significant than the meaningless growth of
plants in winter or the motion of a water wheel winding
down. Or, if he still has some remnant of life, the poet is like
a shipwrecked and dying sailor scratching his last words in the
dust; with the first storm they will vanish. Moreover, in the
little time that remains to him, he cannot begin to compass
the complexity of his theme; he can never record the "worlds
of thoughts" within him.

Ocean to Cynthia registers a mind in disorder, a sensibility
which has lost its coherence:

Lost in the mudd of thos hygh flowinge streames
Which through more fayrer feilds ther courses bend,
Slayne with sealf thoughts, amasde in fearfull dreams,
Woes without date, discumforts without end,
From frutfull trees I gather withred leves
And glean the broken eares with misers hands,

> Who sumetyme did injoy the waighty sheves
> I seeke faire floures amidd the brinish sand.

[17–24]

The "withred leves" and "broken eares" which symbolize the
collapse of his career and the misery of his existence are also
the blighted fragments of poetry which he has managed to
glean from his bitter experience. Fuller and richer forms,
"faire floures" of rhetoric and emotion, are no longer possible,
because the poet's imagination was utterly bound up with the
love of the mistress who has now forsaken him:

> Oh hopefull love my object, and invention,
> Oh, trew desire the spurr of my consayte,
> Oh, worthiest spirrit, my minds impulsion,
> Oh, eyes transpersant, my affections bayte,
> Oh, princely forme, my fancies adamande,
> Devine consayte, my paynes acceptance,
> Oh, all in onn, oh heaven on yearth transparant,
> The seat of joyes, and loves abundance!
> Out of that mass of mirakells, my Muse,
> Gathered thos floures, to her pure sences pleasinge.

[37–46]

His love was his inspiration: "the spurr of my consayte . . .
my minds impulsion." Without this creative force, the kind of
poetry he once wrote ("thos floures, to her pure sences pleas-
inge") is no longer possible. That poetry was part of an imaginative world now irrevocably lost:

> All in the shade yeven in the faire soon dayes
> Under thos healthless trees I sytt alone,
> Wher joyfull byrdds singe neather lovely layes
> Nor Phillomen recounts her direfull mone.
> No feedinge flockes, no sheapherds cumpunye
> That might renew my dollorus consayte,
> While happy then, while love and fantasye
> Confinde my thoughts onn that faire flock to waite;
> No pleasinge streames fast to the ocean wendinge
> The messengers sumetymes of my great woe,
> But all onn yearth as from the colde stormes bendinge
> Shrinck from my thoughts in hygh heavens and below.

[25–36]

The "sheapherds cumpunye" recalls the meeting pictured by
Spenser in *Colin Clouts Come Home Againe* where, by the
banks of a pleasing stream, the Shepherd of the Ocean sang
his "lamentable lay" to Colin. Sorrows in this pastoral world
are shared and transformed into flowing, musical verse, poetry
which pleases and reassures even in expressing "great woe."
For Ralegh, the pastoral represents a human condition ante-
rior to a full consciousness of time, death, and individuality. It
is set against the silent, dead world in which the poet now
lives, the wasteland in which there is neither shared joy nor
shared sorrow, but only aching loneliness and the total isolation of the self:

> But all onn yearth as from the colde stormes bendinge
> Shrinck from my thoughts in hygh heavens and below.

The mind reaches out to make contact with the world, but the
world shrinks back.[36]

For the new human condition of radical isolation, there
must be a new kind of poetry. In the very first lines of *Ocean
to Cynthia,* Ralegh confronts the problem of style:

> Sufficeth it to yow my joyes interred,
> In simpell wordes that I my woes cumplayne,
> Yow that then died when first my fancy erred,
> Joyes under dust that never live agayne.
> If to the livinge weare my muse adressed,
> Or did my minde her own spirrit still inhold,
> Weare not my livinge passion so repressed,
> As to the dead, the dead did thes unfold,
> Sume sweeter wordes, sume more becumming vers,
> Should wittness my myshapp in hygher kynd,
> But my loves wounds, my fancy in the hearse,
> The Idea but restinge, of a wasted minde,
> The blossumes fallen, the sapp gon from the tree,
> The broken monuments of my great desires,
> From thes so lost what may th'affections bee,
> What heat in Cynders of extinguisht fiers?
>
> [1–16]

Poetic style and emotion are all but inseparable. A phrase like
"The broken monuments of my great desires" which refers to

the poet's frustration and despair also suggests the nature of
the verse: the complex syntax, logical discontinuities, sudden
shifts of imagery and leaps in time. C. S. Lewis has observed of
Ocean to Cynthia that "as often happens in the work of an
amateur, what is unfinished is more impressive, certainly more
exciting, than what is finished," [37] but the poem's merits are
not adventitious. Ralegh may have intended to rework certain
verses,[38] but there is no evidence whatever that he would have
altered its basic character. On the contrary, the continual references to things broken, fragmented, withered, and distorted,
to words scratched in the dust by a dying man, to an immense
history begun too late ever to be finished indicate that Ralegh
was remarkably aware of what he was doing. *Ocean to Cynthia* is not only about the death of love but about the death of
a whole imaginative world sustained by that love.

The poet of *Ocean to Cynthia* has no firm ground anywhere
—his mistress' love, the natural world around him, his poetic
style, his very identity, all are subject to instability and uncertainty. Even the names "Ocean" and "Cynthia" seem strangely
ambiguous and inconclusive.[39] By themselves they are splendid and suggestive images for the relationship of subject and
queen: the ocean eternally drawn by the moon but never
reaching her, the moon constantly changing and yet always re-
affirming herself; the ocean restless and immensely powerful,
the moon cold, distant, and beautiful. But Ralegh does not
weave his poem around these images or draw out their latent
meaning. On the contrary, the queen is at one moment the
moon and at the next the sun (see 104–19) and Ralegh, the
"Ocean," is alternately drowning in destructive floods (see
132–42) and dying of fierce thirst (see 237–40, 478–80). Identity is at all times too problematical in this poem for names to
denote anything clearly: the self and the beloved continually
shift in and out of focus, continually assume new qualities that
modify or contradict the old. If the names "Ocean" and "Cynthia" do have any constant meaning in the work as a whole,
it lies only in the suggestion of uncertainty and flux which
they both convey.

Similarly, the recurrent images in the poem—fire, water,

natural fertility—constantly promise a coherent and logical
path through the tangle of shifting emotions, a resolution
which they just as constantly fail to deliver. The imagery is
tantalizingly interwoven in subtle and complex patterns,[40]
but, as in a kaleidoscope, the pieces fall into new and entirely
different configurations as soon as they are perceived. The
constant shifting from a world of dust to a world of mud and
raging waters, from "th'Arabien sande" (478) to the "trobled
ocean" (484), from the fire of destruction to the vestal fire of
love, from the waters of redemption to the waters of death, finally leaves the reader with a sense of disorientation and bewil-
derment.

The instability of the imagery reflects the turbulent flux of
the poet's emotions. The praise of the goddess becomes anguish at the waste of twelve long years in a bitter war; the
beautiful, sweet face untouched by time is transformed into
the cruel mask of an executioner; love itself turns into a curse
bringing despair and death. Adoration and harsh reproach follow so quickly upon each other that at last they are indistinguishable:

> And like as that immortall pour douth seat
> An element of waters to allay
> The fiery soonn beames that on yearth do beate
> And temper by cold night the heat of day,
> So hath perfection, which begatt her minde,
> Added therto a change of fantasye
> And left her the affections of her kynde
> Yet free from evry yevill but crueltye.
>
> [205–12]

As God placed "an element of waters" (Genesis 1 : 7) between
the earth and the sun for the protection of living things, so
perfection has added inconstancy to Cynthia's nature! We
await a resolution, a decisive turn to bitter irony or to love,
but none is forthcoming. Instead, the mind of the poet constantly revolves upon itself, spiraling ever deeper into isolation.

Although in their constant shifts and reorientations, Ra-

legh's images become riddling and elusive, individually they
are quite simple and public. With a few exceptions, they are
drawn from the most conventional stockpile of the period:
falling fruit, dust, fire, ice, blood, streams, grazing flocks, shepherd's pipes, sun, moon, and ocean. One critic has even suggested that Ralegh "is a plain man's poet; his fancy lingers by
the experiences of everyday life, the permanent, the factual."[41]
But the very universality and simplicity of the images only
heightens the sense of the poet's powerful shaping fancy:

> Such is agayne the labor of my minde
> Whose shroude by sorrow woven now to end
> Hath seene that ever shininge soonn declynde
> So many yeares that so could not dissende
> But that the eyes of my minde helde her beames
> In every part transferd by loves swift thought;
> Farr off or nire, in wakinge or in dreames,
> Imagination stronge their luster brought.

[104–11]

The relation between the poet's imagination and the world is
deliberately rendered complex and ambiguous, for the mind
both perceives and half creates. The drama of the poem takes
place not in the realm of "the permanent, the factual," but in
the poet's troubled consciousness, in his shifting perceptions of
the world.

Ralegh's method in *Ocean to Cynthia* is highly personal,
but it is not completely without parallel in the period. For example, in Sidney's famous "Ye Gote-heard Gods," the conventional meanings of the sestina's terminal words are broken
down in the successive stanzas. The mountains, valleys, and
forests that begin as the properties of pastoral poetry and
everyday life gradually become the landscape of the imagination, changing with the emotional moods of the speakers. One
use of a word never completely cancels another—the effect is
cumulative, inclusive, even where meanings are contradictory.
William Empson has followed the metamorphoses of each of
the key words through the poem. For example,

Mountains are the haunts of Pan for lust and Diana for chastity, to both of these the lovers appeal; they suggest being shut in, or banishment; impossibility and impotence, or difficulty and achievement; greatness that may be envied or may be felt as your own (so as to make you feel helpless, or feel powerful); they give you the peace, or the despair, of the grave; they are the distant things behind which the sun rises and sets, the too near things which shut in your valley; deserted wastes, and the ample pastures to which you drive up the cattle for the summer.[42]

The images of *Ocean to Cynthia* have a similar ambiguity: thus, fire suggests the joyous ardor of love and the torments of hell; the searing pain of memory or the means of obliterating the past; the impulse to poetic creation or the destroyer of poetry; the pure, ethereal essence of beauty and the humble means used by the ploughman to destroy the stubble in his fields. In both poems there is no final determination of meaning, no veil to be lifted or essence to be revealed, but only ceaseless turns and returns.

Yet despite these resemblances, "Ye Gote-heard Gods" and *Ocean to Cynthia* are radically different. Sidney's Strephon and Klaius are like the speakers of Ralegh's early poems— virtually anonymous voices, undifferentiated from each other and from the hundreds of other figures just like them. They are not so much characters as convenient devices in the service of the formal structure to which Sidney faithfully and brilliantly adheres. Even at the climax of passion, the emotions never threaten to upset the exquisite balance and order of the form:

> *Strephon.* I wish to fire the trees of all these forrests;
>   I give the Sunne a last farewell each evening;
>   I curse the fidling finders out of Musicke;
>   With envie I doo hate the loftie mountaines;
>   And with despite despise the humble vallies;
>   I doo detest night, evening, day, and morning.
>
> *Klaius.* Curse to my selfe my prayer is, the morning;
>   My fire is more, then can be made with forrests;
>   My state more base, then are the basest vallies;

> I wish no evenings more to see, each evening;
> Shamed I hate my selfe in sight of mountaines;
> And stoppe mine eares, lest I growe mad with Musicke.
>
> [49–60] [43]

For all the despair and violence, there is no straining against the structure. In *Ocean to Cynthia,* on the contrary, the speaker's powerful and individual sense of time constantly erupts into the poem, displaying itself in the explosions and slackenings of meter, the strained or broken syntax, the leaps in logic and meaning. There are traces of control, faded memories of Ralegh's former manner: a penchant for latinate syntax, the frequent use of repetition and parallelism, a division into quatrains (masked in the original manuscript by the absence of regular stanza divisions).[44] But these barely suffice to keep the poem from anarchy. As if reacting to a verse that relies on form almost at the expense of consciousness, Ralegh writes a poem that relies on consciousness almost at the expense of form. *Ocean to Cynthia* seems to occupy that strange interior space between a sensation and the expression of that sensation in words, forever arrested at the moment of coming into being.

The order of Ralegh's poem comes not from quatrains or rhyme or syntax, nor from the principles of duration and repetition that govern poetry as musical expression, nor from the progressive development of images, but from an inner principle of continuity, a core of the self that resists the constant pull toward chaos. This principle—which Ralegh calls "love" —holds together not only the poem but the poet's very mind:

> But in my minde so is her love inclosde
> And is therof not only the best parte
> But into it the essence is disposde. . .
> Oh love (the more my wo) to it thow art
> Yeven as the moysture in each plant that growes,
> Yeven as the soonn unto the frosen ground,
> Yeven as the sweetness, to th'incarnate rose,
> Yeven as the Center in each perfait rounde,
> As water to the fyshe, to men as ayre,

> As heat to fier, as light unto the soonn.
> Oh love it is but vayne, to say thow weare,
> Ages, and tymes, cannot thy poure outrun. . . .
> Thow are the sowle of that unhappy minde
> Which beinge by nature made an Idell thought
> Begon yeven then to take immortall kynde
> When first her vertues in thy spirrights wrought. . . .
> From thee therfore that mover cannot move
> Because it is becume thy cause of beinge.
>
> [426–43]

This love, then, has all but displaced God in Ralegh's world;
the unmoved mover, it grants the poet's soul immortality. And
yet, even as Ralegh speaks of his soul's essence and the essence
of his poem, his statement calls forth a counterstatement:

> Yet as the eayre in deip caves under ground
> Is strongly drawne when violent heat hath rent
> Great clefts therin, till moysture do abound,
> And then the same imprisoned, and uppent,
> Breakes out in yearthquakes teringe all asunder,
> So in the Center of my cloven hart,
> My hart, to whom her bewties wear such wounder,
> Lyes the sharpe poysoned heade of that loves dart,
> Which till all breake and all desolve to dust
> Thence drawne it cannot bee, or therin knowne.
> Ther, mixt with my hart bludd, the fretting rust
> The better part hath eaten, and outgrown. . . .
>
> [450–61]

The love which was the element of unity, coherence, and immortality is now pictured as an explosive, destructive force
hidden at the core of the self, poisoning and corroding the
vital energies until at last it is violently released in the total
annihilation of being.

And then, almost abruptly, the poet's will to continue ques-
tioning, probing, complaining gives way: "Butt stay my
thoughts, make end, geve fortune way" (474). There has been
no resolution; there is no reason to close but the exhaustion reflected in the attenuated rhythm: "Thus home I draw, as

deaths longe night drawes onn" (509). Yet even here, on the
threshold of death, the poet cannot completely free himself
from thoughts of the past. In an extraordinary passage, the
dream of love bursts once again into the verse:

> On Sestus shore, Leanders late resorte,
> Hero hath left no lampe to Guyde her love;
> Thow lookest for light in vayne, and stormes arise;
> Shee sleaps thy death that erst thy danger syth-ed
> Strive then no more, bow down thy weery eyes,
> Eyes, which to all thes woes thy hart have guided.
> Shee is gonn, Shee is lost! Shee is found, shee is ever faire!
> Sorrow drawes weakly, wher love drawes not too.
> Woes cries, sound nothing, butt only in loves eare.
> Do then by Diinge, what life cannot do. . . .
>
> [487–96]

The sudden outburst, "Shee is found, shee is ever faire!" is a
momentary gasp of hope, a split-second vision of the kind of
poem Ralegh would like to have written: a poem in celebration of renewed love. The vision vanishes as abruptly as it
came, and the poet returns to the slow process of dying.

Again and again *Ocean to Cynthia* frustrates the reader's desire for order, tempting him with patterns and forms which
suddenly are interrupted or dissolve or veer away from his
grasp. At the close of the 21st Book, there is one last such experience:

> My steapps are backwarde, gasinge on my loss
> My minds affection, and my sowles sole love,
> Not mixte with fancies chafe, or fortunes dross.
> To God I leve it, who first gave it me,
> And I her gave, and she returned agayne,
> As it was herrs. So lett his mercies bee,
> Of my last cumforts, the essentiall meane.
>   But be it so, or not, th'effects, ar past.
>   Her love hath end; my woe must ever last.
>
> [514–22]

Finally after all his suffering and anxious isolation, the poet,
like Petrarch at the end of the *Canzoniere,* turns to God and

prays for his mercy and comfort. The reader feels relief, a
sense of homecoming—and then the final couplet shatters this
last movement toward transcendence. The "it" in that detached and indifferent phrase "But be it so, or not" is nothing
less than God's mercy. The poet's suffering overpowers God
Himself, and the 21st Book ends not on a note of divine consolation but with an expression of private grief.

Yet the final outcome is not as significant as the process of
the poem, its constant fluctuation of feeling. Cut off from the
traditional principles of stability in his world and in himself,
the poet undergoes a prolonged crisis of identity; conflicting
images of the self and the beloved present themselves on the
stage of his consciousness for a moment and then retire. The
shattered poet of *Ocean to Cynthia* resembles Richard II in
Pomfret Castle, who endlessly shuffles in his mind a set of
symbols that constantly shift their meaning:

> Thus play I in one person many people,
> And none contented. Sometimes am I a king:
> Then treasons make me wish myself a beggar,
> And so I am. Then crushing penury
> Persuades me I was better when a king:
> Then am I king'd again; and by and by
> Think that I am unking'd by Bolingbroke,
> And straight am nothing.
>
> [v, v, 31–38]

As in Shakespeare's play, the tragedy in Ralegh's poem begins
with something external—a fall from power, the destruction
of a social role—and then moves deeper and deeper into the
self. Ralegh sets out to write the conventional "complaint" of
the abandoned lover, the part into which he cast himself after
his disgrace. But the old style, with its timeworn formulas,
strict formal controls, and a clear sense of identity, could not
represent the isolation and the turbulent flux of his consciousness. And so Ralegh moves on his own, falteringly, brilliantly,
toward a new mode of self-representation. The theatricalism
remains, but the stage has been internalized: "My sowle the
stage of fancies tragedye" (144).[45] The critical issue is no

longer the fall from high estate, but the tragedy of the imagination.

Once again, *Ocean to Cynthia* resembles *Richard II*. Shut
up in his dark cell, the deposed king struggles to comprehend
the disintegration of his life:

> I have been studying how I may compare
> This prison where I live unto the world;
> And, for because the world is populous,
> And here is not a creature but myself,
> I cannot do it. Yet I'll hammer it out.
> My brain I'll prove the female to my soul,
> My soul the father; and these two beget
> A generation of still-breeding thoughts;
> And these same thoughts people this little world,
> In humours like the people of this world,
> For no thought is contented.
>
> [v, v, 1–11]

Isolated from the community of men and from his own past,
Richard's mind turns to the fashioning of metaphors—to the
creation of poetry—as his only means of reestablishing a coherent relation between himself and the world. In the past,
such creation came easily to him. Sustained by the ceremonies
of kingship, by the stable role that he had inherited, he had
effortlessly spun a complex web of metaphors. But now, his
isolation has profoundly altered the nature of poetic creation.
He must "hammer out" his metaphors, grapple with his "still-
breeding thoughts," and create a new kind of poetry-in-process. If ultimately he fails to achieve any lasting coherence, he
at least attains a heroic stature in the attempt.

Similarities between Shakespeare's play and *Ocean to Cynthia* are not the result of literary influence but of a common
mood of doubt, a shared vision of the self and the universe as
problematic and crisis-torn. Like *Richard II*, Ralegh's poem
manages to capture that mysterious moment when the old fab-
ric is undone and the new only beginning to be woven. It af-
fords a precious glimpse of a dark and largely uncharted process: change in man's consciousness of himself. Such change is

notoriously difficult to follow, because it almost never occurs
as a cataclysm, but consists rather of a series of small, diverse,
and exceedingly numerous alterations, like the movement of
vast land masses that only rarely is violent enough to be felt as
an earthquake. Thus historians clearly perceive a major alteration in consciousness between the Middle Ages and the Renaissance but cannot pin down the boundaries or even agree on
the critical events. But in Ralegh's life and verse this slow
change seems to be violently compressed. It is as if he entered
history with a slightly archaic consciousness and had suddenly
to catch up.

The 21st Book of *Ocean to Cynthia* is followed in the Hatfield House manuscript by a brief fragment in tercets entitled
"The end of the bookes, of the Oceans love to Scinthia, and
the beginninge of the 22 Boock, entreatinge of Sorrow" (*Poems,*
p. 44). The first nine lines are very much in the spirit of the
preceding book: a declaration of grief by one in the evening
and winter of his life, one whose times, "runn out in others
happines,/Bring unto thos new joyes, and new borne dayes"
(8–9). But the remaining lines turn—with a characteristic syntactical jolt—in a new direction:

> So could shee not, if shee weare not the soonn,
> Which sees the birth, and buriall, of all elce,
> And holds that poure, with which shee first begunn;
> Levinge each withered boddy to be torne
> By fortune, and by tymes tempestius,
> Which by her vertu, once faire frute have borne,
> Knowinge shee cann renew, and cann create
> Green from the grounde, and floures, yeven out of stone,
> By vertu lastinge over tyme and date,
> Levinge us only woe, which like the moss,
> Havinge cumpassion of unburied bones
> Cleaves to mischance, and unrepayred loss.
> For tender stalkes—
>
> [10–22]

The sense of isolation and mortality is undiminished, but
there is a new note of resignation, of near acceptance. In a few

lines, Ralegh sketches the last act of his tragedy, passing from
anguish to a recognition of the larger movement in which his
personal destiny had played only a minute part. He perceives
a power which is at once in time and above it, a power which
brings all things to fruition, leaves them to die, and passes on
undiminished. He cannot share in this eternal process, for he
views it from the time-bound perspective of the suffering individual, of the "withered boddy" and of "unrepayred loss." But
there is a new sense of objectivity in the fragment, an objectivity in the contemplation of his own wretchedness that gives
the closing image of the moss its strange air of detachment. It
is as if Ralegh had passed *through* extreme self-consciousness
to a state which more nearly resembles the consciousness of his
early poems.

The fragment's return to the spirit of the past was prophetic. When a fleet he and others had financed brought back a
fabulously rich Portuguese carrack, the *Madre de Dios,* Ralegh
was released from the Tower.[46] In time, he was partially rec-
onciled with the queen and even reinstated as a favorite. But
the relations between them were never what they once had
been; the intimacy and intensity were gone. The only poem to
the queen which survives from these last years of her reign is
the lyric "Now we have present made," an epilogue to Cynthia.[47] Oakeshott discovered an autograph copy on the flyleaf
of a notebook in which Ralegh assembled material for *The
History of the World,* in other words, a notebook which Ralegh had with him during the years in the Tower from 1603 to
1616. As the lyric was probably written in 1602, it appears
that after Elizabeth's death and Ralegh's imprisonment—after
the collapse of his entire world—he copied out for himself a
poem that he had written a few years earlier which recalled
far happier days.[48] Even when the poem was originally composed, shortly before the queen's death, it recreated an earlier
mode of vision, a recollection of a time before the bitterness of
the Essex rebellion and the melancholy of the closing years of
the reign.

The lyric may have been, as Oakeshott suggests, the epi-

logue to an entertainment held in the queen's honor, which
would help to explain the opening lines. But there is also a
suggestion in the first stanza of a broader retrospect encom-
passing the many images in which Elizabeth had been figured
over the years:

> Now we have present made
> To Cynthia, Phoebe Flora.
> Diana, and Aurora.
> Bewty that cannot vade.

The unpleasant memories of the queen's fickleness and vindic-
tiveness have been purged away. She is once more a goddess, almost completely divorced from human nature:

> A floure of loves own planting
> A patern keipt by nature
> For bewty, forme, and stature
> When shee would frame a darlinge.

Those lines almost certainly recall earlier verses, now lost, to
which Ralegh also alludes in *Ocean to Cynthia:*

> that natures wonder, Vertues choyse,
> The only parragonn of tymes begettinge
> Devin in wordes, angellical in voyse;
> That springe of joyes, that floure of loves own
> settinge [. . .]
> Such didsst thow her longe since discribe.

> [344–47, 351]

Again and again in this final poem to the queen, Ralegh
reaches back into the past, giving form to the underlying
unity of all the poems of his long courtship. "Time conquering all she mast'reth/By beinge alwaye new" (11–12) recalls
both the fragment of the 22nd Book and "Praisd be Dianas
faire and harmles light"; the "elementall fire/Whose food and
flame consumes not" (13–14) is like both the "vestall fier that
burnes, but never wasteth" of the 21st Book (189) and the "durable fyre/In the mynde ever burnynge" of the Walsingham
ballad; the image of the quill drawn from an angel's wing re-

calls the second of Ralegh's introductory sonnets to *The Faerie Queene*.[49] The anguished sense of isolation and mortality which gave *Ocean to Cynthia* its power is missing. Yet this too has left its traces in the poem's closing moments:

> But loves and woes expenc
> Sorrow can only write.

                                                                [31–32]

"Now we have present made" is Ralegh's epilogue to his entire poetic self-dramatization.

4 Theatricalism in Action: The Guiana Voyage of 1595 and the Treason Trial of 1603

In this chapter, I intend to focus upon two crucial events in Ralegh's career: his voyage to Guiana in 1595, with the subsequent attempt to interest the nation in his "discovery," and his performance at the treason trial of 1603. My purpose is to explore the interplay of life and art in these events, and my method, as in chapter 1, is to broaden the subject of critical inquiry so as to include not only explicitly literary works but also pamphlets, letters, speeches, and even actions.

The Guiana voyage has been discussed in many contexts: as part of the European Reconnaissance as a whole and English voyages of discovery in particular, as part of the sporadic search by adventurers beginning in the 1530s for a lost Incan empire, as an outgrowth of English-Spanish relations in the late sixteenth century, and as a realization of Ralegh's long-standing personal interest in colonizing voyages.[1] We must stress another and narrower context: Ralegh's restless discontent in the years following his disgrace. In keeping with one of the most characteristic patterns of his life, the vigorous self-assertiveness manifested in the voyage grew out of his mood of disillusionment and pessimism.

After his release from the Tower and the settlement of the profits from the *Madre de Dios,* Ralegh retired to his estate at Sherborne in Dorset, bitterly resentful of what he felt was the unfair distribution of the spoils. His attitude toward the world may perhaps be gauged from the testimony given in March 1594 at Cerne Abbas during an official investigation into the rumored atheism of Ralegh and certain members of his entourage.[2] In particular, the account given by the chief witness, the Reverend Ralph Ironside, of a "disputacion" reveals some of those qualities in Ralegh which were, so to speak, the negative basis of the voyage. Ralegh appears to have been less interested in a serious discussion, in the "instruccion" he facetiously requested, than in an opportunity to bait Ironside, to attack the "obscure, & intricate" logic of Aristotle and the Schoolmen, and to ridicule the inevitable circularity of "definitions" of God and the soul:

I have benn . . . a scholler some tyme in Oxeforde, I have aunswered under a Bacheler of Arte, & had taulke wth divers, yet heitherunto in this pointe (to witt what the reasonable soule of man is) have I not by anye benne resolved.[3]

Ironside's answer was solidly traditional: "the reasonable soule is a sperituall & immortall substance breathed into man by god, wherby he lyves & moves & understandeth, & soe is distinguished from other Creatures." But Ralegh pressed him further:

[Y]ea but what is that sperituall & immortall substance breathed into man &c. saieth Sr Walter; the soule quoth I., naye then saieth he you aunswer not like a scholler.

Ralegh demanded the kind of definition which Ironside could not possibly give:

[B]ut we have principles in our mathematickes sayeth Sr Walter, as totum est minus quamlibet sua parte. and aske me of it, and I can showe it in the table in the window in a man the whole beinge bigger then the partes of it. I replied first that he showed quod est, not, quid est, that it was but not what it was; secondlye, that such demonstracion as that was against the nature of a mans soule beinge a sperite. for as his thinges beinge sensible were subjecte to the sence; soe mans soule beinge insensible was to be discerned by the sperite. nothinge more certaine in the worlde then that there is a god, yet beinge a sperite to subjecte him to the sence otherwise then perfected it is impossible.

Ironside's response was clearly meant to put an end to the discussion, but Ralegh insisted upon carrying it further:

Marrye quoth Sr Walter these 2 be like for neither coulde I lerne heitherto what god is.

Particularly with the provocative tone in which it was evidently spoken, this was an impudent and, for the late sixteenth century, a dangerous remark. Ironside, eschewing now the authority of Aristotle whom Ralegh had previously challenged, turned to the ultimate authority, the Bible, indeed to the actual voice of God in the Bible: "that god was ens entium a thinge of thinge[s] havinge beinge of him selfe, & geivinge beinge to all creatures, it was most certaine, and confirmed by god him selfe unto moyses." And still Ralegh was dissatisfied:

[Y]ea but what is this ens entium sayeth Sr Walter? I aunswered it is God. And beinge disliked as before Sr Walter wished that grace might be sayed; for that quoth he is better then this disputacion.

Ralegh had the last word, and he left his final attitude ambiguous. It is difficult to believe that he was engaged in a serious attempt to define the essence of God and the soul. If, on the other hand, he was attacking the learning of scholars and theologians in order to exalt faith over reason and speculative inquiry, why did he reject the biblical revelation, or why, for that matter, did he pursue the discussion at all after Ironside had counseled against being overly "curious" in searching out the essence of spiritual things? Ralegh was scornful of both the simplicity of faith and the complexity of Aristotelian scholasticism. Yet apart from praising the clarity of "our mathematickes" and calling for grace to be said, he adopted no other position. His stance certainly does not reveal atheism, but it does suggest a discontent hovering between faith and skepticism.

This discontent lies at the heart of the celebrated poem "The Lie" (*Poems,* pp. 45–47) which probably dates from the same period as the Cerne Abbas inquiry. Lefranc has disputed Ralegh's authorship of the poem and has succeeded in showing that the contemporary attributions are not conclusive, but, in my opinion, Ralegh remains the most likely author (see appendix). "The Lie" epitomizes the mood of disillusionment that was evident in Ralegh's character and his writings from his earliest known letters and his first published poem.[4] It anticipates *The History of the World,* which reverberates with contempt for the false wisdom of the worldly philosophers, the lies of the poets, the insane ambition of kings, and the rottenness of empires.

The poem's religious certainty—"Stab at thee he that will,/no stab they soule can kill" (77–78)—may seem surprising after the conversation with Ironside, but Ralegh's beliefs appear to vary with his rhetorical purpose. In attacking the circular logic and the complacent certainties of clerics, he affects an ignorance of the nature of God and the soul. In giving the world the lie, he speaks with certainty of his immortal soul, setting that truth against the falsehoods he is determined to expose. What is common to both is an attack upon false appearances, upon the established, comfortable way of regarding the world and the divine, upon the easy assurance that things are what they seem to be and that man's institutions and his understanding are fundamentally sound.

This attack grew out of the frustration and bitterness of the years which followed Ralegh's disgrace. It reflected the dark vision of a Cynthia who is a fickle, cruel woman, no longer the perfect goddess above time and mortality, and registered loss of faith in man's power to transform his identity and the world. Its purpose was to unmask:

> Say to the Court it glowes,
>   and shines like rotten wood,
> Say to the Church it showes
>   whats good, and doth no good.

[7–10]

Ralegh had become sensitive to the distance between role and reality; he experienced a revulsion against pretense. In the conversation with Ironside, he sought to expose the university's and the church's presumptuous claims to sure knowledge of God and the soul. In "The Lie" he portrayed a world of sham and posturing where everything is less than it appears to be, where the glittering surfaces hide decay and death. Yet precisely in this period, in the midst of pessimism and disgust, Ralegh kept alive within himself the opposing vision, the conviction that role and reality can come together, so that by the power of the imagination the world is recreated in the image of man's desires. And this vision did not spin itself out in ethereal dreams but found a clear and worldly focus: Guiana.

Guiana was, of course, more than a fantasy of gold and glory. It was the culmination for Ralegh of many years of practical involvement in colonial ventures, from fortified estates in Ireland to three unsuccessful attempts to found a settlement in Virginia. Ralegh understood the ramifications for international diplomacy that must accompany English involvement in territory clearly marked off, if imperfectly held, by Spain. He knew, as well, the hard facts of financing such projects, recruiting the men, and finding and provisioning the ships. He had studied the available documents on Guiana and had spoken with French merchants and captured Spanish conquistadors. In employing Thomas Hariot, he even became, according to E. G. R. Taylor, "the first Englishman to engage a scientific and technical expert to advise him on his colonizing enterprises." Before finally committing himself to a major expedition, he dispatched Captain Jacob Whiddon in 1594 to appraise the situation in Trinidad and to gather more detailed information on Guiana. "So far from being the great romantic of tradition," Taylor writes, "Sir Walter was a hardheaded practical man." [5] Yet we may acknowledge all of the calculations and careful planning without granting this last distinction. For Ralegh, and for his associates John Dee and Thomas Hariot, the conventional antinomies of visionary and down-to-earth, romantic and practical, have little meaning.[6] Ralegh's tough-minded leadership of the Guiana voyage was inextricably bound up with his imaginative conception of heroic action.

The idea of the voyage appears as an image in *Ocean to Cynthia:*

> To seeke new worlds, for golde, for prayse, for glory,
> To try desire, to try love severed farr,
> When I was gonn shee sent her memory
> More stronge then weare ten thowsand shipps of warr,

> To call mee back, to leve great honors thought,
> To leve my frinds, my fortune, my attempte,
> To leve the purpose I so longe had sought
> And holde both cares, and cumforts in contempt.

[61–68]

The immediate reference here is not to Guiana but to Ralegh's recall by the queen's order in 1592 from the command of
an expedition against the Spanish treasure fleet and the Spanish settlement of Panama.[7] This incident is transformed by
Ralegh's poetic imagination from an operation against the
power of Spain to a quest for "new worlds" and a test of the
queen's love. Perhaps, as A. L. Rowse suggests, Ralegh an-
nounced his Guiana intentions in *Ocean to Cynthia* in hopes
that the queen would recall him from this dangerous voyage
as she had recalled him from the expedition of 1592. For
Rowse, the elaborate plans were a kind of charade, a poetic
gesture like the violent fit of hysterics at the sight of the
queen's barge, the passionate expressions in the letter to Robert Cecil, or the imaginary twenty-two books of *Ocean to Cynthia*.[8] Then the queen's silence forced Ralegh to go through
with the voyage. But, while Rowse's theory is plausible, it
slights Ralegh's complex, paradoxical ability both to play a
part and to commit himself completely to that part. The
Guiana voyage was indeed a theatrical gesture calculated to
dazzle the queen and win a return of her favor, but it was also
the fulfillment of a personal vision. It was set against the re-
tirement to Sherborne and the bitter mood of "The Lie" in
the unending dialectic in Ralegh's life between optimism and
despair, between the vision of a world made over in the image
of man's desires and the vision of a world of lies, disappointment, and death.

Not only did the queen do nothing to stop Ralegh's voyage
in 1595, but, upon his return, she shared with the court, the
powerful merchants of the City, and the general public a wry
skepticism about his enthusiastic reports. Ralegh's enemies
spread rumors that he had not been to Guiana at all, but had

hidden in Devon or Cornwall until his ships came home again. Others whispered that, failing to discover any gold in Guiana, he had purchased the specimen ore he brought back on the Barbary Coast.

In response to the doubts and the rumors, in an attempt to vindicate himself, Ralegh turned, as he had in the past, to writing. The excitement and interest he could not generate with his ore samples, he would spark with his pen. In 1596 he published *The Discoverie of the Large, Rich, and Bewtiful Empyre of Guiana, with a relation of the great and Golden Citie of Manoa (which the Spanyards call El Dorado) And of the Provinces of Emeria, Arromaia, Amapaia, and other Countries, with their rivers, adjoyning.*[9] The title, like the entire work, has a triumphant ring which is deceptive, for, quite apart from its failure to excite interest at home, the voyage had been in most respects a disappointment. Ralegh had not discovered El Dorado. He carried home only a tiny quantity of gold and gold-bearing ore. He had inflicted a few minor indignities upon the Spanish while himself suffering considerable losses in his attempts to plunder the towns of the Spanish Main. With all his hardships, he had not explored any new territory. His greatest achievement, the establishment of friendly relations with the Indians, would have meaning only in a concerted effort to expel the Spaniards and establish an English colony, an effort which Her Majesty's Government was entirely unwilling to make.[10]

The *Discoverie* was a calculated performance, a work of propaganda, sharing the aims of the hundreds of books and pamphlets on exploration that were turned out in the late sixteenth and seventeenth centuries to proclaim the great success of an expedition, invite subscriptions for subsequent voyages, attract adventurers and emigrants, and solicit government support.[11] It is pitched to readers with a broad range of motives and interests—curiosity, adventurousness, greed, desire for personal glory, nationalism:

Those that are desirous to discover and to see many nations, may be satisfied within this river, which bringeth forth so many armes and branches leading to severall countries, and provinces, above 2000 miles east and west, and 800 miles south and north: and of these, the most eyther rich in Gold, or in other marchandizes. The common soldier shal here fight for gold, and pay himselfe in steede of pence, with plates of halfe a foote brode, wheras he breaketh his bones in other warres for provant and penury. Those commanders and Chieftaines, that shoote at honour, and abundance, shal find there more rich and bewtifull cities, more temples adorned with golden Images, more sepulchers filled with treasure, then either *Cortez* found in *Mexico,* or *Pazzarro* in *Peru:* and the shining glorie of this conquest will eclipse all those so farre extended beames of the Spanish nation. [p. 71]

Ralegh's sensitivity to his audience may be seen most clearly in his different terms for the profits of the enterprise: "Gold" for the merchant adventurers, "plates of halfe a foote brode" for the common soldiers, and "golden Images," "sepulchers filled with treasure," and "shining glorie" for the commanders.

Throughout the *Discoverie,* Ralegh balances history, speculation on Spanish intentions, anthropological observation, military strategy, topographical description, patriotic appeals, prophecy, and straightforward narrative. His style is likewise flexible, though he stives throughout to maintain a note of authenticity by a confident use of terms and place names familiar to a voyager. The opening sentence is characteristic:

On Thursday the 6 of Februarie in the yeare 1595, we departed *England,* and the sunday following had sight of the North cape of *Spayne,* the winde for the most part continuing prosperous; wee passed in sight of the *Burlings* and the rocke, and so onwardes for the *Canaries,* and fell with *Fuerte ventura* the 17 of the same moneth, where we spent two or three daies, and relieved our companies with some fresh meate. [p. 11]

The sentence moves with that easy, artless matter-of-factness parodied by Swift in *Gulliver's Travels.* This is the style of the eyewitness who does not wish to distort his experience by using "art" in the telling of it: as Ralegh notes in his dedicatory epistle, "I have neither studied phrase, forme, nor fashion" (p. 6). The aura of authenticity is heightened by the great many native words and names that Ralegh records. Instead of simply noting that he freed five local chieftains who had been chained together and tortured by the Spanish governor, Ralegh adds their names: "Those five *Capitaynes* in the chaine were called *Wannawanare, Carroaori, Maquarima, Tarroopanama,* and *Aterima*" (p. 14). Similarly, he recounts, with evident satisfaction, his own use of native words and the names which the Indians gave to Queen Elizabeth:

I made them understand that I was the servant of a Queene, who was the great *Casique* of the north, and a virgin, and had more *Casiqui* under her then there were trees in their iland. . . . so as in that part of the world her majesty is very famous and admirable, whom they now call *Ezrabeta Cassipuna Aquerewana,* which is as much as *Elizabeth,* the great princesse or greatest commaunder. [p. 15]

These strange words do more than heighten the authenticity of the account. With their unfamiliar sounds and cadences they stimulate the reader's imagination, suggesting something rich and strange and grandiose. Arranged in long, sonorous lists, they evoke the world of the epic-romance:

There are besides within the land which are indeed rich and populous, the townes and Cities of *Merida, Lagrita, S. Christofero,* the great Cities of *Pampelone, S. Fede Bogota, Tunia* and *Mozo* where the *Esmeralds* are founde, the townes and Cities of *Morequito, velis, la villa de Leva, Palma, unda, Angustura,* the greate Citie of *Timana, Tocaima, S. Aguila, Pasto, Ivago,* the greate city of *Popaian* it selfe, *Los Remedios,* and the rest. [pp. 5–6]

The suggestions of romance are reinforced by the discussion of Amazons, of the Ewaipanoma who "are reported to have their eyes in their shoulders, and their mouths in the middle of their breasts," and, of course, of El Dorado and the great, golden city of Manoa. But the interweaving of life and art is most thorough and far-reaching in Ralegh's presentation of himself in the dedicatory epistle to Lord Charles Howard and Sir Robert Cecil:

In my more happie times as I did especially honour you both, so I
found that your loves sought me out in the darkest shadow of adversitie, and the same affection which accompanied my better fortune, sored not away from me in my manie miseries: all which
though I cannot requite, yet I shal ever acknowledge: and the great
debt which I have no power to pay, I can doe no more for a time
but confesse to be due. It is true that as my errors were great, so
they have yeelded verie grievous effects, and if ought might have
been deserved in former times to have counterpoysed any part of
offences, the frute thereof (as it seemeth) was long before fallen
from the tree, and the dead stocke onely remained. I did therefore
even in the winter of my life, Undertake these travels, fitter for
boies lesse blasted with mis-fortunes, for men of greater abilitie, and
for mindes of better incouragement, that thereby if it were possible
I might recover but the moderation of excesse, and the least tast of
the greatest plentie formerly possessed. If I had knowen other way
to win, if I had imagined how greater adventures might have re-
gained, if I coulde conceive what farther meanes I might yet use,
but even to appease so powerefull displeasure, I would not doubt
but for one yeare more to holde fast my soule in my teeth, til it
were performed. Of that little remaine I had, I have wasted in effect al herein, I have undergone many constructions, I have been
accompanyed with many sorrows, with labour, hunger, heat, sicknes,
and peril. ... But, if what I have done receive the gratious construction of a painful pilgrimage, and purchase the least remission,
I shall thinke all too little, and that there were wanting to the rest,
many miseries: But if both the times past, the present, and what
may be in the future, doe all by one graine of gall continue in an
eternall distast, I doe not then knowe whether I should bewaile my
selfe either for my too much travel and expence, or condemne my
selfe for doing lesse then that, which can deserve nothing. [pp. 3–4]

The man who in the winter of his life embraces perilous adventures in a strange land is the suffering, abandoned lover of
Ralegh's poetry:

> As in a countrey strange without companion,
> I onely waile the wrong of deaths delaies,
> Whose sweete spring spent, whose sommer well nie don,
> Of all which past, the sorow onely staies.
>
>   ["Farewell to the Court"]

> Love lykes not the fallyng frute
> From the wythered tree.
>
> > [Walsingham ballad]
>
> The blossumes fallen, the sapp gon from the tree,
> The broken monuments of my great desires,
> From thes so lost what may th'affections bee,
> What heat in Cynders of extinguisht fiers?
> . . . .
> To seeke new worlds, for golde, for prayse, for glory,
> To try desire, to try love severed farr.
>
> > [*Ocean to Cynthia*, 13–16, 61–62]

Moreover, the sorrowful cadences of the dedicatory epistle echo much of Elizabethan love poetry,[12] while the image of the old man who sails off to find forgiveness and grace suggests those larger patterns of death and rebirth which are present in many of the great artistic creations of the period. Ralegh crystallizes the poetic overtones of the voyage when he describes it as "a painful pilgrimage"—the same phrase used by the Hermit of Heavenly Contemplation in *The Faerie Queene* to describe the difficult journey to the New Jerusalem (I, x, 61).

Ralegh's *Discoverie,* then, sets the Guiana voyage in the context both of the personal sorrow which had animated his poetry and of some of the major religious and national myths of his age. Perhaps "religious" is too strong; the pilgrimage is almost wholly secular. Ralegh makes no mention of bringing the true faith to the pagan or even of combating the Roman Catholicism of Spain. Instead, like Montaigne, he finds the natives worthy of admiration and respect:

notwithstanding the moistnes of the aire in which they live, the hardnes of their diet, and the great labors they suffer to hunt, fish, and foule for their living, in all my life either in the Indies or in Europe did I never behold a more goodlie or better favoured people, or a more manlie. [p. 39] [13]

Their dignity and simplicity render their harsh treatment at the hands of the Spanish all the more atrocious and provide the English with a moral mission: to undertake a war of liberation on behalf of an oppressed people. As in Book v of *The Faerie Queene,* Spain is the terrible, devilish enemy who must be fought with force and guile and whose final defeat is the great destiny of the English nation:

And I farther remember that *Berreo* confessed to me and others (which I protest before the Majesty of God to be true) that there was found among prophecies in *Peru* (at such time as the Empyre was reduced to the Spanish obedience) in their chiefest temples, amongst divers others which foreshewed the losse of the said Empyre, that from *Inglatierra* those *Ingas* shoulde be againe in time to come restored, and delivered from the servitude of the said Conquerors. [p. 75]

And just as the Red Crosse Knight and Calidore are granted the splendid visions of the New Jerusalem and Mount Acidale, Ralegh twice glimpses the wonderful serenity and beauty of the New World:

On both sides of this river, we passed the most beautifull countrie that ever mine eies beheld: and whereas all that we had seen before was nothing but woods, prickles, bushes, and thornes, heere we beheld plaines of twenty miles in length, the grasse short and greene, and in divers parts groves of trees by themselves, as if they had been by all the art and labour in the world so made of purpose: and stil as we rowed, the Deere came downe feeding by the waters side, as if they had beene used to a keepers call. [p. 42]

I never saw a more beawtifull countrey, nor more lively prospectes, hils so raised heere and there over the vallies, the river winding into divers braunches, the plaines adjoyning without bush or stubble, all faire greene grasse, the ground of hard sand easy to march on, eyther for horse or foote, the deare crossing in every path, the birds towardes the evening singing on every tree with a thousand several tunes, cranes and herons of white, crimson and carnation pearching on the rivers side, the ayre fresh with a gentle easterlie wind, and every stone that we stooped to take up, promised eyther golde or silver by his complexion. [pp. 54–55]

These brief moments of luminous simplicity and beauty are rendered the more precious by being hard-won. The first vi-

sion is the unexpected reward of a harrowing search along a
branch of the Orinoco for a friendly village where Ralegh and
his men hoped to find food and drink. When they realized
how far they had come from the main river and their galley,
they suspected their Indian pilot of treachery:

At the last we determined to hang the Pilot, and if we had well
knowned the way backe againe by night, he had surely gone, but our
owne necessities pleaded sufficiently for his safetie: for it was as
darke as pitch, and the river began to narrow it selfe, and the trees
to hang over from side to side, as we were driven with arming
swordes to cut a passage thorow those branches that covered the
water. [p. 41]

Only after this journey through a hostile landscape do the
men glimpse for a moment the serene beauty of the land, with
the promise of security embodied in the deer that "came
downe feeding by the waters side, as if they had been used to
a keepers call." But the vision is fragile, and a moment later
the company once again faces danger and hardship. Similarly,
the second Edenic scene, won by a tedious trek to which Ralegh himself objected, is quickly followed by mention of "that
lodging, watching, care, perill, diseases, ill savoures, bad fare,
and many other mischiefes that accompany these voyages" (p.
55). Indeed, in this latter case, the very sentence of description
turns away slightly from the idyll, as it concludes "and every
stone that we stooped to take up, promised eyther golde or silver by his complexion." The final clause is slightly detached
from the preceding clauses by its syntactic independence and
by the elevation of diction. This detachment gives greater
weight to the climactic wonder of Guiana—its abundance of
precious metals—but it also suggests that the gold and silver
are of a different order from the green grass, the deer, the
beautiful birds, and the fresh, gentle air. We feel a slight jar
when we reach the end of the sentence; we sense that the
terms of thought and feeling have suddenly shifted. After all,
Ralegh himself had written of the Spanish king that "It is his
Indian Golde that indaungereth and disturbeth all the nations of Europe, it purchaseth intelligence, creepeth into

Councels, and setteth bound loyalty at libertie, in the greatest Monarchies of Europe" (p. 9). This belief, of course, was no hindrance to the English search for some "Indian Golde" of its own—quite the reverse—and yet the uneasiness remains.

It is unlikely that Ralegh was ever conscious of the tension between his primitivism and his plans for the exploitation of Guiana. But that tension nonetheless existed, and it appears subtly in the style of the *Discoverie*. Consider, for example, Ralegh's summation:

To conclude, *Guiana* is a Contrey that hath yet her Maydenhead, never sackt, turned, nor wrought, the face of the earth hath not beene torne, nor the vertue and salt of the soyle spent by manur-ance, the graves have not beene opened for gold, the mines not broken with sledges, nor their Images puld down out of their tem-ples. [p. 73]

The meaning seems clear—all of Guiana's riches are still intact—and the required course is obvious: "the conquest of Guiana" (p. 73). And yet there is something disquieting in the tone of this passage, a note of regret and dread running counter to the dominant assertion. The words are too strong, their connotations too unpleasant to enable us to translate them into a positive course of action for England: *sackt, turned, wrought, torne, spent, broken, puld down.* The images of the virgin land and of an earth whose face has not yet been torn by the plough recalls Ovid's description of the Golden Age: "The earth herself, without compulsion, untouched by hoe or plowshare, of herself gave all things needful." [14] This is the landscape of wish-fulfillment, the unspoiled world of man's imagination, and its image subverts the ethic of empire and aggressive capitalism. As in *Ocean to Cynthia,* what began as a theatrical gesture, a work intended to attract attention and achieve practical results, itself became a stage on which oppos-ing forces within Ralegh struggled for dominance.

Though it was a popular success, the *Discoverie* failed to ex-cite significant government interest, and the Guiana enterprise

was allowed to lapse. Ralegh's martial spirit and will to command found a focus in such adventures as the attack upon
Cadiz in 1596 when, responding to each firing of the enemy
guns with a blare of a trumpet, his ship sailed into the harbor
at the head of the English fleet.[15] His dreams of a Golden
World gave way in the last years of Elizabeth's reign to a partial, autumnal return to the spirit of the early period of the
queen's favor. Cynthia once again became the focus, at least
superficially, of the strain of visionary optimism in his nature.

Though these were years of wealth and influence, Ralegh's
life as a courtier in the twilight of the Tudor dynasty seems
strange and even dreamlike. Isolated as always, dependent
upon the queen's favor and upon her increasingly erratic
moods, he played his old, slightly tarnished role. The queen,
nearly seventy years old, obstinately refused the anxious appeals from her counselors and from Commons to name a successor, insisting almost fiercely upon a constant reiteration of
the rituals of the past. Alternately grave and girlish, madden-
ingly independent of mind, stingy, cautious, and astonishingly
energetic, she was still the Virgin Queen of old, dressing herself gorgeously, restlessly moving about the country, flirting
with her handsome courtiers. But the romance was now gro-
tesque, the attempt to transcend time and mortality increasingly pathetic and desperate. "Time conquering all she
mast'reth/By beinge alwaye new," wrote Ralegh at the turn of
the century, adapting lines he had written years before, but
others knew better. In secret correspondence with King James
VI of Scotland, Robert Cecil and Henry Howard worked to
assure themselves a place in the new government and plotted
the downfall of dangerous rivals like Ralegh. Howard's letters
reveal an almost pathological hatred of Ralegh, while Cecil's
are more subtle and indirect—and perhaps more effective in
poisoning the mind of the king:

Let me, therefore, presume thus far upon your Majesty's favour
that, whatsoever he [Ralegh] shall take upon him to say for me,
upon any new humour of kindness—whereof sometimes he will
be replete, upon the receipt of private benefit—you will no more

believe it . . . be it never so much in my commendation. . . . Would
God I were as free from offence towards God in seeking, for private
affection, to support a person whom most religious men do hold
anathema.[16]

This was Ralegh's great friend and ally, the man he trusted
and relied upon for advice. The ground was carefully being
laid for an accusation of high treason, and Ralegh walked as if
in a dream.

A few months after the accession of James to the English
throne, the trap was sprung. One morning between the 13th
and the 15th of July 1603, as Ralegh was waiting on the ter-
race at Windsor for the king to appear and mount for the
hunt, Robert Cecil approached and told him "as from the
King" that he was to stay, and present himself before the
Lords in Council. "They have some questions to ask you." [17] A
few days later, Ralegh was imprisoned in the Tower, impli-
cated, with Lord Cobham and others, in a complex plot to
kill the king, place Arabella Stuart on the throne, and make
peace with Spain. It is difficult to take seriously the Crown's
charges against Ralegh; the conduct of the investigation and
trial suggests that the prosecutors themselves were far from
convinced by the tissue of circumstantial evidence, hysterical
accusations quickly withdrawn, and rancorous gossip. The actual details of the plot and the obscure nature of Ralegh's involvement do not concern us here. But his behavior throughout this miserable affair strikingly reinforces the conception of
Ralegh as a self-dramatizer, deliberately shaping his identity.

On July 27, Ralegh stabbed himself in an apparent suicide
attempt. Cecil's account in a letter to the English ambassador
in Paris is probably the most reliable:

Although lodged and attended as well as in his own house, yet one
afternoon, while divers of us were in the Tower, examining these
prisoners, Sir W. Ralegh attempted to have murdered himself.
Whereof when we were advertised, we came to him, and found him
in some agony, seeming to be unable to endure his misfortunes, and
protesting innocency, with carelessness of life. In that humour he
had wounded himself under the right pap; but no way mortally,

being in truth rather a cut than a stab. . . . He is very well cured, both in body and mind.[18]

Taking up Cecil's hint, Agnes Latham has suggested that Ralegh's stab "was merely a feint, a dramatic gesture indicating desperation, and carefully timed when the commissioners were actually in the Tower." [19] We may place this gesture in the context of his by now familiar recourse to self-dramatization at moments of crisis. Yet to view the incident as nothing more than a clever scenario may be to overlook the substantial reality of the passions and anguish expressed in Ralegh's act and in his suicide note:

For my selfe I am left of all men, that have done good to many. All my good turnes forgotten, all my errors revived, and expownded to all extremitie of ill. All my services, hazardes, and expences, for my Countrie; plantinges, discoveries, fightes, Councells, and whatsoever ells, malice hath nowe covered over. I am nowe made an enemie and traytor by the word of an unworthie man; he hath proclaimed me to be a partaker of his vaine imaginacions, notwithstanding the whole Course of my life hath approved the contrarie, as my death shall approve it. . . . Oh intollerable infamie. Oh god I cannot resiste theis thoughtes, I cannot live to thincke how I am deryded, to thincke of the expectacion of my enimyes, the scornes I shall receive, the crewell words of Lawyers, the infamous tauntes and dispightes, to be made a wonder and a spectacle. O death hasten the[e] unto me, that thowe maiste destroye the memorie of theis, and laye me up in darke forgetfullnes. O death destroye my memorie which is my Tormentor; my thoughts and my life cannot dwell in one body.[20]

This is the actor emoting before his audience, but then, like the dedicatory epistle in the *Discoverie*, Ralegh's suicide note is the work of a man who seems to conceive of his identity as a dramatic role. The stab was probably an act, as Latham suggests, but acting was one of Ralegh's modes of self-consciousness. In the suicide attempt, he acted out his crushing self-pity and loneliness, his dark, fearful vision of oblivion, and perhaps a genuine longing for death. Paradoxically, he may also have intended his act to express heroic self-affirmation, the unwillingness of a Brutus "to be made a wonder and a spectacle" for his enemies. In *The History of the World,* despite his general avoidance of unorthodoxy, Ralegh praises Demosthenes for taking his own life,

> rather choosing to doe the last execution upon himselfe, than to fall into the hands of such as hated him. Only this act of his (commendable, perhaps, in a Heathen man) argued some valour in him. [IV, iii, 6, p. 221]

That this admittedly pagan heroism was the interpretation Ralegh wished to be put on his action is reinforced by the French ambassador's dispatch to his king on August 13:

> Sir Walter Ralegh is said to have declared that his design to kill himself arose from no feeling of fear; but was formed in order that his fate might not serve as a triumph to his enemies, whose power to put him to death, despite his innocency, he well knows.[21]

The French envoy's report is a reminder that the great advantage of the feigned suicide, as Latham observes, is that Ralegh himself could be around to point the moral.

The part Ralegh was to play in the next months was less spectacular than the suicide attempt but far more effective in changing public opinion. From narrowly escaping dismemberment at the hands of a mob, he became, by the end of his trial, a symbol of the innocent man abused by harsh, unjust laws and wicked, timeserving men. Of course, Ralegh probably *was* an innocent man. But to communicate this innocence to a hostile populace took all of his powers of self-presentation and dramatic timing. The success of Ralegh's performance at his trial on 17 November 1603 is confirmed by many spectators. Dudley Carleton's account is typical:

> Sir Walter Ralegh served for a whole act, and played all the parts himself. . . . He answered with that temper, wit, learning, courage, and judgment, that, save it went with the hazard of his life, it was the happiest day that ever he spent. And so well he shifted all advantages that were taken against him, that were not *fama malum gravius quam res,* and an ill name half hanged, in the opinion of all men, he had been acquitted.[22]

In the face of the vindictive attacks of Edward Coke, the attorney general, Ralegh maintained a quiet dignity, asserting his innocence firmly yet without arrogance, patiently requesting his legal rights and pointing out distortions in the state's case against him, refusing to beg abjectly for his life or to humble himself before his accusers and the king. Again and again, Coke attempted to move the accused in some way, either to anger or outrage or self-pity or fear, but Ralegh steadfastly remained calm and self-controlled, as he was to do years later on the scaffold.

Two plots had been discovered, the "Bye" or "Priest's Plot" and the "Main." Ralegh was charged only with the latter, but Coke quickly set about to implicate him in both. Ralegh objected:

RALEGH. I pray you, Gentlemen of the Jury, remember I am not charged with the *bye,* which was the treason of the priests.

COKE. You are not; but your Lordships will see that all these treasons, though they consisted of several points, closed in together, like Sampson's foxes, which were joined in the tails, though their heads were severed. . . . I shall not need, my Lords, to speak anything concerning the King, nor of the bounty and sweetness of his nature; whose thoughts are innocent, whose words are full of wisdom and learning, and whose works are full of honour. But to whom, Sir Walter, did you bear malice? To the royal children?

RALEGH. Mr. Attorney, I pray you to whom, or to what end speak you all this? I protest I do not understand what a word of this means, except it be to tell me news. What is the treason of Markham and the priests to me?

COKE. I will then come close to you; I will prove you to be the most notorious traitor that ever came to the bar; you are indeed upon the *main,* but you have followed them of the *bye* in imitation; I will charge you with the words.

RALEGH. *Your* words cannot condemn me; my innocency is my defence. I pray you go to your proofs. Prove against me any one thing of the many that you have broken, and I will confess all the indictment, and that I am the most horrible traitor that ever lived, and worthy to be crucified with a thousand torments.

COKE. Nay I will prove all; thou art a monster; thou hast an English face, but a Spanish heart.[23]

In repeated exchanges of this kind, the whole tenor and meaning of the trial shifted, from the case of the people against a
dangerous traitor to the spectacle of the vast powers of the
state and the law arrayed against a courageous, innocent individual. Coke's bitter and intemperate attacks helped to bring
about this shift, but the primary credit was Ralegh's. His arguments and replies were not only brave and intelligent, but
they powerfully conjoined his individual case and the condition of all mankind, transforming the particular into the universal. This transformation is characteristic of Ralegh
throughout his career: from the flatterer of the queen to the
awestruck worshipper of Diana, from the disgraced favorite to
man in search of himself and of true, undying love, from the
adventurer in Guiana to the seeker of the Golden World, and,
at the end of his life, from the condemned traitor to man con-
fronting time and death. Again and again in the trial of 1603,
as Ralegh replies to Coke, we hear this resonance of the universal in the words of the individual:

If you proceed to condemn me by bare inferences, without an oath,
without a subscription, without witness, upon a paper accusation,
you try me by the Spanish inquisition. [p. 418]

By the law of God, therefore, the life of man is of such price and
value, that no person, whatever his offence is, ought to die, unless
he be condemned on the testimony of two or three witnesses. [p.
419]

[I]f witnesses are to speak by relation of one another, by this
means you may have any man's life in a week. [p. 429]

I will challenge nothing to myself, nor expect anything of you but
what reason, religion, and conscience ask for every man: only this
let me say to every one of you in particular;—remember what St.
Augustine saith, 'So judge as if you were about to be judged yourselves, for in the end there is but one Judge and one Tribunal for
all men.' That Judge must judge both me and you; before that Tribunal both you and I must stand. Now if you yourselves would like
to be hazarded in your lives, disabled in your posterities—your
lands, goods and all you have confiscated,—your wives, children

and servants left crying to the world; if you would be content all
this should befal you upon a trial by suspicions and presumptions,
—upon an accusation not subscribed by your accuser,—without the
open testimony of a single witness, then so judge me as you would
yourselves be judged! [p. 442]

Ralegh was found guilty of treason and sentenced to death,
but his words and his demeanor had made an ineradicable
and deeply disturbing impression that did more than simply
change the attitude of the populace toward the once-hated favorite.[24] He transformed his life into a symbol of the lives of
all men threatened by an overwhelmingly powerful system:
"by this means you may have any man's life in a week." He exposed the hypocrisy of a legal system which prided itself upon
its humane abjuration of torture, the instrument of the Spanish Inquisition, while using the threat of torture to abstract
confessions:

RALEGH. For that you tell me of Kemys, I never sent him on any
such message [to Lord Cobham]. I know not what you might draw
from myself for fear of torture, for this poor man hath been a close
prisoner these eighteen weeks, and hath been *threatened with the
rack to make him confess;* but I dare stand upon it he will not say
it now.

LORD HENRY HOWARD. No circumstance moveth me more than
this; *Kemys was never on the rack,* for the King gave charge that no
rigour should be used.

COMMISSIONERS. We protest before God there was no such matter
intended to our knowledge.

RALEGH. Was not the keeper of the rack sent for, and he threatened with it?

SIR W. WADE. When Mr. Solicitor and myself examined Kemys,
we told him he deserved the rack, but did not threaten him with it.

COMMISSIONERS. That was more than we knew. [pp. 433–34]

Above all, he suceeded in simplifying and polarizing the issues
to a conflict between the individual and the state:

RALEGH. Mr. Attorney, have you done?

COKE. Yes, if you have no more to say.

RALEGH. If you have done, then I have somewhat more to say.

COKE. Nay, I will have the last word for the King.

RALEGH. Nay, I will have the last word for my life!

COKE. Go to, I will lay thee upon thy back for the confidentest traitor that ever came to the bar! [p. 443]

In such exchanges, Ralegh dramatized before the whole nation the radical alienation of the individual from the state which was to become so important in the reign of the Stuarts. The groundwork was being laid for the belief that the state was hostile to the deeper values of religion and the individual, the belief that would eventually bring James's son to the scaffold. Echoes of Ralegh's voice may be heard, for example, a half-century later in the impassioned words of the radical John Lilburne:

. . . for what is done to any one, may be done to every one: besides, being all members of one body, that is, of the English Commonwealth, one man should not suffer wrongfully, but all should be sensible and endeavor his preservation; otherwise, they give way to an inlet of the sea of will and power, upon all their laws and liberties, which are the boundaries to keep out tyranny and oppression.[25]

It was no accident that the Puritans later made Ralegh a martyr for the liberties of England; he had prepared the way for this transformation.

As long as he was on the stage before the public, Ralegh held up his heroic role. Even when the dread sentence was read—"you shall be drawn upon a hurdle through the open streets to the place of execution, there to be hanged and cut down alive, and your body shall be opened, your heart and bowels plucked out, and your privy members cut off and thrown into the fire before your eyes. Then your head to be stricken off from your body, and your body shall be divided into four quarters, to be disposed of at the King's pleasure"— even then, he refused to cringe and beg for mercy in public, only privately requesting that the lords "be suitors in his behalf to his Majesty, that, in regard of the places of honour which he had theretofore held, the rigour of his sentence might be qualified, and his death be honourable and not ignominious." [26] But when his great moment had passed, Ralegh's spirit suddenly seemed to break as his role shattered. In the ensuing weeks he wrote to the king and the lords begging for his life or at least "one yeare to geve to God in a prison." [27] All that remains of the splendid prisoner at the bar in these self-abasing letters is the will to live; the heroism and self-control are gone.

But when these desperate appeals were ignored, when the priests, Watson and Clarke, had been hanged and Lord Cobham's brother, George Brooke, had been beheaded, when the day of his own execution neared, Ralegh's mood changed once again. "Gett those letters (if it bee possible) which I writt to the Lords, wherein I sued for my lief," he wrote to his wife. "God knoweth that itt was for you and yours that I desired it, but itt is true that I disdaine myself for begging itt. And know itt (deare wief) that your sonne is the childe of a true man, and who, in his own respect, despiseth Death, and all his misshapen and ouglie formes" (*Letters*, pp. 286–87). As he made himself ready for the final scenes, Ralegh mastered his fear. His spirit was not that of the saint who goes to the block firm and happy in his belief in the sacred cause, for he did not think himself a martyr for anything; he knew that he was the victim of malice and lies. But still less was his mood that of the writer of the "suicide" note, the hysteric who, in his self-pity and frustrated rage, longs for death to free him from the memory of his wrongs and the taunts of his enemies. Ralegh's famous letter of farewell and consolation to his wife, written shortly before his expected execution, reveals in him a rare spirit of faith—not the aggressive piety of a Puritan saint but the simple faith of a pilgrim:

Love God, and beginne betymes to repose yourself on Him; therein shall you find true and lastinge ritches, and endles comfort. For the rest, when you have travelled and wearied your thoughts on all sorts of worldly cogitacions, you shall sit downe by Sorrow in the end. Teach your sonne alsoe to serve and feare God, while he is young; that the feare of God may grow upp in him. Then will God be a husband unto you, and a father unto him; a husband and a father which can never be taken from you. . . .

I cannot wright much. God knowes howe hardlie I stole this tyme, when all sleep; and it is tyme to separate my thoughts from the world. Begg my dead body, which living was denyed you; and either lay itt att Sherborne if the land continue, or in Exiter church, by my father and mother. I can wright noe more. Tyme and Death call me awaye.

The everlasting, infinite powerfull, and inscrutable God, that Almightie God that is goodnes itself, mercy itself, the true lief and light, keep you and yours, and have mercy on me, and teach me to forgeve my persecutors and false accusers; and send us to meete in His glorious kingdome. My true wief, farewell. Blesse my poore boye; pray for me. My true God hold you both in His armes. [*Letters*, pp. 285–87]

It does not detract from the beauty and pathos of these expressions to observe here the workings once again of role-playing, the dynamic principle of Ralegh's response to crisis, nor does it detract from his sincerity, for we have seen how deeply committed he could become to the role he consciously or unconsciously adopted. An awareness of the histrionic sensibility simply enables us to understand, far better than any notion of a last-minute "conversion," the unexpected appearance in Ralegh of these religious feelings and, still more, his ability to express them in such a compelling, dramatic form. The moving words of farewell reflect his profound sense of the self as an actor, his strange, paradoxical detachment at moments of the deepest emotion.

This same yoking of engagement and detachment is at the heart of a famous poem of this period which a strong manuscript tradition assigns to Ralegh, "The Passionate Mans Pilgrimage": [28]

> And this is my eternall plea,
> To him that made Heaven, Earth and Sea,
> Seeing my flesh must die so soone,
> And want a head to dine next noone,
> Just at the stroke when my vaines start and spred
> Set on my soule an everlasting head.

The strange tone of this passage and of the entire poem, the mingling of faith, cold gallows humor, and the fascination with the awful moment of death, reflects Ralegh's capacity for intense self-dramatization, for being both within and outside the self. The religious imagery, however, is unprecedented in his poetry and has led Philip Edwards and Pierre Lefranc to dispute Ralegh's authorship.[29] Of course, their argument is weakened by the simple possibility that Ralegh might well have written a wholly "uncharacteristic" poem, particularly under the pressure of approaching death, but in fact "The Passionate Mans Pilgrimage" accords very well with the role to which Ralegh had committed himself in what he believed were his last days. The difference between the hope that God will "send us to meete in His glorious kingdome" and the visionary pilgrimage is great, but it may be the difference between a letter and a poem, between role-playing in life and in art. Ralegh's poems fully realize and elaborate roles which are, of necessity, only partially acted out in life. As the anguish of *Ocean to Cynthia* has its roots in the feelings of rejection expressed in the letter to Cecil ("My heart was never broken till this day"), and as the driving, bitter attack of "The Lie" seems to originate in the mood of disillusionment that followed his disgrace in 1592, so the religious vision of "The Passionate Mans Pilgrimage" reflects Ralegh's spiritual mood in the days before his impending execution.

The role of pilgrim was not new to Ralegh's imagination. Years before, in a brilliant translation of a poem by Phillippe Desportes, he had pictured himself "Like to a Hermite poore" (*Poems*, pp. 11–12), and later he had used the motif of pilgrimage in the Walsingham ballad. Still later, in 1596, Ralegh had hoped that the queen would view his voyage to Guiana as a "painful pilgrimage." From this role, I believe, follow the images that strike Edwards and Lefranc as uncharacteristic. Thus in the translation of Desportes, there are many of the same attributes—gown, staff, food and drink—only used as images of sorrow rather than salvation. Likewise, Rosemond Tuve has noted that "in a *Horae* MS bearing Ralegh's signa-

ture . . . the illumination picturing St. James furnishes this
palmer par excellence with the *scallop-shell, staff, gown* of
Ralegh's poem." [30] And the sensuous images of the middle
stanzas, the "Seelings of Diamonds, Saphire floores,/High
walles of Corall and Pearle Bowres" need not demonstrate, as
Edwards believes, that "The Passionate Mans Pilgrimage" is
the work of a Roman Catholic, but may simply reflect the
same traditions that later in the century led Milton to give his
heaven a "bright/Pavement, that like a sea of jasper shone"
and Bunyan to picture the Heavenly City "builded of pearls
and precious stones, also the street thereof . . . paved with
gold." [31] As for the uncharacteristic sense of personal intimacy
with Christ that Edwards finds especially strong in the lines

> Christ pleades his death, and then we live,
> Be thou my speaker taintles pleader,
> Unblotted Lawer, true proceeder,
> Thou movest salvation even for almes:
> Not with a bribed Lawyers palmes

that sense is considerably qualified by restoring the lines to
their context, a satirical attack on the English courts and the
king's attorney:

> From thence to heavens Bribeles hall
> Where no corrupted voyces brall,
> No Conscience molten into gold,
> Nor forg'd accusers bought and sold,
> No cause deferd, nor vaine spent Jorney,
> For there Christ is the Kings Atturney.

If we recall that the king's attorney was Sir Edward Coke and
that throughout his trial Ralegh contrasted the mercy of God
with the "barbarous" proceedings of men, Ralegh's claim to
"The Passionate Mans Pilgrimage" is further strengthened.

   In the years between his disgrace in 1592 and his imprisonment in 1603, Ralegh moved restlessly back and forth between
despair and heroic self-assertion, disillusionment and fervent
optimism. The role of pilgrim resolved the conflicting visions
within him, the Golden World and the world of death. A bit-

ter contempt for the world, its hopes and institutions, is linked with a vivid, highly sensuous conception of heaven, the landscape of wish-fulfillment:

> Then the holy paths weele travell
> Strewde with Rubies thicke as gravell,
> Seelings of Diamonds, Saphire floores,
> High walles of Corall and Pearle Bowres.

For a moment, Ralegh is able to unite both the dark truth of "The Lie" and the riches and glory of the romanticized Guiana voyage. But even within "The Passionate Mans Pilgrimage" itself, this resolution shows strains and potential rifts. The deliberate naiveté of the pilgrim's vision of heaven jars with both the worldly satire upon the courts and the strange detachment of the final stanza. The tenuous union of optimism and despair is already dissolving. When Ralegh's sentence was commuted to life imprisonment—an imprisonment that actually was to last for nearly thirteen years—the role of visionary pilgrim altogether crumbled away.

Even this picture of conflict and tension is, of course, oversimplified. I have selected aspects of Ralegh's life in this period which reveal most clearly his penchant for self-dramatization and mark those extremes between which he oscillated. But there is much that does not neatly fit into this pattern: an extremely active parliamentary career, complex litigation and financial maneuvering, his functioning in various offices, and above all those countless small incidents which dominate the lives of us all. The themes I have chosen to discuss do in fact relate to many of these things, but rather obliquely, and I have naturally concentrated only on incidents and writings where they are crucial.

Moreover, even in discussing the interplay of life and art in Ralegh's career, I have not stressed certain distinctions which should nonetheless be noted. There is clearly a difference between the self-dramatization involved in a grand and complicated scheme like the Guiana voyage and the self-dramatization manifested in a one-man-show like the suicide attempt, just as there is a difference between the poetic image of the self created in action and the poetic image of the self created in words. In the more highly controlled situations, Ralegh's powers of self-fashioning had freer and more direct play. If I have not constantly reminded the reader of these distinctions, it is because I think they are obvious and finally less important than the continuity between the various modes of self-dramatization.

5 The History of the World

O eloquent, just, and mighty Death!

At the close of a moving passage in the 21st Book of *Ocean to Cynthia*, Ralegh acknowledges the impossibility of ever completing his vast poetic undertaking, of ever recording the "worlds of thoughts" within him:

> As if when after Phebus is dessended
> And leves a light mich like the past dayes dawninge,
> And every toyle and labor wholy ended
> Each livinge creature draweth to his restinge
> Wee should beginn by such a partinge light
> To write the story of all ages past
> And end the same before th'aprochinge night.
>
> [97–103]

Characteristically, his admission of defeat is at the same time a heroic assertion. In comparing the story of his life and "the story of all ages past," the poet implies that the record of his shifting emotions is as grand and complex as the history of the world. For a moment, we glimpse all of Ralegh's massive egotism. But the prevailing mood is helplessness; the immense expanse of universal history is incommensurate with a few twilight minutes of feverish activity. For each living creature, the "aprochinge night" is a time of rest before another day of labor, but for the poet there will be no dawn. For him the night is death, the obliteration of all his complex memories and emotions, the endless sleep of which Catullus wrote in lines that Ralegh translated and placed in *The History of the World:*

> The Sunne may set and rise:
> But we contrariwise
> Sleepe after our short light
> One everlasting night.
>
> [I, ii, 5, p. 31]

127

The image of writing "the story of all ages past" is an astonishing premonition of the *History*, but it is highly unlikely that Ralegh had seriously considered writing a universal history in 1592. The work probably existed as an image or theme in Ralegh's poetic imagination long before it existed in fact, just as the voyage to Guiana was perhaps prefigured in the line "To seeke new worlds, for golde, for prayse, for glory." But while the search for the Golden World was a form of wish-fulfillment (and a very conventional one at that), writing the *History* was the realization of a much more complex idea, an image of both grandeur and futility, a symbol of the astonishing breadth of man's vision and the hopelessness of his ever achieving his goals. Indeed, the *History* succeeds nearly perfectly in embodying simultaneously—in *acting out*—the two conflicting traditions which, as we have seen, underlie Ralegh's dramatic sense of life.

Just as the projected length of *Ocean to Cynthia* precluded the possibility of its completion, so the scope of the *History*, as Ralegh conceived it, was far beyond the powers of a single man. Had the work, he writes in the Preface,

beene begotten then with my first dawne of day, when the light of common knowledge began to open it selfe to my yonger yeares: and before any wound received, either from Fortune or Time: I might yet well have doubted, that the darknesse of Age and Death would have covered over both It and Mee, long before the performance. For, beginning with the Creation: I have proceeded with the History of the World. . . . [Pref., sig. A1ʳ]

Ralegh almost suggests here what we may well believe, that he had been drawn to his immensely ambitious project precisely because he knew it was impossible to complete, precisely to dramatize the "time of day" as he puts it, "the day of a tempestuous life drawne on to the very evening ere I began." The expression takes us back to *Ocean to Cynthia* with its symbol of human aspiration and hopelessness—the enormous task undertaken in the "partinge light" of evening.

This sense of unrelenting time is a bridge between the *His-*

tory, written in the Tower from 1609 to 1614, and Ralegh's poetry, which was for the most part composed before the death of Elizabeth. The figure of Time stalks through almost all his poems, destroying the "passionate shepherd's" pastoral dreams, undermining love and nature, causing man's hopes to wither and die:

> Time drives the flocks from field to fold,
> When Rivers rage, and Rocks grow cold,
> And Philomell becommeth dombe,
> The rest complaines of cares to come.
>
> > [*Poems*, p. 16]

> So fraile is all thinges as wee see,
> So subject unto conquering Time.
>
> > [*Poems*, p. 20]

> But Time which nature doth despise,
> And rudely gives her love the lye,
> Makes hope a foole, and sorrow wise,
> His hands doth neither wash, nor dry,
> But being made of steele and rust,
> Turnes snow, and silke, and milke to dust.
>
> > [*Poems*, p. 21]

> [A]ll thos flames that rize
> From formes externall, cann no longer last,
> Then that thos seeminge bewties hold in pryme
> Loves ground, his essence, and his emperye,
> All slaves to age, and vassalls unto tyme
> Of which repentance writes the tragedye.
>
> > [*Poems*, p. 31]

Significantly, on the night before his execution, Ralegh recalled his apostrophe to Time in "Nature that washt her hands in milke" and made it his epitaph.

Ralegh's preoccupation with time dominates the *History*. As we have seen, his consciousness of the gap between his vast undertaking and the brief time of life left to him seems to be part of the very impulse behind the work; its echoes may be heard in his reflections on the time of empires, dynasties, and reigns, the time of ideas and works of art, the time of the ancient gods:

> The Fire, which the *Chaldaeans* worshipped for a God, is crept into
> every mans chimney, which the lacke of fewell starveth, water quen-
> cheth, and want of aire suffocateth: *Jupiter* is no more vexed with
> *Junoes* jelosies; Death hath perswaded him to chastitie, and her to
> patience; and that Time which hath devoured it selfe, hath also
> eaten up both the bodies and images of him and his: yea, their
> stately Temples of stone and durefull Marble. The houses and
> sumptuous buildings erected to *Baal,* can no where bee found upon
> the earth; nor any monument of that glorious Temple consecrated
> to *Diana.* There are none now in *Phoenicia,* that lament the death
> of *Adonis;* nor any in *Lybia, Creta, Thessalia,* or elsewhere, that
> can aske counsaile or helpe from *Jupiter.* The great God *Pan* hath
> broken his Pipes. . . . [I, vi, 8, p. 96]

The tone is ironic, of course, but there is also a surprising
note of nostalgia, not so much for the lost pagan beauty which
Milton half-consciously mourns in the Nativity Ode as simply
for all things which have been devoured by time.

Behind this and many similar passages is the tragic sense of
the individual life which ends in death, the sense of time
which tormented the poet of *Ocean to Cynthia:*

> But as the feildes clothed with leves and floures
> The bancks of roses smellinge pretious sweet
> Have put ther bewties date, and tymely houres,
> And then defast by winters cold, and sleet,
> So farr as neather frute nor forme of floure
> Stayes for a wittnes what such branches bare,
> Butt as tyme gave, tyme did agayne devoure
> And chandge our risinge joy to fallinge care;
> So of affection which our youth presented,
> When shee that from the soonn reves poure and light
> Did but decline her beames as discontented
> Convertinge sweetest dayes to saddest night;
> All droopes, all dyes, all troden under dust
> The person, place, and passages forgotten
> The hardest steele eaten with softest ruste,
> The firme and sollide tree both rent and rotten.

[241–56]

The seasonal imagery and even the rhythms here appear again and again in the *History* as Ralegh reflects upon the contrast between the human life cycle, with its terrible finality, and the natural cycle of death and rebirth:

For this tide of mans life, after it once turneth and declineth, ever runneth with a perpetuall ebbe and falling streame, but never floweth againe: our leafe once fallen, springeth no more, neither doth the Sunne or the Summer adorne us againe, with the garments of new leaves and flowers. . . . [A]s the sappe and juyce, wherein the life of Plants is preserved, doth evermore ascend or descend: so is it with the life of man, which is alwaies either encreasing towards ripeness and perfection, or declining and decreasing towards rottennesse and dissolution. [i, ii, 5, pp. 31–32]

This sense of the "tide of man's life" lies at the heart of the entire *History*. Its particular expressions are often highly conventional, the long, resounding cadences reaching back through centuries of histories, sermons, and orations to the Bible and to classical moralists, but the effect of the whole is profoundly personal. No matter how far Ralegh may seem to move away from the self and toward the anonymity of religious and political orthodoxy, the vital pulse of the work always emanates from his inner anxieties. The *History* may have "recapitulated the entire sixteenth-century development" or English historical thought,[1] it may have laid the groundwork for the English revolution,[2] its Preface may have been the "culminating document of Renaissance historiography in England,"[3] but it is first of all a work of the individual imagination, vitally related to the tensions, concerns, and sense of self that shaped Ralegh's actions and his poetry. My purpose in this chapter will be to examine the presence of Ralegh in his work. Naturally, in dealing with so massive an achievement—2,700 pages in the 1829 reprint—I shall have to be highly selective, and I do not pretend to offer an exhaustive reading. But I believe there is much to be gained from viewing the *History* in the light of the themes I have discussed thus far, particularly in the light of Ralegh's characteristic response to crisis. For the *History* was in its origin a histrionic gesture, and, like similar gestures in his career, it was soon transformed into a stage on which were enacted his inner conflicts.

When Ralegh was imprisoned in 1592, he turned to poetry as a tactic to regain the queen's favor. That poetry should be his medium followed from the nature of Ralegh's relationship with the queen: an intense, highly poetic courtship often carried on in verse. More generally, poetry reflected the nature of Elizabeth's court with its carefully controlled atmosphere of poetic love and adoration, its romantic myths designed to enhance royal power, and its frequent histrionic performances by the queen herself. When Ralegh was imprisoned in 1603, the situation had changed. The charges against him and the punishment were immeasurably more serious—indeed, Ralegh narrowly escaped with his life. Moreover, with the accession of James, the atmosphere of the court had radically altered. Ralegh could not understand the king, despised his policies so far as he understood them, and disliked the new courtiers and favorites. Many of the old unwritten codes and values upon which Ralegh had based his life-style were swept away by the new regime. His life-imprisonment was both the result and the perfect symbol of his alienation from the state. He was cut off not only from the centers of power but from the entire community of men. Alienation so extreme was a form of death— and Ralegh *was* legally dead. As he wrote to the king after his conviction:

The lief which I had, most mighty Prince, the law hath taken from mee, and I am now but the same earth and dust out of which I was made. . . . Name, bloud, gentillety or estate, I have none; no, not so mich as a beeing; no, not so mich as *vita plantae*. [*Letters*, p. 296]

A work like *Ocean to Cynthia*, an exploration of the currents of passion, despair, and remorse, was no longer possible. The intimate expressions and the special language intended for a very select, knowing audience were now pointless. When Ralegh finally turned to a vast writing project, as he had done during his first, relatively brief imprisonment, it was not to poetry but to universal history, the most public of forms.[4] But for all the apparent objectivity, the *History*, like the poems, was his attempt to come to terms with his situation, both as a tactic to obtain his release and as a mode of self-exploration and understanding.

Ralegh knew that his release, if it could ever be obtained, would come not from the bounty of the king, but from the good graces of James's eldest son. Prince Henry admired his father's prisoner and, according to Ralegh, encouraged him to write the *History*.[5] No doubt there was more than personal affection and fascination behind the prince's regard. The young heir was at the center of a militantly Protestant, anti-Spanish faction which opposed the policies of the king. As it was widely believed that Ralegh had been martyred in 1603 to the pro-Spanish and pacific policy of James, the prisoner was a ready-made symbol of opposition. The *History* itself reads at times like a factional tract directed squarely against the king.[6] Ralegh, of course, denied any satirical intention and larded his work with fulsome flattery of James, but even the flattery is heavily tinged with irony. For example, can Ralegh, imprisoned in the Tower on a trumped-up charge of treason, be fully serious when he writes that James "never tooke revenge of any man, that sought to put him beside" the crown? or when he praises *"His Majesties* temperate, revengelesse, and liberall disposition"* (Pref., sig. B2ᵛ)? or when he says, of a king who was notorious for showering vast sums upon his minions, that "His Majesty hath had more compassion of other mens necessities, than of his owne Coffers" (Pref., sig. B2ᵛ)? Furthermore, a number of seemingly innocuous passages of the *History* conceal bitter and insolent attacks upon the king. James himself was said to have been stung by the portrait of Ninias, the successor of the powerful and glorious Queen Semiramis, a weak king "esteemed no man of warre at all, but altogether feminine, and subjected to ease and delicacie" (ii, i, 1, p. 217).

But more important and damaging than any specific passage of irony or satire was the general orientation of the *History*, the unending examples of God's just punishment of wicked kings:

Oh by what plots, by what forswearings, betrayings, oppressions, imprisonments, tortures, poysonings, and under what reasons of State,
and politique subteltie, have these forenamed Kings, both strangers,
and of our owne Nation, pulled the vengeance of Goᴅ upon themselves, upon theirs, and upon their prudent ministers! [Pref., sig.
C2ʳ]

[T]he hand of God was extended against the body of this wicked
King, smiting him with a grievous disease in his bowells, which left
him not untill his guts fell out. [ɪɪ, xx, 4, p. 524]

Leontius laid hold upon the Emperor *Justine,* cut off his nose and
eares, and sent him into banishment: but Gods vengeance rewarded
him with the same punishment, by the hands of *Tiberius;* to
whose charge hee had left his owne men of warre. *Justine,* having
recovered forces, lighted on *Tiberius,* and barbed him after the
same fashion. *Philippicus,* commanding the forces of *Justine,* murdered both the Emperour and his sonne. *Anastasius,* the vassal of
this new Tyrant, surprised his Master *Philippicus,* and thrust out
both his eyes [etc., etc.]. [v, vɪ, 2, pp. 716–17]

Often God's vengeance strikes just when the tyrant feels himself most secure, most godlike in his power and freedom. Then
too, if by chance the malefactor himself escapes punishment,
God is merely preparing a still more terrible fate for his children.

James, who was morbidly fearful of violence and death and
also extremely sensitive to criticism, can have missed very few
of the concealed threats and attacks. Sensitive, too, to public
opinion, he was alarmed by the *History*'s popularity, which
was virtually unprecedented for a work of its size, learning,
and cost. He is reported to have ordered the book called in
"for divers exceptions, but specially for beeing to sawcie in
censuring princes," but the order does not appear to have
been carried out.[7]

Friendless, powerless, shut up in the Tower without pros-
pects of release, Ralegh devised a way to strike out at his per-
secutor without incurring further punishment. Indeed, Lefranc argues that the whole *History of the World* is a polemic
written for that portion of the English public increasingly op-

posed to the royal prerogatives and policies. He suggests that
Ralegh turned to history as a form of surrogate action and accordingly narrowed his history's field of vision to serve a massive, only half-concealed attack on the king: Providence is reduced to justice, justice constantly limited to punishment,
punishment reserved principally for tyrants, and those tyrants
all presented as archetypes of James I.[8] Yet, though the polemical side of the *History* must not be overlooked, the work's
real centers of interest and passion and intelligence are, in my
opinion, at once more personal and more universal.

In the *History,* as in *Ocean to Cynthia,* beneath the tactics
and calculation, lies an attempt to come to terms with the crisis of the self and to reestablish continuity with the past and
the future. The poem's focus is clearly upon the isolated individual, torn between conflicting visions of reality. In the *History,* the focus shifts to the vast theater of the world where the
great conquerors, self-styled gods-on-earth, appear like shadows
for a brief moment and then vanish. But the mind and experience of the individual in the present remain central to the
work.

Ralegh knew and acted instinctively upon the principle, recently reaffirmed by Collingwood, that the concern of the historian is not the past in general, but "the past of this present,
the present in which the act of imagination is going on as here
and now perceived." [9] But one must quickly add that Ralegh
also believed that the order of history was in the universe itself, not solely in the mind of man. This conviction is the cor-
nerstone of the *History:*

[T]he same just God who liveth and governeth all thinges for ever,
doeth in these our times give victorie, courage, and discourage,
raise, and throw downe Kinges, Estates, Cities, and Nations, for the
same offences which were committed of old, and are committed in
the present: for which reason in these and other the afflictions of *Israel,* alwaies the causes are set downe, that they might bee as pre-
cedents to succeeding ages. [II, XIX, 3, pp. 508–09]

To Ralegh, any notion of the complete interpenetration of
subjective and objective in history would no doubt have

seemed chaotic and dangerous, permitting the individual to disregard all those things which run counter to his own will. For he argued in the *History* that it was precisely the malignant disease of man to try to force the shape of his intellect and will upon the universe. That Ralegh's whole active life was in fact just such an attempt is not for the moment relevant, though we shall return to this paradox. In the *History* he tirelessly attacks the presumption of those who attempt to set up their will as supreme and to make themselves the measure of the universe. History is the unending demonstration of the futility of this attempt:

This wise and politique King, who sold Heaven and his owne Honour, to make his sonne, the Prince of *Spaine,* the greatest Monarch of the world: saw him die in the flower of his yeares. [Pref., sig. C1^r]

GOD hath said it and performed it ever: *Perdam sapientiam sapientum,* I will destroy the wisdome of the wise. [Pref., sig. C2^r]

God derideth the wisedome of the worldly men, when forgetting the Lord of all power, they relie on the inventions of their owne most feeble; and altogether darkened understanding. [II, iii, 3, p. 250]

This was that *Seleucia,* whereto *Antigonus the great* who founded it, gave the name of *Antigonia:* but *Seleucus* getting it shortly after, called it *Seleucia;* and *Ptolemie Evergetes* having lately won it, might, if it had so pleased him, have changed the name into *Ptolemais.* Such is the vanitie of men, that hope to purchase an endlesse memoriall unto their names, by workes proceeding rather from their greatnesse, than from their vertue; which therefore no longer are their owne, than the same greatnesse hath continuance. [v, v, 2, p. 646]

Politicians, for Ralegh, have no conception of history, no sense of the past: "It is in the present time, that all the wits of the world are exercised" (Pref., sig. C2^r).

But though Ralegh believed that the universe had an objective order which resisted man's will and which was revealed in history, that order did not lie in facts which had simply to be set out in writing. It lay rather in a vision of the meaning of human life in time, that meaning ultimately deriving from the will of God. The true historian was a kind of visionary, who brought all of his experience, passion, and imagination to bear upon the eloquent expression of his insights. The writing of history entailed the full involvement of the individual, not the stifling of the personal and subjective. Far from suppressing references to his own time or even to his own career, Ralegh allows them full play, not inadvertently, not because he could not bring himself to write "objectively," but because such references are essential to his conception of history.

The interaction of ancient and modern begins early in the work. A description of Eden reminds Ralegh of the landscape he had seen in Guiana, the fertility of the soil in Babylonia recalls Spanish accounts of the valley of Mexico, Moses' account of the Flood in Genesis is clear to anyone who has seen the terrible waterspouts in the Indies (I, vii, 6, p. 107). Speculation that the Tree of Knowledge was the Indian fig tree takes Ralegh back to the Orinoco:

I my selfe have seene twentie thousand of them in one Valley, not farre from *Paria* in *America*. . . . I have seene five hundred Oysters hanging in a heape thereon; whereof the report came, that Oysters grew on trees in India. But that they beare any such huge leaves, or any such delicate fruit I could never finde, and yet I have travailed a dozen miles together under them. [I, vi, 2, pp. 67–68]

Most of the personal references in the early sections of the *History* are to his experiences in the New World simply because the subject of those sections is what he calls the "plantinge of nations," the migration of peoples and the rise of government. With his strong sense of the interplay of the past and the present, Ralegh saw his Guiana and Virginia schemes as just such a "plantinge": for him the Western Hemisphere was truly a "new world." Later, when the subject of the *History* shifts to political and military concerns, the contemporary references shift accordingly. The occupation of Jerusalem by the king of Judah recalls the occupation of Florence by Charles VIII of France (II, xxii, 1, p. 554); the rebellion of the Greeks against Persia is like the Irish rebellion (III, v, 7, p. 54); the enormous

and hopelessly cumbersome army that Xerxes led into Greece
against the advice of his counselor Artabanus is the very
match of "the enterprise of *Philip* the second upon England in
the yeare 1588, who had belike never heard of this Counsell of
Artabanus to *Xerxes,* or forgotten it" (III, vi, 2, p. 62). Likewise, the personal reminiscences shift from the New World to
war and diplomacy:

I saw in the third civill Warre of *France* certain caves in *Langue-
doc,* which had but one entrance, and that very narrow, cut out in
the mid-way of high Rocks, which we knew not how to enter by any
ladder or engine, till at last by certaine bundells of straw let downe
by an yron chaine, and a waightie stone in the middest, those that
defended it were so smothered, as they rendred themselves with
their plate, monie, and other goods therein hidden. [IV, ii, 16, pp.
197–98]

Many such examples of perfidious dealing have I noted in other
places, and can hardly forbeare to deliver unto memorie the like
practises, when they meete with their matches: That which hapned
unto *Monsieur de Piles,* was very sutable to this treacherie, wherewith *Dionysius* pursued *Himilco.* I was present, when *De Piles* related the injurie done unto him. [v, i, 4, pt. 4, p. 336]

In the longest of these reminiscences, Ralegh defends the land-
ing of the English at Fayal under his command, but in this
instance the historical topic—"How the Romans having lost
their fleet by tempest, resolve to forsake the Seas" (v, i, 9, p.
357)—merely serves as a pretext for the self-justification.

The History of the World is permeated on many levels with
Ralegh's personality and experiences—from historical parallels
intended to clarify puzzling events of the past to the bitter
masked polemic against James, from personal reminiscences to
a less obviously personal interest in certain kinds of problems
and approaches (geography, national migrations, ship build-
ing, naval strategy, alchemy, etc.),[10] from a marked involvement with explorers, inventors, and public servants who are
unjustly hated by the multitude or betrayed by their rulers (in
other words, figures in whom Ralegh could see himself)[11] to a
profound concern with the ravages of time. Indeed the very

act of conceiving and writing a universal history had a complex symbolic significance for him, significance which he envisaged as early as *Ocean to Cynthia*. But the heart of his personal involvement in the *History* is that which is often adduced as the most orthodox and conventional aspect of the work: the conception of the ultimate meaning of history.

Broadly speaking, for Ralegh that meaning is God's will, a view which is, of course, entirely traditional. In its providentialism, the *History* is heir to a venerable line tracing its English ancestry back at least as far as Ranulph Higden's *Polychronicon* in the early fourteenth century and continuing unbroken through the Reformation.[12] But God's Providence, like Christianity itself, was not a monolithic doctrine. Ralegh had a range of options open to him: he could present history as the theater of God's justice, vengeance, or mercy; he could show God participating directly in human events or working His will from an immense distance; he could find in the workings of Providence evidence for man's blessedness or man's wretchedness, for human progress through the ages or for decay and dissolution.

As the force of *Ocean to Cynthia* lies largely in the transition from image to image and emotion to emotion, so in the *History* Ralegh's intellectual and spiritual anxieties are most powerfully recorded in the shift from one conception of historical causation to another. Every one of the *History*'s numerous versions of God's Providence—down to the subtlest shades and variations—has its sources and analogues. The power of the work—its fusion of the deeply personal and the universal—is less in any individual idea than in its great evolving flow, its changes, tensions, and contradictions. To be sure, those contradictions themselves were inherent in the historical tradition, but Ralegh had identified himself with the search for the meaning of history, just as he had linked his personal destiny with the search for El Dorado. The inner tensions and conflicting world-views that we have examined in his poetry and his career reappear tied to his shifting interpretation of history.

The *History* is riddled with uncertainties, ambiguities, and outright contradictions. As the vast work slowly unfolds, with its thousands of names, places, authorities, and dates, with its mass migrations, half-forgotten dynasties, and bloody rebellions, the perspective and meaning ceaselessly change. There is scarcely an issue on which Ralegh's position is not ambiguous. Fortune is dismissed as a vain superstition and then is quietly reinstated as a major force in human events; [13] we read histories, Ralegh states, "to informe our understanding by the examples therein found," and yet "where God hath a purpose to destroy, wise men grow short lived"; [14] eclipses may foretell an "alteration in civil affairs" or then again they may not; [15] the soul is called immortal, and yet there is almost no mention of an afterlife in the entire work; [16] primitive man may have been a creature of remarkable virtue by comparison to men of the present, or he may have been a savage tamed only by the rise of governments; [17] the world and all its goods may be worthless and vain, and yet it is not only "lawful to rejoyce in those good things, wherwith God hath blessed us; but a note of much unthankfulnesse to entertaine them with a sullen and unfeeling disposition;" [18] for all his godlike airs, the king is just the same as the beggar, indeed the man of wealth and power is likely to be far more corrupt than the poor man, and yet "God himself, by his eternal providence . . . ordaynded Kings"; [19] Ralegh speaks of Galileo's recent discovery of the phases of Venus, the decisive proof of Copernicus' theory, and yet the cosmology of the *History* is unreservedly Ptolemaic.[20]

Above all, God Himself enters and exits and reenters the scene. At certain moments, history for Ralegh is filled with the presence of God who shapes all events with miraculous power, sometimes allowing the wicked to prosper briefly only to punish them more severely, sometimes testing with adversity the pious and good, illuminating the chosen with His wisdom, blinding those He has determined to destroy. The instruments of His will are infinite:

There is not . . . the smallest accident, which may seeme unto men as falling out by chance, and of no consequence: but that the same is caused by God to effect somewhat else by: yea, and oftentimes to effect things of the greatest worldly importance, either presently, or in many yeares after, when the occasions are either not considered, or forgotten. [II, v, 10, p. 310]

This is said of God's merciful care of Moses, but it applies as well to the far more frequent examples of God's vengeance:

Now seemed the affaires of *Greece* likely to bee setled in better order, than they had ever beene since the beginning of the *Peloponnesian* Warres, yea or since the *Persian* Invasion: when God, who had otherwise disposed of these matters, hindred all, with a draught of cold water, which *Cleomenes* dranke in a great heat, and thereupon fell extreme sick. [v, ii, 6, p. 406]

At other moments, however, God seems immensely distant from the actual events of history: "The Heavens are high, farr off and unsearcheable . . ." (Pref., sig. C2ᵛ). From this perspective, for example, the rise of so many tyrants throughout history is due not to God's desire to scourge wicked nations but to man's nature:

[I]n Mankind there is found, ingrafted even by Nature, a desire of absolute dominion: whereunto the generall custome of Nations doth subscribe; together with the pleasure which most men take in flatterers, that are the basest of slaves.

This being so, we finde no cause to mervaile, how Tyrannie hath beene so rife in all ages, and practised, not onely in the single rule of some vicious Prince, but ever by consent of whole Cities and Estates. [v, ii, 2, pt. 4, p. 385]

Likewise, the fall of tyrants is due to the natural return of violence and rapacity on their own heads.

In the great mass of the *History*, however, God is neither the totally immanent being that determines the shape and outcome of all events nor the distant principle to be politely acknowledged and ignored. There is a deep tension throughout much of the work, a tension that finds expression in paragraphs and even single sentences that begin in one position and end in quite another:

[That Moses] forbare to enter *Arabia* being then in sight thereof, it seemeth to proceede from three respects; the first two naturall; the third divine. [II, iii, 7, p. 258]

That the wickednesse of King *Manasses* was the cause of the evill, which fell upon his Kingdome and Person, any Christian must needes beleeve: for it is affirmed in the Scriptures. Yet was the state of things, in those parts of the World, such, at that time, as would have invited any Prince (and did perhaps invite *Merodach,* who fulfilled Gods pleasure, upon respect borne to his owne ends) desirous of enlarging his Empire, to make attempt upon *Juda.* [II, xxvii, 2, p. 615]

To this end came all the travailes of the worthie Generall, *Eumenes;* who had with great wisedome, fidelitie, and patience, laboured in vaine, to uphold the family which God purposed to cast downe. He is reckoned among the notable examples of Fortunes mutabilitie, but more notable was his government of himselfe in all her changes. Adversitie never lessened his courage, nor Prosperitie his circumspection. But all his vertue, industrie, and wit, were cast away, in leading an Armie, without full power to keepe it in due obedience. [IV, iv, 7, p. 250]

Hee therefore made a journie against *Arsaces* founder of the *Parthian* kingdome: wherein his evill fortune, or rather Gods vengeance, adhered so closely to him, that he was taken prisoner. [v, v, 1, p. 643]

   That the tension manifested here never erupts into open conflict is probably due to Ralegh's reliance on the traditional distinction between primary and secondary causes. God is the First Cause of all things, but He almost always acts through second causes. The First Cause remains fixed and unchanging throughout time, but second causes are numerous and time-conditioned, and it is to these causes that the historian applies all of those techniques which sixteenth-century historiographers had refined: source study and criticism, geography, chronology, ethnography, and, not least important, common sense.[21] This distinction does nothing to resolve the major philosophical problems of providential history; it does not lead to a clearer conception of God's judgments or of man's freedom; it fails to explain the relationship between an eternal deity and a time-bound world; it cannot help man find the way to accord his will to the will of God. Rather it simply permits the historian to operate in radically contradictory modes without ever directly facing the consequences: Ralegh may speak with harsh cynicism about political realities and respond sympathetically to all those intellectual forces in the sixteenth and early seventeenth century undermining traditional historiography, but in an instant he can be back in the strictest orthodoxy, condemning the shallow wisdom of the worldly and exhorting his readers (and himself) to turn toward the First Cause of things.

At times, it seems that there is no order in all of this, but gradually out of the tension and turmoil, a movement or pattern of meaning does emerge in the *History*. Book I opens with a vision of a God who is all things, infinitely remote and utterly present, in nature and yet apart from nature, inaccessible to the human understanding and invisible to corporeal sight and yet plainly manifested in this visible world "which is also the understood language of the Almightie" (I, i, 1, p. 2). Whatever has life in the universe, has it from Him; whatever happens, happens in accordance with His will:

God worketh by Angels, by the Sunne, by the Starres, by Nature, or infused properties, and by men, as by severall organs, severall effects; all second causes whatsoever, being but instruments, conduits, and pipes, which carrie and disperse what they have received from the head and fountaine of the Universall. For as it is Gods infinite power, and every-where-presence (compassing, embracing, and piercing all things) that giveth to the Sunne power to draw up vapours, to vapours to be made cloudes, cloudes to contayne raine, and raine to fall: so all second and instrumentall causes, together with Nature it selfe, without that operative facultie which God gave them, would become altogether silent, vertuelesse, and dead. [I, i, 10, p. 13]

This seems to settle at a stroke the question of the ultimate meaning of history, but it does so at the expense of human volition: a conduit or pipe can hardly be said to have a will. As

Ralegh becomes involved in the narration of human actions and as those actions become less fabulous, the second causes which seem so mechanical in the beginning increasingly detach themselves from "the head and fountaine of the Universall." In describing relations between Israel and Judah, Ralegh can write:

To say that God was pleased to have it so, were a true, but an idle answere (for his secret will is the cause of all things) . . . Wherefore we may boldly looke into the second causes. [ii, xix, 6, p. 512]

Still, with certain notable exceptions,[22] the chapters that deal with biblical history are concerned with the relation between the events of history and God's judgments. Those judgments are always manifested in the world—there is occasional mention of angels and the devil, but no sense of heaven or hell—and if a tyrant escapes punishment during his own lifetime, he will be punished through his posterity, even unto the third or fourth generation. Ralegh's God is, for the most part, the stern and jealous God of the Old Testament, ever watchful for disobedience to His commandments. Were it not that there are almost no elect in the *History*, the vision of men and nations would strongly resemble that held by the Puritans.[23] But Ralegh could not view history as the struggle between the forces of good and evil, the struggle to establish God's kingdom on earth, because he saw so few traces of the good and holy in human life, particularly in the life recorded by historians. Milton had his one just man, bearing the image of Christ even in the darkest of times,[24] but Ralegh's good men—and they are very few—do not participate in any enduring pattern or leave any lasting impression behind them. Indeed the good are likely to have little to do with the world at all, for in the early books of the *History*, Ralegh regards all great and successful actions in the world as almost inevitably corrupting:

For whosoever shall tell any great man or Magistrate, that he is not just, the Generall of an Armie, that he is not valiant, and great Ladies that they are not faire, shall never be made a Counseller, a Captaine, or a Courtier. Neither is it sufficient to be wise with a wise Prince, valiant with a valiant, and just with him that is just, for such a one hath no estate in his prosperitie; but he must also change with the successour, if he be of contrary qualities, saile with the tide of the time, and alter forme and condition, as the Estate or the Estates Master changeth: Otherwise how were it possible, that the most base men, and separate from all imitable qualities, could so often attaine to honour and riches, but by such an observant slavish course? These men having nothing else to value themselves by, but a counterfait kinde of wondring at other men, and by making them beleeve that all their vices are vertues, and all their dustie actions cristalline, have yet in all ages prospered equally with the most vertuous, if not exceeded them. . . . so as whosoever will live altogether out of himselfe, and studie other mens humours, and observe them, shall never be unfortunate; and on the contrary, that man which prizeth truth and vertue (except the season wherein he liveth be of all these, and of all sorts of goodnesse fruitfull) shall never prosper by the possession or profession thereof. [i, i, 15, p. 21]

"Whosoever will live altogether out of himselfe"—Ralegh's criticism of the successful counselor, captain, or courtier is a criticism of the flexible man, the man who has mastered the art of self-fashioning and learned how to "alter forme and condition, as the Estate or the Estates Master changeth." "If one could change one's nature with time and circumstance, fortune would never change," Machiavelli wrote, and it is precisely this protean self that Ralegh finds incompatible with virtue:

Whosoever therefore will set before him *Machiavels two markes to shoote at* (to wit) riches, and glorie, must set on and take off a backe of yron to a weake wooden bow, that it may fit both the strong and the feeble: . . . that man which prizeth vertue for it selfe, and cannot endure to hoise and strike his sailes, as the divers natures of calmes and stormes require, must cut his sailes, and his cloth, of meane length and breadth, and content himself with a slow and sure navigation, (to wit) a meane and free estate. [i, i, 15, p. 21]

Ralegh rejects then that "dramatic sense of life" which we found in Machiavelli, that sense of identity as a role to be shaped and controlled. Or rather, at this point he accepts Ma-

chiavelli's assessment of what is required to achieve success in
the world, and for this very reason rejects the pursuit of such
success. But, of course, the early books of the *History* go on to
ascribe worldly failure expressly to those who disobey God:

Thus it commonly falls out, that they who can find all manner of
difficulties in serving him, to whom nothing is difficult, are in stead
of the ease and pleasure to themselves propounded by contrarie
courses, over-whelmed with the troubles which they sought to avoid,
and therein by God whom they first forsooke, forsaken, and left
unto the wretched labours of their owne blinde wisdome, wherein
they had reposed all their confidence. [ii, xxi, 2, p. 531]

Ralegh has it both ways: the common link is simply that nothing virtuous or lasting can come of man's own efforts. The
only true success is that which is ascribed directly to God's
will.

As biblical history draws to a close, however, Ralegh's vision
of history changes. God gradually retreats from the stage of
human affairs into the role of the remote First Cause, to be
evoked now and then for rhetorical effect. With this change,
the style of the *History* likewise alters. In the first two books,
we frequently find long, loose, sonorous periods:

In this time it is, when (as aforesaid) we, for the most part, and
never before, prepare for our eternall habitation, which we passe on
unto, with many sighes, grones, and sad thoughts, and in the end,
by the workemanship of death, finish the sorrowfull businesse of a
wretched life, towards which we alwayes travaile both sleeping and
waking: neither have those beloved companions of honour and
riches any power at all, to hold us any one day, by the promises of
glorious entertainments; but by what crooked path so ever wee
walke, the same leadeth on directly to the house of death: whose
doores lie open at all houres, and to all persons. [i, ii, 5, p. 31]

The sentence might have stopped at "habitation," again at
"thoughts," and certainly at "life," but instead it continues
with a member that is syntactically parallel to the earlier rela-
tive clause. The parallelism only emphasizes the period's asym-
metry, which is then further intensified by the syntactically

new member beginning "neither." Finally, the sentence once
again breaks new syntactic ground with the clause beginning
"but." This final clause seems to glance at the style itself: the
crooked path has led back directly to the "eternall habitation"
of the opening. The unity of the sentence comes not from
tight grammatical construction, but from its internal echoes
and its ultimate goal. This style is characteristic of Ralegh's
prose of meditation: it improvises, crosses syntactic boundaries
and then returns upon itself, bending and shifting as the mind
muses on human time and God's eternal will. The prose of
the later books, on the other hand, is far more concerned with
clear historical narration and with the formulation of political
maxims. The sonorous passages of meditation are fewer, and
the style becomes tighter, sparer, more inclined to aphorism:

But where unsound advice finding bad proofe, is obstinately pursued, neither *Pallas* nor *Fortune* can be justly blamed for a miserable issue. [iii, viii, 8, p. 99]

It was therefore *Machiavels* counsell, that he which resolveth to defend a passage, should with his ablest force oppose the Assailant.
[iv, ii, 3, p. 172]

Surely, if adventurous natures were to be commended simply, wee
should confound that vertue with the hardinesse of Theeves, Ruffi-
ans, and mastife Dogges. [iv, ii, 23, p. 211]

It is truely said, He that faineth himselfe a sheepe may chance to
be eaten by a Wolfe. [iv, iii, 1, p. 213]

Wheresoever the Prince doth hold all his Subjects under the condition
of slaves; there is the conquest easie, and soone assured: Where
ancient Nobilitie is had in due regard, there is it hard to winne all,
and harder to keepe that which is wonne. [iv, v, 8, p. 264]

Crueltie doth not become more warrantable, but rather more
odious, by being customarie. [v, i, 8, p. 356]

There is no precise point where the shift in evidence here
may be said to take place; the concise style and the increasing
independence of the historical agents begin well within the
confines of biblical history, while echoes of the meditative

style and the traditional providentialism may be heard
throughout the later books. But it would be hard to overesti-
mate the profound effect on Ralegh of leaving behind the
shelter of the Bible, that compendium of God's judgments recorded for posterity "by those happy hands which the Holy
Ghost hath guided" (Pref., sig. A2ᵛ), and plunging into classical history. There were, to be sure, interpretive problems in
dealing with the Bible. Indeed, almost the entire first book of
the *History* consists not of narrative but of extended discussions of such problems: "Of the meaning of *in principio*,"
"How it is to be understood, that *the Spirit of God moved
upon the waters*," "That there was a true locall Paradise, East-
ward, in the Countrie of *Eden*," "Of *Becanus* his opinion, that
the Tree of Knowledge was *Ficus Indica*," and so forth. With
the aid of commentaries such as Pererius' great *Commentar-
iorum et disputationum in Genesin,* Ralegh cites scores of authorities, weighs their conflicting arguments, and attempts to
reach conclusions.[25] But at least the Bible remains an absolutely unassailable source, and the events recorded in it are
the clear realization of God's secret purpose.

When the prop of the infallible Scriptures is removed, Ralegh's whole response to human actions changes. Where in the
first two books he counsels a retired life, "a slow and sure navigation," in the books treating classical history he reserves his
warmest tributes for men of *virtù* like the Theban Epaminon-
das:

His Justice, and Sinceritie, his Temperance, Wisedome, and high
Magnanimitie, were no way inferiour to his Militarie vertue; in
every part whereof hee so excelled, That hee could not properly
bee called a Warie, a Valiant, a Politique, a Bountifull, or an In-
dustrious, and a Provident Captaine; all these Titles, and many
other, beeing due unto him, which with his notable Discipline, and
good Conduct, made a perfect composition of an Heroique Generall. [III, xii, 7, p. 153]

The lessons drawn from history in the later sections of the
work do not relate to an awareness of God's overarching plan,

but to such things as "The great advantages of a good fleet in warre, between Nations divided by the Sea," "the defence of hard passages," and "The dangers growing from the use of mercenarie Souldiers, and forraigne Auxiliaries." The latter discussions are taken directly from the *Discourses* and *The Prince,* and, in general, there is a sharp increase in quotations from and allusions to Machiavelli. Whereas in Book I Ralegh condemns Machiavellian "policy," in Book IV he suggests, echoing a famous passage from the *Prince,* that "a Foxe-taile doth sometimes helpe well to peece out the Lions-skinne, that else would be too short" (IV, ii, 18, p. 204). Moreover, in the later books, though he was by no means a republican, Ralegh seems to share with Machiavelli a passion for political liberty. He is bitter in his scorn and pity for those who "are now so patient of a forraigne yoke, that like Sheepe or Oxen, they suffer themselves to be distributed, fought for, wonne, lost, and again recovered, by contentious Masters; as if they had no title to their owne heads . . ." (IV, v, 8, p. 264).[26] And he celebrates "the husbandman & the yeoman of *England*" as "the freest of all the World," observing that "it is the freeman, & not the slave, that hath courage, & the sense of shame deserved by cowardise" (v, i, 2, p. 315, note b).[27]

This is not to suggest, of course, that God is entirely banished from the later books of the *History.* On the contrary, generations of pious readers, and especially the Puritans, treasured Ralegh's work as an invaluable demonstration of the divine purpose in human events. Having accepted the strict providentialism of the early books, the reader who is so inclined can easily view the whole work as a chronicle of God's harsh judgments on individuals and nations. Such a reader may not even register the startling absence in Ralegh's work of a sense of the Incarnation.[28] To be sure, this absence may be traced, in part, to the simple fact that the narrative breaks off in 146 B.C. What is missing, however, is not the event itself but the meaning which radiates from that event, giving direction and purpose to the flux of human actions. There is no mediator in Ralegh's history between the increasingly remote will of God and the victories and defeats of earthbound men; the Word does not become flesh.

And as the *History* lacks the sense of the coming of Christ, so too it lacks the sense of grace and redemption which provided traditional universal history with its *telos*. For all the vast expanse of Ralegh's work, there is a feeling of claustrophobia, of being locked in history, which contrasts sharply with the continual glimpses of the realm beyond time provided by earlier universal historians. Thus in the twelfth century, Otto of Freising, reflecting upon the death of Alexander the Great, turns away from the spectacle of treachery and defeat to the contemplation of the City of God:

The dominion of the Macedonian empire which had its beginning in him came to an end with him at his death. But we who love the world, who desire to cleave to it as though it were something eternal and abiding, do not consider such things as this. We fall with the falling, slip with the slipping, roll with the rolling, in a word, perish with the perishing. The City of Christ, however, founded upon a firm rock, is not shaken by the misfortunes and tempests of the world, but continuing immovable and unshaken, gains an eternal kingdom and an eternal crown.[29]

But reflecting upon the same event, Ralegh contemplates only the human wreckage that such "Troublers of the World" leave behind them and concludes bleakly with Seneca's judgment upon both Alexander and his father Philip: " 'That they were no lesse plagues to mankinde, than an over-flow of waters, drowning all the levill; or some burning droughth, whereby a great part of living creatures is scorched up' " (IV, ii, 23, pp. 211–12).

With the initial vision of history as the theater of God's will giving way to a historiography in which the human agents appear increasingly to draw upon their own inner sources of energy, Ralegh's work seems to be moving steadily toward modern history with its conception of the secular state, its concern for power, and even, as I have suggested, its ideal of political liberty. This is not, however, the direction that the *History* finally takes. The dwindling of God's presence in history ultimately leaves Ralegh with a sense of bitterness and emptiness instead of liberating him intellectually and emotionally. The practical lessons of politics and war seem increasingly useless, for, by the end of the work, history seems little more than the record of nations set upon enslaving other nations and doomed to enslavement themselves. Ralegh has none of the humanist's veneration of Greece and Rome, and he sees in classical history only a bitter chronicle of the ruthless destruction of liberty. For him, Athenian democracy was nothing but the rule of "the rascal multitude" who "in all ages have beene more stirred up with fond Prophecies and other like superstitious fooleries, than by any just cause or solide reason" (III, v, 8, p. 57). The Romans were "those Ravens and spoilers of all Estates, disturbers of Common-weales, usurpers of other Princes Kingdomes: who with no other respect led than to amplifie their owne glorie, troubled the whole world: and themselves, after murthering one another, became a prey to the most salvage and barbarous Nations" (II, IX, 1, p. 369). The whole last book of the *History* presents the spectacle of an immensely powerful, ambitious, and ruthless Roman empire yoking the once proud and independent Greeks. Like the discontented Israelites in the wilderness who wish to return to Egypt,[30] most of the Greeks seem to embrace their own humiliation and enslavement, vying with each other in petty ambition, stupidity, and cowardice, while the few free spirits are destroyed. The deepest shame is reserved for the Athenians:

Only the Athenians, once the most turbulent Citie in *Greece,* having neyther subjects of their own that might rebell, no [r] power wherewith to bring anie into subjection; for want of more noble argument wherein to practise their eloquence that was become the whole remainder of their ancient commendations, were much delighted in flattering the most mightie. So they kept themselves in grace with the *Romans,* remained free from all trouble, untill the warre of *Mithridates:* being men unfit for action, and thereby innocent; yet bearing a part in many great actions, as Gratulators of the *Roman* victories, and Pardon-cravers for the vanquished. Such were the *Athenians* become. [V, vi, 4, p. 727]

There is no sense of God's plan here, no triumphant demonstration of God's vengeance and justice. Even the sense of
God as the remote First Cause has all but vanished. But at the
same time, the concern for political and military wisdom that
had characterized Books III and IV of the *History* seems to
have diminished; there are few, if any, practical lessons to be
learned from this bitter chronicle of folly, destruction, and
death. The crisp aphorisms gradually die out in Book V, along
with the digressions on special questions of strategy and tactics. Almost imperceptibly, the *History* changes its course once
again and slowly moves toward a final vision of death.

Perhaps the darkening of Ralegh's historical vision may be
traced to the death of Prince Henry.[31] The Prince's death on
6 November 1612 robbed Ralegh of his most powerful friend,
his only substantial hope for the future. It robbed him, too, of
the most important potential reader of his history, a reader
who could grasp its lessons and translate them directly into
national policy. After 1612, those lessons must have seemed increasingly futile to Ralegh.

By the close of Ralegh's work, the landscape of history has
become that wilderness which the Angel Michael described to
Adam in the closing books of *Paradise Lost,* that world "to
good malignant, to bad men benign,/Under her own weight
groaning" (XII, 538–39). But it is precisely here that Milton's
Angel offers fallen man the consoling vision:

> Under her own weight groaning till the day
> Appear of respiration to the just,
> And vengeance to the wicked, at return
> Of him so lately promis'd to thy aid
> The Woman seed, obscurely then foretold,
> Now amplier known thy Saviour and thy Lord,
> Last in the Clouds from Heav'n to be reveald
> In glory of the Father, to dissolve
> *Satan* with his perverted World, then raise
> From the conflagrant mass, purg'd and refin'd
> New Heav'ns, new Earth, Ages of endless date
> Founded in righteousness and peace and love
> To bring forth fruits Joy and eternal Bliss.
>
> [XII, 539–51]

Ralegh's world, too, cries out for judgment and redemption, but *The History of the World* ends not with the coming of Christ but with the apotheosis of death, the death which, as Ralegh's brother Carew had remarked years before, comes to all, sinner and righteous alike. Even the terrible vengeance of the Lord is better than this valley of dry bones:

It is therfore Death alone that can suddenly make man to know himselfe. He tells the proud and insolent, that they are but Abjects, and humbles them at the instant; makes them crie, complaine, and repent, yea, even to hate their forepassed happinesse. He takes the account of the rich, and proves him a begger; a naked begger, which hath interest in nothing, but in the gravell that filles his mouth. He holds a Glasse before the eyes of the most beautifull, and makes them see therein, their deformitie and rottennesse; and they acknowledge it.

O eloquent, just and mightie Death! whom none could advise, thou hast perswaded; what none hath dared, thou hast done; and whom all the world hath flattered, thou only hast cast out of the world and despised: thou hast drawne together all the farre stretched greatnesse, all the pride, crueltie, and ambition of man, and covered it all over with these two narrow words, *Hîc iacet.* [v, vi, 12, p. 776]

With this, and a final sentence lamenting the untimely death of Prince Henry, *The History of the World* comes to a close.

Lefranc suggests that this invocation to death is a final thrust at King James, a veiled threat of revolution and regicide,[32] but this does not seem to be the mood and tenor of the passage. After moving in the course of his work from providentialism to the growing political awareness of the Renaissance, Ralegh does not emerge triumphantly into the rebellious seventeenth century, ready to drag James or his son to the scaffold, but he retreats into a dark personal vision. The closing passage glances mockingly at the rich and the great; its brilliantly ironic language parodies their pretensions and reduces their far-stretched greatness to nothing. But the deepest ironies turn inward. In his preface, Ralegh proudly declared that history "hath triumphed over time, which besides it, nothing but eternity hath triumphed over," and

claimed further that "wee may gather out of History a policy
no lesse wise than eternall; by the comparison and application
of other mens fore-passed miseries, with our owne like errours
and ill deservings" (Pref., sig. A2). At the close of his work,
after the hundreds of great men and events, the mass migrations, wars, broken treaties, discoveries, and conquests, Ralegh
renounces his own exalted pretensions: "It is therfore Death
alone that can suddenly make man to know himselfe." In
terms of the play metaphor, we have reached an extreme of
dramatic irony—the players can know nothing about their
roles or the play they are acting in; they perform in complete
ignorance or rather in an arrogant illusion of knowledge, until
they are "cast out of the world and despised." In terms of Ralegh's histrionic sensibility, we have also reached an extreme—
the grand gesture of projecting the mind beyond the prison
walls to embrace the whole history of the world has ended in
nothingness; the assertion of human power has turned into a
bitter assertion of human emptiness. The bitterness is mingled
with a strange, mocking humor, the brittle laughter of a man
who has abandoned all faith in human achievement. History
itself is no longer possible, and the work simply breaks off,
never to be resumed.

6   Ralegh's Second Guiana Voyage

A mountain . . . covered with gold and silver ore

The vision of death with which *The History of the World* closes is the culmination of a dark and bitter side of Ralegh's nature, a deep vein of pessimism which exerted a powerful force upon his imagination even in his days of greatest prosperity and favor. All human fame and achievement are seen as doomed to oblivion, all endeavors worthless, all ambition tainted. In Sidney's terms, man's "erected wit" can grasp the principles of right conduct, but his "infected will" always turns toward evil and destruction. By the end of the *History,* Ralegh seems to hold, with Calvin, that "Because of the bondage of sin by which the will is held bound, it cannot move toward good, much less apply itself thereto." But whereas Calvin immediately proceeds, "for a movement of this sort is the beginning of conversion to God, which in Scripture is ascribed entirely to God's grace," Ralegh mentions neither conversion nor grace.[1] Instead, he finds not only that the human will is hopelessly corrupt, but that man is trapped in a cycle from which there is no escape, a natural cycle of growth and decay that leads inevitably to death. Death is the ultimate affront to human dignity; it is extinction, nothingness. For Ralegh, death is not bound up with any doctrine of sin or hope of redemption. It is an absolute in his universe, a simple, terrible, inexorable fact.

But pessimism is only one term of a dialectic fundamental to Ralegh's existence. Always opposed to the dark vision was a passionate belief in man's powers, the power to conquer, to discover, to restructure the world as he sees fit and to transform the self into a work of art. This conviction burst forth in Ralegh's gorgeous clothing and haughty demeanor, his poetic courtship of the queen, his aggressive foreign policy, his attempts to plant colonies in Virginia and discover El Dorado in

Guiana, his chemical experiments, and even his choice of associates. He was a patron to both Thomas Hariot and John Dee,
who were not only brilliant mathematicians and practical inventors, but were also England's greatest Renaissance magi in
the Hermetic tradition, men who believed that through magic
they could harness immense cosmic forces to the service of
mankind. Such men, as Frances Yates has observed, helped to
bring about "the momentous step which western man took at
the beginning of the modern period of crossing the bridge between the theoretical and the practical, of going all out to
apply knowledge to produce operations." [2] That Ralegh consciously pursued precisely this end is attested to by his distinguished contemporary, Richard Hakluyt, in the dedication of
the 1587 edition of Peter Martyr's *De orbe novo:*

Ever since you perceived that skill in the navigator's art, the chief
ornament of an island kingdom, might attain its splendour amongst
us if the aid of the mathematical science were enlisted, you have
maintained in your household Thomas Hariot, a man preeminent
in those studies, at a most liberal salary in order that by his aid you
might acquire those noble sciences in your leisure hours, and that
your own sea-captains, of whom there are not a few, might link
theory with practice, not without almost incredible results. [3]

As Hakluyt suggests, Ralegh was directly involved in
"operations"—among them, shipbuilding, medicine, and car-
tography, as well as navigation. Moreover, his large collection
of Hermetic books indicates that he may have dabbled in the
occult sciences under Hariot's tutelage. [4] Throughout his years
of favor, there were dark rumors to this effect, rumors

Of Sir Walter Rawleys school of Atheisme . . . & of the Conjurer
that is M [aster] thereof, and of the diligence used to get yong gentlemen to this schoole, where in both Moyses, & our Savior, the
olde, and the new Testamente are jested at, and the schollers
taughte, among other thinges to spell God backwarde. [5]

Such slander probably had little or no relation to reality, but
it reflects the disturbing aura that Ralegh bore about him, the
sense that he embodied the passionate—and, in this instance,

dangerous—energies of his entire generation.[6] This aura was, as I have suggested, in part consciously generated by Ralegh himself. Thus, a revealing letter survives from Hakluyt to Ralegh in 1586 regarding the dedication cited above:

I heare nothinge from yow of the acceptation of my dedication of that noble historie of the eight decades of Peter Martyr, which will cost mee fortie french crownes, and five monethes travayle with that which is to come before yt be finished, which wilbe aboute the beginning of march. Yf her majestie have of late advanced yow, I wold be gladde to be acquaynted with yor title, and if there be any thinge else that yow wold have mentioned in the epistle dedicatorie, yow shal doe wel to let mee understand of yt betimes.[7]

Hakluyt's praises, like so many other seemingly artless manifestations of the queen's favorite, were actually manipulated by Ralegh.

Even during the long years in the Tower under a guard determined to curb all his activities, Ralegh retained traces of his old vitality and power. He won Prince Henry's favor, advising the boy on naval warfare and diplomacy. His medical experiments became famous, so famous in fact that the convicted traitor's Great Cordial was administered to the dying Crown Prince. In his makeshift laboratory, Ralegh practiced alchemy and "natural magic" as well.[8] These arts, which Ralegh took pains to defend in the *History*,[9] were a means of reaching out beyond the prison walls and remaking the world in the image of man's desires. The *History* was itself a powerful assertion of the grandeur and range of the human mind, however pessimistic the final vision of the work. And, above all, at the same time that he was recording his despairing conclusions about life, Ralegh was nursing deep within him the fantastic dream that had obsessed him throughout the late 1580s and 1590s, the dream of national and personal glory, of unlimited riches, of a vast English empire far surpassing the Spanish and owing its existence to himself alone.

Ralegh had never given up the idea of Guiana.[10] A few months after his own return in 1595, he sent back his faithful

lieutenant, Laurence Keymis, to discover the exact location of
Manoa, the city of El Dorado, and to secure a good quantity
of gold ore from the mines which were believed to exist near
the banks of the Caroni. Neither objective was achieved, but
Keymis did bring back one potentially valuable piece of information, the location of a gold mine that he himself had seen
and was certain he could find again. Still the queen and her
advisers were not convinced, and the substantial government
and private support needed for a major expedition was not
forthcoming. But Ralegh did not lose interest or hope. The
dream was too promising, too important to abandon. After
1603, there were few promising dreams left to Ralegh.

Images of the New World haunted Ralegh in the Tower.
When he came to describe Eden in the *History,* his imagination turned repeatedly to what he had himself seen in Guiana:

[T]hose regions [in America] have so many goodly rivers, foun-
taines and little brookes, abundance of high *Cedars,* and other
stately trees casting shade, so many sorts of delicate fruites, ever
bearing, and at all times beautified with blossome and fruit, both
greene and ripe, as it may of all other parts bee best compared to
the *Paradise* of *Eden.* [I, iii, 8, p. 46]

But there were dangers in the New World as well as beauty
and riches, and, in keeping with the spirit of quietism that
marks the early sections of the *History,* Ralegh decries adventurous voyagers, repudiating by implication his own past. The
fables of the cyclops "receive this moral":

That if those men which fight against so many dangerous passages
for gold, or other riches of this world, had their perfect senses, and
were not deprived of halfe their eye-sight (at least of the eye of
right reason and understanding) they would content themselves
with a quiet and moderate estate; and not subject themselves to
famine, corrupt aire, violent heate, and cold, and to all sorts of miserable diseases. [I, viii, 15, pt. 5, p. 176]

Much later, when God's judgments have receded and the
pious quietism has given way to an ethic of heroism and stren-
uous endeavor, Ralegh takes just the opposite tack, without
minimizing any of the dangers:

We seldome or never finde, that any Nation hath endured so many misadventures and miseries, as the *Spaniards* have done, in their *Indian Discoveries*. Yet persisting in their enterprises, with an invincible constancie, they have annexed to their Kingdome so many goodly Provinces, as burie the remembrance of all dangers past. Tempests and shipwracks, famine, overthrowes, mutinies, heat and cold, pestilence, and all manner of diseases, both old and new, together with extreme povertie, and want of all things needfull, have beene the enemies, wherewith every one of their most noble Discoverers, at one time or other, hath been encountred. Many yeares have passed over some of their heads, in the search of not so many leagues: yea more than one or two, have spent their labour, their wealth, and their lives, in search of a golden Kingdome, without getting further notice of it, than what they had at their first setting forth. All which notwithstanding, the third, fourth, and fift undertakers, have not beene disheartned. Surely, they are worthily rewarded with those Treasuries, and Paradises, which they enjoy; and well they deserve to hold them quietly, if they hinder not the like vertue in others, which (perhaps) will not be found. [v, i, 10, p. 367]

"Vertue"—the word in this context does not have the moral significance it had at the beginning of the *History* [11] but the meaning which Machiavelli gave to *virtù* in *The Prince,* the heroic strength of will that strong men exercise to oppose envious fortune. This was the power that Ralegh was summoning to combat the long imprisonment and his vision of death.

At least as early as 1607, Ralegh was seeking permission and support for another voyage to Guiana to work the gold mines that his Indian guides had promised to show him in 1595, the mines that Keymis claimed to have actually seen. In an urgent letter to Robert Cecil, now Lord Treasurer Salisbury, Ralegh, begging for financial backing for such a voyage, claims that a sample of ore he had brought back on his first voyage over ten years before had just then been found to contain gold. To be sure, Ralegh admits, he had promised the assayer ("a man very skillful but poore") twenty pounds if he could find gold or silver in the ore, but the findings are not the less true. If Cecil fears that once set free on the high seas, Ralegh will become a "runagate," let him to as a private man and let the captain have orders to cast him into the sea if he "but perswade[s] a contrary course" (*Letters*, p. 390). And finally, as for the Spanish, who were known to have a settlement near the reputed location of the richest mine and who claimed title to all of Guiana for their king, they would not be disturbed or even seen "except they assayle us." Cecil and the Privy Council were interested, but the details of the expedition could not be agreed upon, and the negotiations were halted.

But his dream of a "golden Kingdome," of "Treasuries and Paradises," did not die. Two years later we find Ralegh writing to John Ramsey, Viscount Haddington, with essentially the same scheme; only now the mine has swelled to a mountain, "covered with gold and silver oare" (*Letters*, p. 393). Again the results were negative. Also in 1609, Ralegh invested a large sum in the Guiana expedition of Sir Thomas Roe who returned over a year later without discovering either the City of Manoa or gold, although he had heard the same stories of rich gold mines further inland. Still Ralegh was not deterred. In 1611, his pleading and promising and cajoling recommenced, with letters to Cecil, to the Privy Council, and even to the king and queen. At one moment, Ralegh pictures himself as Columbus turned away by the foolish councilors of Henry VII, at the next as "an ould, and Sorrowe-worne Man"; [12] now as a miserable wretch with nothing to live for and now as a proud and careful man aware that "the imprysonm^te of a longe Navigac'on is ffarr more greivous then the Tower of London" and willing to undertake the dangerous enterprise only out of deep love for His Majesty King James.[13] In all the letters he passionately denies the suspicions against him and disclaims the rumors that the mine did not exist. Would he, to purchase a few miserable years of liberty in a strange country, disgrace his wife and children and his own name forever after? To be sure, the mine, which only Keymis had actually seen, would not be easy to locate; yet, Ralegh assures the Council,

though itt be a difficult matter—of exceeding difficulty—for any man to find the same acre of ground againe in a country desolate and overgrowne which he hath seene but once, and that sixteene yeares since (which were hard enough to doe upon Salisbury Plaine), yett that your Lordshipps may be satisfied of the truth I am contented to adventure all I have, but my reputacion, upon KEEMISHE's memory. [*Letters,* p. 338]

As in 1607, there was considerable interest in these proposals, especially because the king was now in extreme financial difficulty, but again the negotiations fell through. In the following years, there were more schemes to free Ralegh from the Tower—the king of Denmark, James's brother-in-law, wanted Ralegh as his admiral; the Huguenot Prince de Rohan requested his services as commander of a fleet intended to capture the Spanish Plate Fleet—but James refused to release his prisoner. Finally, in 1615, the political climate shifted in Ralegh's favor: a number of influential enemies had died in the preceding years (including Robert Cecil [14] and, more important, Henry Howard); the king had a new favorite, George Villiers, whose influence could be acquired; Sir Ralph Winwood, one of the leaders of the militantly anti-Spanish faction, had become secretary of state. V. T. Harlow argues that this faction was the crucial force behind the decision to allow Ralegh to go ahead with the Guiana voyage.[15] Less interested in gold than in provoking a rupture—perhaps even a war—with Spain, they counted on a clash between Ralegh's men and the Spanish at S. Thomé, a settlement near the supposed location of the mine. That Ralegh himself would be dishonored and ruined in such a clash was of no concern to the anti-Spanish faction.

James's motives for allowing the voyage to take place are more obscure, and his behavior throughout the affair is riddled with conflicts and inconsistencies. At least one important factor is that by 1615 the Crown's finances were in a truly desperate state,[16] and Ralegh's vision of limitless and easy wealth—a whole mountain covered with gold and conveniently located near a river for easy transport—seemed irresistible. Moreover, James may have been willing to strain considerably his relations with Spain for the sake of a strategic foothold in Guiana. But, at the same time, the king was under

the powerful influence of the subtle and brilliant Spanish ambassador, Gondomar. Furious at the approval granted to so
blatant a provocation of Spain and unable to force James to
rescind his permission entirely, Gondomar induced the king to
bind Ralegh to a series of impossible conditions. Ralegh had
to pledge his life that he would not "inflict the least injury in
the world" upon any Spanish subject and vow that he would
not set foot on Spanish territory—though Spain claimed the
whole Orinoco region. He had, moreover, to state his destina-
tion in writing and submit a chart designating the precise lo-
cality and a list of the ships composing the fleet. All of this information was secretly handed over by the king to Gondomar,
who promptly forwarded it to the Madrid authorities who in
turn sent warnings to the Spanish at S. Thomé.[17] And further,
Ralegh was denied a free pardon and thus remained under
law a convicted traitor.

Under the best of conditions, the odds against success in the
expedition Ralegh proposed would have been extremely high.
Even if the mine existed, could Keymis find that precise plot
of land in a strange country he had visited twenty years before? And what assurance was there that the mine was so very
rich—a few ounces of gold discovered under dubious circumstances in a piece of ore from an entirely different deposit and
a few rumors about the existence of mines further inland,
mines which no Englishman had ever seen? And if, by some
lucky chance, such a rich mine was found, would the Spanish,
who were known to have a settlement nearby and who
claimed all of the Orinoco for themselves, be likely to sit back
and watch the English carry away the treasure? Now, shackled
with the conditions that reflected the king's profound distrust
of him and unwillingness to offend Spain, Ralegh had almost
no chance for success well before he set sail from England.
Why, then, did he go through with the voyage?

The official government "Declaration," published after Ralegh's execution, argues that he had simply lied about the mine
to achieve his own ends:

first, To secure his liberty, and then to make new fortunes for himself, casting abroad only this tale of the Mine as a lure to get ad-

venturers and followers, having in his eye the Mexico fleet, the sacking and spoil of towns planted with Spaniards, the depredation of ships, and other such purchase; and making account, that, if he returned rich, he would ransom his offences . . . and, if otherwise, he would seek his fortune by flight, and new enterprises in some foreign country.[18]

But this theory is inconsistent with virtually all the evidence. All of Ralegh's letters, plans, and hopes centered on the mine; the conditions he agreed to, upon forfeit of his life, bound him to work the mine and attempt nothing else; more important, all of his actions during the voyage suggest his utter reliance upon the existence of the mine. Ralegh was often a liar, but about the fabulous gold mine he seems to have been thoroughly convinced.

A far more plausible suggestion has been made by Harlow: that Ralegh and the king had a tacit understanding on the validity of an English claim to the right bank of the Orinoco, that therefore a mine on such territory was English property and all Spaniards in the area were interlopers.[19] Thus the success of the expedition, while extremely difficult to achieve, would not be rendered totally unattainable by the king's conditions. According to Harlow, Ralegh must have calculated on the basis of this tacit understanding that if the mine proved rich enough, James would be willing to go to war with Spain to protect the English claim. Ralegh would then have succeeded in freeing himself with honor, restoring the fame and fortune of his family, enriching the government, and setting England on a grand imperial course to the glorification of the Protestant cause and the eventual defeat of the hated Spanish empire. "At the back of his mind," suggests Harlow, "he may have envisaged the marching of a great Indian army, commanded by English leaders, to hammer at the gates of Manoa and receive the homage of El Dorado, the Gilded King." [20] But this entire grand structure rested on the mine. If the anti-Spanish faction believed that a clash with the Spanish in Guiana for any reason whatever would suffice to shift the whole of English policy and commit the king to war, they had grossly and inexcusably misunderstood the king's intentions and character. Ralegh knew better. He understood that without the mine—and not just a mine but an incredibly rich deposit of almost pure gold—any struggle with the Spanish would mean his own ruin and the end of all hope for an English empire in South America, for James would certainly give up the English claim to the right bank of the Orinoco. Much later, when the expedition had failed miserably and he was struggling for his life, Ralegh argued that mine or no mine the land belonged to England, but this was only an argument born of desperation, and James quite naturally ignored it. In Guiana, when Ralegh received word that the mine had not been found, and that a Spanish town had been destroyed with heavy loss of life, he knew immediately that he was ruined. The complex secret negotiations that Ralegh was engaged in with the French government, the struggle of pro- and anti-Spanish factions within the English government, the diplomatic maneuvers of Gondomar, the conflict in the conscience of the king, the dreams of an "Anglo-Manoan" empire—all rested in the end upon the existence of that mountain covered with gold and silver ore in which Ralegh so passionately believed.

The official "Declaration," in justifying the king's permission of the enterprise, acknowledges the almost magical force of Ralegh's conviction:

Sir Walter Ralegh had so enchanted the world, with his confident asseveration of that which every man was willing to believe, as his majesty's honour was, in a manner, engaged, not to deny unto his people the adventure and hope of so great riches, to be sought and atchieved, at the charge of volunteers; especially for that it stood with his majesty's politic and magnanimous courses, in these his flourishing times of peace, to nourish and encourage noble and generous enterprises, for plantations, discoveries, and opening of new trades.[21]

"That which every man was willing to believe"—Ralegh's dream was the dream of an age, the dream first articulated perhaps by Marlowe's Jew of Malta and brilliantly satirized by Jonson in Volpone and Sir Epicure Mammon: ingots of pure

gold borne in argosies from the New World, enough to buy
and sell whole nations, to dominate Europe, to transform life
into something rich and strange. Gone was the medieval quietism, the sense of absolute limits set upon man and the world,
the belief in the unreality of all things earthbound and the
sinfulness of ambition. Riches and glory and far-stretched
greatness awaited the man of *virtù*, the man bold enough to
defy fortune, to reach out and seize the prize.

In 1616, this dream was perhaps a bit tarnished—Cortez
and Pizarro were already legends, Drake and Hawkins were
dead, the age of great discoveries was giving way to the age of
patient colonization. Those who searched for paradise increasingly looked not to the gold of the New World but to the
"paradise within." [22] The energies of faith which the Puritans
released were truly explosive, but in a far different way from
the heroic energies of a man like Ralegh. At sixty-four years
old, Ralegh belonged to a past age, and his Guiana enterprise
was a slight anachronism—not, of course, in its ultimate goal
of empire, but in its fabulous mine, its aura of the spectacular
and theatrical. The thousand men who signed up for the voyage were not the well-disciplined crew of the first Guiana voyage twenty years before but a violent, mutinous rabble, some
of them quite as eager to turn pirate as search for the mine
and unwilling to return to England for fear of imprisonment
once they had safely fled its shores.[23] For, though the enterprise excited the imagination of the people, it had about it,
even in the early days of wild hopes and speculation, a feverish air of desperation, and it attracted mostly those with nothing to lose.

Ralegh's own attitude may be gauged by the name he gave
to the fine ship he had built especially for this voyage—the
Destiny. He must have known that, one way or another, this
would be his last voyage—he would return either an enor-
mously rich man to spend his remaining years in power and
honor or a miserable, bankrupt traitor. "Ther is no middle
course but [perish] or prosper," he wrote to Sir Richard Boyle
at the outset of the adventure.[24] As a token of his faith in a

successful outcome, Ralegh took with him his eldest son Wat. Perhaps he dreamed that Wat would share his destiny and inherit the command of the great empire that he was about to found. Despite the careful preparations, the maps and charts and orders drawn up, the secret deplomatic negotiations and the financial arrangements, there is a pervasive sense of fantasy in Ralegh's whole conception of the enterprise. For Ralegh, the voyage was a complex, living memory. In poetry, he was continually drawn to his earlier works, recalling, revising, adding to them. Here, this principle becomes operative in life itself. Bound up in this last adventure is the memory of his first voyage to Guiana, not so much of the actual voyage as of that experience imaginatively transformed first in the *Discoverie* and then in his dreams during the long years of imprisonment, dreams of lost empires, of ancient migrations, of Eden. The use of this kind of memory is to translate the present into the past even as it is being lived—a crucial principle for the transformation of life into art, for memory permits rough and formless experience to be artfully shaped by the imagination. Ralegh acted again and again as if his very actions had already been transformed by memory.

In most of the histrionic performances that marked his extraordinary career, art was clearly in the service of life: the early poems of adoration and sorrow were part of the courtier's role and helped to attract the queen's attention; the theatrical letters and spectacular dress similarly set him apart from the crowds of ambitious young men and gave him a public personality; the overtones of romance in the *Discoverie* heightened the Edenic quality of the New World and hence attracted support for Ralegh's schemes of colonization. But imprisonment, where the control of life was no longer Ralegh's, seemed to alter the relation between reality and imagination. During or shortly after the brief imprisonment of 1592, Ralegh wrote *Ocean to Cynthia,* a poem of an entirely different order from the lovely, conventional lyrics of the earlier years, a poem whose complexity and intensity went far beyond any pragmatic designs. Similarly, in the long years in the Tower after 1603, Ralegh devoted himself to the massive *History of the World,* the scope of which again transcended all realistic goals. Then climactically he turned to the wild gamble of his last voyage. On the strength of his belief in his unique destiny to find a mountain of pure gold and redeem his entire life, Ralegh marshaled a thousand men and a fleet and sailed to Guiana with only the slightest rational chance for success. That mountain would *have* to exist because it was the key to the fulfillment of a vision, a vision of man's greatness which would dispel forever the dark vision of death.

The fusion of life and art was the source of Ralegh's great strength, but it was also the fatal weakness that led finally to his ruin. His vision could never accommodate more than a single consciousness—his own. He lacked a sense of the other, and his life consequently is a record of misunderstanding and faulty judgments. Ralegh prided himself on his knowledge of the world, his understanding of Machiavelli, his cynical realism, and yet he constantly misplaced his confidence and trust —Robert Cecil, Lord Cobham, Faige and Belle, Manourie, "Judas" Stukeley. He understood one side of Queen Elizabeth —her penchant for the histrionic—better than any other man in the realm, but his inability to understand her whole complex personality is reflected in his failure to attain a place in the Privy Council and in his part in the debacle of 1592. He hopelessly misunderstood King James. Ralegh's foreign policy, too, with its grandiose visions of war with Spain, mountains of gold, and lost cities, reflects an imaginative distortion of reality, though its imperial design was prophetic.

In 1616, the force of Ralegh's imagination won his release from the Tower and carried him all the way to the Orinoco, but there it clashed violently with reality. The first jolt came when a fever raged through the ships and rendered Ralegh himself so weak as to prevent him from going with the party in search of the mine.[25] The men he sent in his place— Keymis, his nephew George Ralegh, and his son Wat—were singularly ill-suited for the difficult task: another instance of Ralegh's inability to judge others. At the first crisis, Keymis and George Ralegh panicked and were incapable of action, while the impetuous Wat did just the opposite, with disastrous consequences. If the official account may be believed, Wat led his soldiers on a mad charge on the town of S. Thomé, using "these or the like words: 'Come on, my hearts, here is the mine that you must expect; they that look for any other mine are fools.' " [26] The king's "Declaration" interprets these words as clear evidence that the elder Ralegh did not himself believe in the existence of the mine, but they suggest far more plausibly that Wat did not share his father's vision, that he had his own violent destiny to pursue. The town was taken, but young Ralegh lay dead at the gates. And with Spaniards killed and Spanish property seized against all the conditions and oaths under which the fleet had sailed, the elder Ralegh's life was as good as forfeit. There was still one shred of hope—the mine. But, of course, this was the last terrible reality which Ralegh's imagination had almost swept away —the mine did not exist.[27]

After a few weeks of unsystematic and increasingly desperate searches for the mine, Keymis and his men fired S. Thomé and made their way back to the ships where Ralegh awaited them. Having already received word that his son was dead and that S. Thomé had been taken, Ralegh was awaiting them. Keymis tried somehow to explain and apologize to the man he had loyally served for so many years and whom he had utterly ruined. And in Ralegh's reply there is all of the fanatical self-absorption, the lack of a sense of the other, which had led him to the disaster: "I told him, that, seing my sonne was lost, I cared not if he had lost an hundred more in opening the mine, so my credite had been saved" (*Letters*, p. 356). Small wonder that the men refused to go when Ralegh proposed to lead them back for another search! As for Keymis, Ralegh has left his own account of his lieutenant's end:

Afterwards he [Keymis] came to me in my Cabbin . . . and prayed me for to allowe of his Appollogie. But I told him that he had undone me by his obstinacie, and that I would not favour or colour in any sort his former follie. He then asked me, whether that were my resolution; I told him it was: he then replyed in these words, "I knowe then, Sir, what course to take," and went out of my Cabbin upp into his owne, into wch he was noe sooner entered but I heard a pistol goe of [f]. I sent up (not suspecting any such thing as the killing of himselfe) to know who shott the pistoll; Kemish himselfe made answere, lyeing on his bedd, that he had shott it of [f], because it had bene longe charged, with wch I was satisfied. Some halfe an hower after this, his boye goeing into his Cabbin, found him dead, haveing a longe knife thrust under his lefte pappe through his heart, and the pistoll lyeing by him, with wch it appeared he had shott himselfe; but the bullett, lighting upon a ribb, had but broken the ribb, and went noe further.[28]

In all he wrote of Keymis's death, there is that same mark of inhuman coldness bred not only of despair but of the fusion of life and art. Ralegh was living deep within his own imagination. Other human beings seemed to have very little independent reality for him. Even in the terrible, searing letter informing his wife of their son's death, the tragedy is focused more upon himself and his miseries than upon the young man buried by the Orinoco: "Comfort yor heart (deare Bess), I shall sorrow for us bothe; and I shall sorrowe the lesse because I have not long to sorrowe, because not long to live" (Harlow, p. 243). "Not long to live"—he refers to his fever and his despair, but on a deeper level Ralegh was already preparing himself for his last great scenes: the defense of the Guiana voyage and the execution. And if there is something frightful in his use of even this letter as a platform for histrionic self-justification—"I am sure there is never a base slave in the fleete hath taken the paines and care that I have done; hath sleppt so little, and travilled soe much"—there is also something profoundly heroic.

Throughout his career, Ralegh sought to give his life the quality of art, to raise his actions and his sufferings from the level of the private individual to the level of the universal. In his poetry and prose, the crises of his life were transformed into the crises of his age and of all men. Conversely, through an immense effort of the imagination and the will, his life itself was infused with the symbolic power of art. Although the cost to himself and to those near him was high, he ultimately succeeded in making his life his greatest work of art. With the ruins of his last great adventure all around him—his lands and fortune gone, his son dead, his dream of empire shattered —Ralegh ascended the scaffold with a strange air of triumph. He had fashioned the perfect, paradoxical resolution of the conflicting visions that had tormented and impelled him all his life. In his final gesture of command and his last words, "Strike, man!", Ralegh united heroic assertion and death. The work of art was complete.

Appendix: The Authorship of "The Lie"

"The Lie" is probably the best known of all the poems ascribed to Ralegh and the one most frequently cited to exemplify his characteristic mood of disillusionment and contempt. But recently, Pierre Lefranc has emphatically argued against the inclusion of the poem in the Ralegh canon. Lefranc's argument is basically twofold: first, that "The Lie" is so badly written, so clumsy and tedious, that a poet of Ralegh's stature could not possibly have written it ("C'est, tout d'abord, un poème médiocrement écrit et plus méchamment versifié. . . . Même ses premiers efforts en vers, et parmi eux ses poèmes à refrain ou basés sur des répétitions de tournures, eurent d'emblée plus d'élégance"); [1] and second, that the poem was unquestionably the work of a Puritan ("Dans chacune de ses condamnations et de ses strophes, 'The Lie' est un poème puritain"),[2] a sect for which Ralegh expressed only dislike and derision. For the contemporary attributions of the poem to Ralegh and the attacks upon him as its author,[3] Lefranc has an ingenious explanation: Ralegh's enemies, the followers of Essex, perceiving that, though of Puritan origin, "The Lie" could be read as nihilist and atheistical, ascribed it to Ralegh in order to encourage the rumors of his atheism and so to discredit him. In support of this conspiracy theory, Lefranc points out that after the execution of Essex and particularly at the time of Ralegh's arrest in 1603, there were circulated a number of poems and letters falsely ascribed to Ralegh in order to slander him.[4] Finally, Lefranc believes he has found the real author of "The Lie" in Dr. Richard Latworth (or Latewar), a Fellow of St. Johns College, Oxford, and later chaplain to Charles Blount, Lord Mountjoy. A number of manuscripts assign the poem to Dr. Latworth, including one entitled "W. R. farewell made by D: Lat:"; [5] this title is taken by Lefranc as confirmation of the conspiracy's existence, and he finds Latworth's claim to "The Lie" further supported by a poem entitled "Dr. Latworth upon his death Bed," which expresses a similar contempt for the world.

I find Lefranc's argument unconvincing at a number of points. It is not impossible that the Essex faction ascribed "The Lie" to Ralegh to damage his reputation, but, like Lefranc's theory about *The Phoenix Nest* poems being a veiled threat to the queen, it is improbable. The Essex faction, an important part of whose support was Puritan, would be unlikely to use as slander a poem that could be interpreted as Puritan. The other extant poems and letters which are mentioned above as falsely ascribed to Ralegh are of a very different kind. They are either confessions of heinous crimes against the martyred Earl of Essex, King James, and the Christian religion or expressions of blatantly Machiavellian doctrines:

> [F]or I his [God's] word & service did despise,
> esteeminge them of noe more worthe then weeds;
> from which most vile conceite theise woes proceede.
> 　For now I find, & findinge, feare to rue,
> 　theire is a god which is both just and true.
> 　　　　*   *   *
> Then did I hold Religion but a Jest;
> farr more esteeminge my owne pollicie,
> Whereby I framed my accions as a beast.
> 　　　　*   *   *
> Then som sage man among the vulgarr
> knowing that lawes could not in quiet dwell
> unles they were observed did first devyse
> the name of god, religion, heaven, and hell . . .
> onely bugberes to keepe the worlde in feare.[6]

All these false attributions follow upon Ralegh's arrest for treason in 1603, whereas "The Lie," which was probably written in 1594–95, seems to be associated with Ralegh's name at least as early as 1599. None of these other writings resembles "The Lie" with its faith in the immortal soul and its deep contempt for the insolence and presumption of worldly men and institutions.

As for the attribution to Dr. Latworth, Agnes Latham has pointed out that the mention of Latworth in "MS. Rawlinson Poetry 212" may refer to the nine answering verses which are incorporated into this copy of the poem, not to "The Lie" itself.[7] Still, this argument is not decisive, and it appears that on the basis of manuscript evidence alone Latworth has as strong a claim as Ralegh. Far less convincing are Lefranc's arguments from internal evidence—that the poem is by a Puritan and that it is too badly written to be by Ralegh:

Est-ce, avant la lettre, le siècle, et même le pays, un nihiliste outrancier, moins amer que rempli de haine, et pour qui plus rien ne vaut hors sa révolte personnelle? Nous n'y sommes pas. Le thème central de "The Lie," celui qui, au-delà de l'avalanche et du désordre des condamnations successives, donne au morceau la seule unité qu'il possède, est celui de la vertu partout bafouée dans le spectacle de la société humaine. Toutes choses, dans ce poème, ne sont pas rapportées à leur néant, mais à l'idée que l'auteur se fait de la vertu, et déclarées scandaleuses par rapport à celle-ci. Dans chacune de ses condamnations et de ses strophes, "The Lie" est un poème puritain.[8]

This is a peculiar argument, to say the least. If a wholly negative reading of the poem was so very far from the mentality of the period and the country and is only imposed by giving "The Lie" "couleurs post-romantiques et modernes," [9] why does Lefranc then expect us to believe that the Essex faction wished to evoke precisely such a reading in attributing the poem to their enemy Ralegh? But, of course, in the passage we have cited, Lefranc is not engaged in that part of his argument, but simply in proving that the poem must have been written by a Puritan. To prove this, he pushes the options to extremes—if "The Lie" was not written by a doctrinaire Puritan, it could only have been the work of a "nihiliste outrancier" engaged in a mad personal revolt against the universe. In the 1590s, however, when the poem appears to have been written, satire was in vogue in England, and practically everyone with an interest in literature tried his hand at the new fashion.[10] The relentlessness, the sense that "The Lie" has been written at white heat, even the roughness and lack of elegance that Lefranc deplores are all highly characteristic of satire in this period. And there is little in the substance of "The Lie" that could not be found in the works of Marston and Hall, or even Donne and Jonson, none of them Puritans. Even the ambiguity which Lefranc emphasizes, the fact that the poem can be read either as religious or irreligious, orthodox or seditious, is a problem common to all satire—witness the controversies which have continued to our own day over precisely this problem in Pope and Swift.[11]

Given the widespread popularity of satire, all that can possibly be said is that the poem *could* have been written by a Puritan. But does this by itself exclude the possibility of Ralegh's authorship, as Lefranc argues? Ralegh despised the Puritan (and the Anabaptist, Brownist, etc.) as a "contentious and ignorant person clothing his fancie with *the Spirit of God,* and his imagination with the gift of Revelation" (*H.W.,* II, v, 1, p. 297), but he shared the Puritan's disillusionment with the practices of the world and the desire to expose the self-delusion and pretensions of the great. In Ralegh this mood was derived not so much from the doctrines of Calvin as from an almost medieval *contemptus mundi.* But in the late sixteenth century, the resemblance between Puritanism and medieval pessimism is often striking.[12]

There is nothing in "The Lie" that is inconsistent with Ralegh's writings or with what is known of his thought. His tendency toward melancholy, his special cause for bitterness in the years following the disgrace of 1592, his notorious boldness, all reinforce the manuscript attributions in his favor. One suspects that the underlying basis for Lefranc's challenge is his dislike of the poem, his belief that it is badly written. Of course, even if it were, we would have no reason to decide that it was not written by Ralegh, however high our estimate of his talent. It seems hardly necessary to point out that Ralegh could have written a bad poem, and bad in an entirely different way from his other failures. But, in fact, "The Lie" is a successful poem, and the excitement it has provoked from the

1590s to the present is not due to an "optical illusion" [13] to its happening to satisfy some romantic image of Ralegh or the age—but to its own concentrated power of expression.

In the taut, angry verse of "The Lie" there is no trace of the syntactical complexity, the suggestive turbulence of *Ocean to Cynthia*. Gone, too, is the elegance of early lyrics like "Praisd be Dianas faire and harmles light," the musical expression of cosmic harmony and adoration. The tight verbal control and the relentlessly repetitive form of "The Lie" are the cutting edges of the poet's energy, his determination to strip away the masks of hypocrisy and expose the corruption that lies beneath. Elegant variation of rhythm and expression has no place here. The tireless repetition of the scornful formula suggests a ritual of cursing and exorcism reaching back to the primitive origins of satire, while the verbal repetitions within the stanzas reflect the spirit of irony that infuses the work:

> Tell Potentates they live
>   acting by others action,
> Not loved unlesse they give,
>   not strong but by affection.
> If Potentates reply,
>   give Potentates the lie.

Ralegh uses the elevated, latinate "Potentates" to heighten the exposure of those who fancy themselves masters of the earth: by the third repetition within the tight stanza, the word, like the mortals it designates, seems impossibly pompous. He achieves the same ironic effect with the pretentious phrase "men of high condition,/that manage the estate," followed by a swift unmasking: "Their purpose is ambition,/their practise onley hate." Both of these passages are cited by Lefranc as instances of the poet's ineptitude; [14] they seem to me instances of his use of irony. The poet repeatedly and deftly turns praise into condemnation:

> Say to the Court it glowes,
>   and shines like rotten wood,
> Say to the Church it showes
>   whats good, and doth no good.

Equally deft is the poem's tightly controlled diction:

> Tell wit how much it wrangles
> in tickle points of nycenesse,
> Tell wisedome she entangles
> her selfe in over wisenesse.
> And when they doe reply
> straight give them both the lie. [. . .]
>
> Tell Arts they have no soundnesse,
> but vary by esteeming,
> Tell schooles they want profoundnes
> and stand too much on seeming.
> If Arts and schooles reply,
> give arts and schooles the lie.

The language, like the poem itself, is lean, mocking, and effective.

Notes

PREFACE

1 Quoted in Harlow, p. 310. See my chapter 1, nn. 7 and 23.
2 Joan Webber, "Stylistics: A Bridging of Life and Art in Seventeenth-Century Studies," *New Literary History* 2 (1971) : 296.
3 *Rambler* 68, in *The Yale Edition of the Works of Samuel Johnson*, vol. 3, ed. W. J. Bate and Albrecht B. Strauss (New Haven, 1969), p. 359.
4 For a survey of the concept of role in social psychology, with an extensive bibliography, see Anne-Marie Rocheblave-Spenlé, *La notion de rôle en psychologie sociale* (Paris, 1969).
5 Francis Osborne, *Historical Memoires on the Reigns of Queen Elizabeth, and King James* (London, 1673), pt. 2, p. 477. (First published in 1658.)
6 Pierre Lefranc, *Sir Walter Ralegh, Ecrivain* (Quebec, 1968), p. 570.
7 Philip Edwards, *Sir Walter Ralegh* (London, 1953), p. 174. See also A. L. Rowse, *Ralegh and the Throckmortons* (London, 1962), pp. 163, 182, 304.

CHAPTER 1

1 "The bringing *Sir WALTER RALEGH* to Execution," in Harlow, p. 302. For a slightly different version of the King's Bench proceedings, see David Jardine, *Criminal Trials* (London, 1832), 1 : 499–502; also *The Arraignment and Conviction of Sir Walter Rawleigh . . . Coppied by Sir Thomas Overbury* (London, 1648).
2 Quoted in William Stebbing, *Sir Walter Ralegh* (Oxford, 1891), p. 230. Sir William Waad, who was in charge of transferring Ralegh from plague-ridden London to Westminster for the trial of 1603, wrote to Robert Cecil on November 13: "I protest to yo[u]r L[ordship] it was hab or nab whether Sir Walter Rawley should have ben brought a live thorow such multytudes of unruly people as did exclayme Against him. He that had seen it would not thinck ther had ben any sicknes In London. We

took the best order we could in setting watches through all the streets both in London and for the suburbes. If one harebrain fellow emongst so great multytydes had begonne to set upon him as they were very neer to do it, no intreaty or meanes could have prevayled the fury of the People was so great" (quoted in Lefranc, p. 401).

3   "The Commissioners to the King (18th October, 1618)," in Harlow, p. 295; also in James Spedding, *The Letters and the Life of Francis Bacon* (London, 1872), 6 : 361. The draft is in the handwriting of Sir Edward Coke, Ralegh's prosecuter in 1603.

4   "The King's Reply," in Harlow, p. 296; also Spedding, p. 363. The conclusion, of course, was foregone: "And then after the sentence for his execution which hath been thus long suspended, a declaration be presently put forth in print, a warrant being sent down for us to sign for his execution" (Harlow, p. 297; Spedding, p. 364).

5   For the following, see Harlow, pp. 302–04.

6   From "A Declaration of the *Demeanour and Carriage* of *Sir Walter Ralegh,* Knight, as well in his voyage, as in and sithence his return; and of the true motives and inducements which occasioned his majesty to proceed in doing justice upon him, as hath been done" (London, 1618), in Harlow, p. 349; also in *The Harleian Miscellany* (London, 1745), 3 : 26; Arthur Cayley, *Life of Sir Walter Ralegh, Knt.* (London, 1806), vol. 2, app. 21, p. 437; Spedding, 6 : 404. The "Declaration" is believed to have been written, at least in part, by Bacon (cf. Spedding, 6 : 379–83). See also T. N. Brushfield, "Raleghana, Part VII," *Report and Transactions of the Devonshire Association* (Plymouth, 1906), 38 : 416–90.

7   From Ralegh's speech on the scaffold, in Harlow, p. 308. Several versions of this speech have survived. See, for example, R. H. Bowers, "Ralegh's Last Speech: The 'Elms' Document," *R.E.S.* 2 (1951) : 209–16. In the "Elms" document, Ralegh's self-justification is as follows: "David a man after Gods hart, yet for safety of his lyfe fayned himselfe madd and lett the spittle falle downe upon his beard, And I fynd not that yt is recorded as a fault in David" (p. 213). The reference is to 1 Samuel 21 : 13.

8   "*A proclamation* declaring his *Majesties* pleasure concerning *Sir Walter Rawleigh,* and those who adventured with him (9th June, 1618)," in Harlow, pp. 245–46; also in Cayley, vol. 2, app. 18, pp. 410–11.

Harlow contends that Ralegh argued as he did in the *Appol-ogie* "because it was the strongest card in his hand. He had made precisely the same assertion to the King himself before setting out, and he was reminding him of that vital fact as di-rectly as he dared" (p. 38). But even if there had been some sort of tacit agreement between Ralegh and the king before the expedition had set out, it would have been of no use what-soever to Ralegh upon his return. Any agreement would have been based at the very least on the condition that Ralegh find and bring back the gold he had promised. With no gold to back it up, Ralegh's anti-Spanish position could only infuriate the king and convince him that the mine was a fabrication from the first. See my chapter 6.

9 *"Sir Walter Raghleys Large Appologie* for the ill successe of his enterprise to *Guiana,"* in Harlow, p. 328.

10 "De Warranto Speciali pro Decollatione *Walteri Ralegh,* Mili-tis, A.D. 1618," in Harlow, p. 305.

11 John Chamberlain to Sir Dudley Carleton, October 31, 1618, in *The Letters of John Chamberlain,* ed. Norman E. McClure (Philadelphia, 1939), 2 : 177.

12 John Pory to Sir Dudley Carleton, November 7, 1618, in Wil-liam S. Powell, "John Pory on the Death of Sir Walter Ra-leigh," *William and Mary Quarterly* 9 (1952) : 538.

13 Dr. Robert Tounson to Sir John Isham, November 9, 1618, in *Letters,* p. 490.

14 Cf. G. B. Harrison, *The Life and Death of Robert Devereux, Earl of Essex* (New York, 1937), pp. 322 ff.; also Beach Langs-ton, "Essex and the Art of Dying," *H.L.Q.* 13 (1950) : 109–29.

Tounson was, of course, simply performing his duty as a min-ister to a man near death. Elizabethan handbooks on the art of dying counseled ministers to bring the sick man to a full con-viction of his sinfulness before showing him God's great mercy. In the case of prisoners, special care was to be taken to point out that "the offense, which you have committed against the Magistrate, is also against God" (Caspar Hueber, *A Riche Storehouse . . . for the Sicke* [1578], cited in Langston, p. 116).

15 Bodleian "MS. Eng. Hist. C. 272," fol. 49^v, cited by Latham in *Poems,* p. 154. Two very early manuscripts, one dated October 29 and the other November 2, 1618, are reported by Lefranc, pp. 81–82, n. 32.

16 Some of the manuscripts give only the first, second, and fourth

stanzas (cf. Latham, p. 119). Lefranc (p. 79) suggests that the longer version may be later than 1592, so perhaps Ralegh returned to the poem more than once.

17 The resemblance to Spenser is noted by Philip Edwards, *Sir Walter Ralegh* (London, 1953), p. 73.

Throughout this book, I shall use the name *Ocean to Cynthia* to refer to the poems entitled "The 21th: and last booke of the Ocean to Scinthia" and "The end of the bookes, of the Oceans love to Scinthia, and the beginninge of the 22 Boock, entreatinge of Sorrow."

18 T. N. Brushfield, "Ralegh Miscellanea," *Report and Transactions of the Devonshire Association* (Plymouth, 1909), 41 : 207.

19 Lefranc, p. 163.

20 For "joys," cf. in *Poems,* "Sweete ar the thoughtes," line 2; "Farewell to the Court," line 1; "The Nimphs reply," line 22; "As you came from the holy land," line 34; *Ocean to Cynthia,* line 4, etc. For "dust," cf. "A Poem put into my Lady Laiton's pocket," line 16; "A Vision upon this conceipt of the Faery Queene," line 4; *Ocean to Cynthia,* lines 4, 91, etc. In his discussion of the poetry (pp. 486–524), Lefranc has an analysis of the associations of many of Ralegh's favorite words.

21 Both quoted in *Poems,* p. 154. (See also *Letters of John Chamberlain,* 2 : 179; and Lorkin, in Harlow, p. 311.)

22 George Cavendish and William Roper, *Two Early Tudor Lives,* ed. R. S. Sylvester and D. P. Harding (New Haven, 1962), p. 198. For a discussion of role-playing in More's early works, see R. S. Sylvester, *"A Part of His Own:* Thomas More's Literary Personality in His Early Works," in *Moreana* 4 (November 1967) : 29–42.

J. H. Adamson and H. F. Folland (*The Shepherd of the Ocean* [Boston, 1969], p. 439), note a similarity between a jest said to have been made by Ralegh and one made by More.

23 *Letters,* p. 491. I have emended Edwards's reading "if" to "it".

Accounts of Ralegh's execution include Tounson to Isham (November 9, 1618), Pory to Carleton (October 31, 1618, and November 7, 1618), Lorkin to Puckering (November 3, 1618), Chamberlain to Carleton (October 31, 1618), MS in Public Record Office (S.P. Dom. ciii, 53), Spanish agent Ulloa to King Philip, Tanner MSS (Bodleian, Oxford, Archbishop Sancroft's collection), and *The Arraignment and Conviction of Sir Walter*

Rawleigh . . . Coppied by Sir Thomas Overbury (London, 1648).

24   Thomas Lorkin to Sir Thomas Puckering, in Harlow, p. 312; also in Cayley, vol. 2, app. 20, pp. 414–15.

25   S. R. Gardiner, *History of England from the Accession of James I to the Outbreak of the Civil War, 1603–1642* (London, 1883–84), 3 : 150 n.

26   *Letters*, pp. 222–23: "Lose not your advantage; if you do, I rede your destiney."

27   Both are quoted in Edward Thompson, *Sir Walter Ralegh* (New Haven, 1936), pp. 386, 382.

28   Lorkin to Puckering, in Harlow, p. 313; also in Cayley, vol. 2, app. 20, p. 417. Cf. also Chamberlain to Carleton (in *Letters of John Chamberlain*, 2 : 177): "He had geven order to the executioner that after some short meditation when he stretcht forth his handes he shold dispatch him. After once or twise putting foorth his handes, the fellow out of timerousnes (or what other cause) forbearing, he was faine to bid him strike."

Chapter 2

1   Cf. also from the same letter (to Robert Cecil, 1604): "And while I know that the best of men are but the spoyles of Tyme and certayne images wherwith childish Fortune useth to play,— kisse them to-day and break them to-morrow,—and therfore can lament in my sealf but a common destiney, yet the pitifull estate of thos who ar altogether healpless, and who dayly wound my sowle with the memory of their miseries, force mee, in dispight of all resolvedness, bothe to bewayle them and labor for them" (*Letters*, p. 312).

2   It is touching that fifteen years later, when Ralegh was really brought to execution, Lady Ralegh echoed a phrase from this letter: "The Lordes have geven me his ded boddi, thought [*sic*] they denied me his life" (*Letters*, p. 413).

3   Cf. Jonas A. Barish, "The Antitheatrical Prejudice," *Critical Quarterly* 8 (1969) : 329.

4   *Poems*, p. 24 l. 1–25. The poem appears in Ralegh's own handwriting in MS Hatfield (Cecil Papers, 144) along with "If Synthia be a Queene, a princes, and supreame," The 21th: and last booke of the Ocean to Scinthia," and "The end of the

bookes, of the Oceans love to Scinthia, and the beginninge of
the 22 Boock, entreatinge of Sorrow." An attempt to assign a
much later date to this group of poems has recently been made
by Katherine Duncan-Jones in "The Date of Raleigh's '21th:
and Last Booke of the Ocean to Scinthia,' " *Review of English
Studies,* new series 21, 82 (1970): 143–58. It is extremely difficult to imagine that the cruel mistress of these poems is dead.

5   Robin Grove has suggested that "My boddy in the walls captived" reveals a disparity between style and feeling: "Even as he
complains of his fettered mind, 'of liberty deprived,' he is writing a sonnet where his skill denies his complaint. To write in
this way, however, necessitates a transformation of personal
feeling into conventional attitudes, of real distress into 'destinies dispightful'. . . . If the sonnet is, ostensibly, the conventional plaint of the displaced courtier or rejected lover, its real
action is to judge the worthiness of the life that sustains these
conventions" ("Ralegh's Courteous Art," *Melbourne Critical
Review,* 7 [1964] : 107). Grove has, I think, misunderstood Ralegh's use of convention. Ralegh is not trapped in the conventional role but rather embraces it: for him literary convention
is not an artificial mold imposed on real feelings struggling to
emerge but a means of fashioning and manipulating the self.
There may, however, be a criticism of the courtly life buried—
perhaps unconsciously—in the poem: "Such prison earst was so
delightfull" suggests that the relationship was a prison even
when the poet's "keeper" was his love. The poet has been
locked away all along; only now with the loss of those things
that made captivity seem delightful, he feels himself "close
keipt."

6   Cf. Anne Righter, *Shakespeare and the Idea of the Play* (London, Penguin Books edition, 1967), p. 76: "In sermons and
song-books, chronicles and popular pamphlets, Elizabethans
were constantly being reminded of the fact that life tends to
imitate the theatre. Comparisons between the world and the
stage were so common as to become, in many instances, almost
automatic, an unconscious trick of speech. . . . The play metaphor was for Elizabethans an inescapable expression, a means
of fixing the essential quality of the age."

7   "Jest" in this context suggests not only a trifling joke but an
"amusing or entertaining performance: a pageant, masque, mas-

querade, or the like" (*O.E.D.*). For a useful survey of the back-ground of the play metaphor, see Jean Jacquot, " 'Le Théâtre du Monde'," *Revue de Littérature Comparée*, 31 (1957): 341–72. Jacquot emphasizes the continuity of the major themes: "le rôle de l'humanisme a principalement résidé dans sa transmission et sa diffusion" (p. 371). For a study emphasizing the special preoccupations of the Renaissance, see Richard Bernheimer, "Theatrum Mundi," *Art Bulletin*, 38 (1956) : 225–47.

Ralegh's epigram is highly conventional in form as well as content. Cf., for example, epigram by Richard Barnfield (1574–1627):

> Mans life is well compared to a feast,
> Furnisht with choice of all Varietie:
> To it comes Tyme; and as a bidden guest
> Hee sets him downe, in Pompe and Majestie;
> The three-folde Age of Man, the Waiters bee.
> > Then with an earthen voyder (made of clay)
> > Comes Death, & takes the table clean away.
> [*Complete Poems*, ed. A. B. Grosart (London, 1876), p. 194.]

8   *Ennead* iii, ii, 15, in *The Enneads*, trans. Stephen MacKenna, 3rd ed. (London, 1956), p. 173.

9   I have followed the 1829 edition of Ralegh's *Works* in emend-ing the original "of the least wormes" to "as the least wormes."

10 John of Salisbury, *Frivolities of Courtiers and Footprints of Philosophers*, trans. Joseph B. Pike (Minneapolis, 1938), 175–76. The reference to Petronius is to *Satiricon* 80 (Cam-bridge, Mass., Loeb edition, 1930) : 160.

11 *Frivolities*, 172–73. Perhaps *tyrannorum*, which Pike translates as "rulers," should, in this context, be read as "tyrants"—"non modo tyrannorum sed et principum" (*Policraticus*, ed. Clemens C. I. Webb [Oxford, 1909], 1 : 192).

12 "None the less those departing hence have been kindly dealt with in that they are not taken from this drama of fortune to be cast into exterior darkness, where there shall be weeping and gnashing of teeth. . . . Kindly have they been dealt with in that they await their Elysian Fields, which the sun of justice il-luminates with his light" (*Frivolities*, 176–77). John even goes so far as to affirm that the world has its own Elysian Fields, "stretching away with the broadness of good souls to whom it

has been granted by the Father of lights to devote their entire energy to the knowledge and love of good" (p. 177).

13   Epistles LXXVI and LXXVII, in Seneca, *Epistulae Morales,* trans. R. M. Gummere (Cambridge, Mass., Loeb edition, 1962), 2 : 165, 181.

14   Job and Ecclesiastes seem to have been Ralegh's favorite books of the Bible. *The History of the World* closes with a passage from Job: "besides many other discouragements, perswading my silence; it hath pleased GOD to take that glorious *Prince* out of the world, to whom they [the volumes of the *History*] were directed; whose unspeakable and never enough lamented losse, hath taught me to say with JOB, *Versa est in Luctum Cithara mea, & Organum meum in vocem flentium."*

15   *Fabula de homine,* trans. Nancy Lenkeith, in Ernst Cassirer, Paul Oskar Kristeller, and John Herman Randall, Jr., eds., *The Renaissance Philosophy of Man* (Chicago, 1956), p. 389. Cf. Io. Lodovici Vivis Valentini, *Opera* (Basel, 1555), pp. 269–72.

16   *De hominis dignitate,* trans. Elizabeth Livermore Forbes, in *Renaissance Philosophy of Man,* ed. Cassirer *et al.,* p. 225.

17   That last observation may glance at the heresy charges leveled at certain of Pico's nine hundred theses, in conjunction with which the *Oration* was written.

18   *The Book of the Courtier,* trans. Charles Singleton (New York, Anchor Books edition, 1959). All citations in the text to *The Courtier* are to this translation.

19   Joseph Anthony Mazzeo has suggested that Castiglione may have derived the term "grace" from Alberti's *Trattato della Pittura,* so that there is precedent for its use as an aesthetic term (*Renaissance and Revolution* [New York, 1966], p. 160, n. 11). Even so, it is remarkable that Castiglione could have reapplied it to the description of man's most precious quality without introducing or even implying religious doctrine.

   I am indebted in this chapter to Mazzeo's discussions of Castiglione and Machiavelli.

20   For a sense of these rehearsals, masked in *The Courtier* by Castiglione's mastery of his own precepts, we must turn to the cruder manuals, such as *The Courte of Civill Courtesie* (London, 1577). This is a handbook designed to help its reader thread his way successfully through the labyrinth of social dis-

tinctions and win at the game of rank. For example, if a host of equal or lower social rank seats a gentleman below an inferior, the author suggests that the gentleman casually sit down two or three places *below* even his assigned place; then if his host tries to move him back, he should say nonchalantly, "As long as I finde good meat, I never use to study for my place." The point, of course, is that this is spoken by someone who has intensely studied for his place.

21 Thomas Greene has suggested that the portrait of the perfect prince in Book IV "betrays less the habit of courtly flattery than the terrible need, within the Italian court, for a governor of character and skill" ("The Flexibility of the Self in Renaissance Literature," in Peter Demetz, Thomas Greene, and Lowry Nelson, Jr., eds., *The Disciplines of Criticism* [New Haven, 1968], p. 254). I have drawn upon Greene's valuable article throughout this discussion.

22 Sir Philip Sidney, "The Defense of Poesie" (1583), in Allan H. Gilbert, ed., *Literary Criticism: Plato to Dryden* (Detroit, 1962), pp. 427–28. For other uses of this *topos,* see (also in Gilbert) Trissino, "Poetica" (1529), p. 213; Mazzoni, "On the Defense of Comedy" (1587), p. 380; Tasso, "Discourses on the Heroic Poem" (1594), p. 468; Guarini, "The Compendium of Tragicomic Poetry" (1599), p. 523.

23 Lucretius, *On the Nature of Things,* IV, 11–25, quoted by Mazzoni, in Gilbert, *Literary Criticism,* p. 380: "Even as healers, when they essay to give loathsome wormwood to children, first touch the rim all round the cup with the sweet golden moisture of honey, so that the unwitting age of children may be beguiled as far as the lips . . . I have desired to set forth to you my reasoning in the sweet-tongued song of the muses, as though to touch it with the pleasant honey of poetry."

24 Jacob Burckhardt, *The Civilization of the Renaissance in Italy,* trans. S. G. C. Middlemore (New York, 1958), 1 : 143. For criticism of Burckhardt, see Wallace Ferguson, *The Renaissance in Historical Thought* (Boston, 1948), chaps. 7–11.

25 For a valuable discussion, from a different perspective, of some of the issues raised here, see Barish, "The Antitheatrical Prejudice," and "Exhibitionism and the Antitheatrical Prejudice," *ELH,* 36 (March 1969) : 1 ff. Cf. also Harry Berger, Jr., "The Ecology of the Mind," *Centennial Review,* 8 (Fall

1964) : 409–34, and "The Renaissance Imagination: Second World and Green World," *Centennial Review,* 9 (Winter 1965) : 36–78.

26 Niccolò Machiavelli, *The Prince and the Discourses* (New York, Modern Library, 1950), p. 56. *The Prince* is translated by Luigi Ricci, revised by E. R. P. Vincent; *The Discourses* by Christian E. Detmold. All citations of Machiavelli are to this edition.

27 Cf. A. Bartlett Giamatti, "Proteus Unbound: Some Versions of the Sea God in the Renaissance," in *The Disciplines of Criticism,* ed. Demetz *et al.,* pp. 437–75.

28 Greene, "Flexibility," p. 257.

29 "TO THE KINGS most Excellent Majestie. The humble petition and information of Sir Lewis Stucley, Knight, Vice-admirall of Devon, touching his owne behaviour in the charge committed unto him, for the bringing up of Sir Walter Raleigh, and the scandalous aspersions cast upon him for the same" (London, 1618), p. 2. Cf. 2 Corinthians 11 : 14—"for Satan himself is transformed into an angel of light."

Stukeley was eventually hounded from London and retired to the Isle of Lundy where he died a lunatic some years later.

30 Cf. Barish, "The Antitheatrical Prejudice," esp. pp. 330–32 on Tertullian.

31 "*Judicious and Select Essayes and Observations.* By that Renowned and Learned Knight, Sir Walter Raleigh." (London, 1650), sig. [A3ʳ]. Moseley's source appears to be not Suetonius, who first told the story, but Francis Bacon, whose phrases are almost exactly copied (cf. *Advancement of Learning,* ii, xxiii, 12).

32 The most moving of the historical examples in *The Prince* concerns the failure of Cesare Borgia to maintain his power: "And he [Borgia] told me on the day that Pope Julius II was elected, that he had thought of everything which might happen on the death of his father, and provided against everything, except that he had never thought that at his father's death he would be dying himself" (p. 29). In fact, Borgia was only ill and did not die until some years later, but Machiavelli, in the manner of a literary craftsman, twists the historical events to show that if Borgia's "measures were not successful, it was through no fault of his own but only by the most extraordinary

malignity of fortune" (p. 24). (At the end of the same chapter, however, Machiavelli reverses himself and finds fault with Borgia's failure to create a Spanish pope.)

33 See George R. Kernodle, *From Art to Theatre* (Chicago, 1944), pp. 130–53; Francis Fergusson, *The Idea of a Theater* (Princeton, 1949), pp. 116 ff.; Alvin B. Kernan, *"Hamlet* and the Nature of Drama," in *Report of the 13th Yale Conference on the Teaching of English* (New Haven, 1967), p. 3. For a somewhat different view of the symbolism of the theater, see Frances A. Yates, *Theatre of the World* (London, 1969), p. 189; Bernheimer, "Theatrum Mundi," on Camillo's magic theater.

34 *Platonic Theology*, trans. Josephine I. Burroughs, in *JHI* 5 (April 1944) : 235. See Paul Oskar Kristeller, *The Philosophy of Marsilio Ficino* (New York, 1943), pp. 92–100, 407–10.

The fascinated interest in models continued throughout the Renaissance. See, for example, the admiration in *The Faerie Queene* for Merlin's wonderful mirror: "Forthy it round and hollow shaped was,/Like to the world it selfe, and seemd a world of glas" (iii, ii, 19). Georges Poulet, in *The Metamorphoses of the Circle* (English trans., Baltimore, 1966), notes the importance of models in seventeenth-century consciousness (p. 17).

35 *An Apology for Actors* (1612), ed. Richard H. Perkinson (New York, 1941), sig. D3^r.

36 Quoted in E. K. Chambers, *The Elizabethan Stage* (Oxford, 1923), 3 : 72. See also Serlio's "Trattato Sopra le Scene," in Chambers, vol. 4, esp. pp. 355–56.

37 *Platonic Theology*, p. 236. Ficino quotes a saying ascribed to Hermes Trismegistus. Cf. Pico, *Oration,* in *Renaissance Philosophy of Man*, ed. Cassirer, *et al.* p. 223.

38 Cf. Kernan, *"Hamlet* and the Nature of Drama," p. 5. All quotations of Shakespeare are from *Works,* ed. George Lyman Kittredge (Boston, 1936).

39 Quoted in J. E. Neale, *Elizabeth I and her Parliaments, 1584–1601* (London, 1965), 2 : 119. Subsequent citations are in the text as "Neale." "She is a Princess," the French ambassador remarked of Elizabeth, "who can act any part she pleases" (quoted in J. E. Neale, *Queen Elizabeth I* [New York, Anchor Books edition, 1957], p. 263). Cf. Francis Osborne, *Historical Memoires on the Reigns of Queen Elizabeth, and King James*

(London, 1673, first published in 1658), pt. 2: "Her sex did bear out many impertinences in her words and actions, as *her making Latine Speeches in the Universities,* and professing her self in public *a Muse,* then thought something too Theatrical for a Virgin Prince . . ." (p. 441).

40 Plowden and Coke quoted in Ernst H. Kantorowicz, *The King's Two Bodies* (Princeton, 1957), p. 13. Cf. Righter, *Shakespeare and the Idea of the Play,* pp. 113–16; G. K. Hunter, *John Lyly* (London, 1962), p. 7.

41 Witness, in the Vestarian Controversy, her staunch support, against the opposition of most of her advisers, for the old ecclesiastical ornaments and clothing.

42 See John Nichols, *The Progresses and Public Processions of Queen Elizabeth,* 3 vols. (London, 1823); David M. Bergeron, *English Civic Pageantry, 1558–1642* (London, 1971); Frances A. Yates, "Queen Elizabeth as Astraea," *JWCI* 10 (1947) : 27–82, and "Elizabethan Chivalry: The Romance of the Accession Day Tilts," *JWCI* 20 (1957) : 4–25; Roy C. Strong, "The Popular Celebration of the Accession Day of Queen Elizabeth I," *JWCI* 21 (1958) : 86–103.

43 Godfrey Goodman, Bishop of Gloucester, *The Court of King James the First* (London, 1839), p. 163 (italics mine). Perhaps the phrase "ordinary public appearance" is misleading here— we would do well to remember that in 1588 any royal appearance before a crowd was a courageous act, as there was great and justified fear of assassination attempts.

44 *The Quenes majesties passage through the citie of London to westminster the day before her coronacion* [1559], ed. James M. Osborn (New Haven, 1960), pp. 28, 46. On Queen Mary's accession, see *The Chronicle of Queen Jane and of Two Years of Queen Mary,* ed. John Nichols, Camden Society, 48 (1850) : 14—"The queenes grace stayed at Allgate-streete before the stage wheare the poore children stood, and hard an oration that one of them made, but she sayd nothinge to them."

45 From John Dowland, *The Second Book of Songs or Airs* (1600), in E. C. Wilson, *England's Eliza* (Cambridge, Mass., 1939), p. 206. Cf. Yates, "Queen Elizabeth as Astraea," p. 75: "The bejewelled and painted images of the Virgin Mary had been cast out of churches and monasteries, but another bejewelled and painted image was set up at court, and went in progress through the land for her worshippers to adore."

46 Ralegh, "Now we have present made," in Walter Oakeshott, *The Queen and the Poet* (London, 1960), p. 205. See E. C. Wilson, *England's Eliza;* Roy C. Strong, *The Portraits of Queen Elizabeth I* (Oxford, 1963).

47 Sir Anthony Bagot, quoted in Edward Thompson, *Sir Walter Ralegh* (New Haven, 1936), p. 33.

48 John Aubrey, *Brief Lives,* ed. O. L. Dick (London, 1950), p. 254.

49 All quoted in Thompson, pp. 34, 176–77, 187, 164. Cf. John Clapham, "Certain Observations Concerning the Life and Reign of Queen Elizabeth" [1603], ed. E. P. Read and Conyers Read, *Elizabeth of England* (Philadelphia, 1951), p. 93: Ralegh "was a man of a very bold spirit and of a quick conceit, in adversity not altogether dejected; insolent in prosperity and ungrateful to such as had supplied his wants in his first and mean estate. He was commonly noted for using of bitter scoffs and reproachful taunts which bred him much dislike. He was so far from affecting popularity, as he seemed to take a pride in being hated of the people, either for that he thought it a point of policy, of else that he scorned the approbation of the multitude."

50 Quoted in Edward Edwards, *Life,* 1 : 154.

51 There are a few brief and guarded moments of detachment verging on cynicism—as when he writes in a letter to his "Cussen George" that "The Queen thincks that George Carew longes to see her; and therefore see her" (*Letters,* pp. 42–43)—but on the whole, Ralegh seems to have taken the cult of Elizabeth with complete seriousness.

CHAPTER 3

1 *Poems,* p. xxiv.

2 Cf. J. W. Saunders, "The Stigma of Print," *Essays in Criticism,* 1 (1951) : 139–64. There were only five poems which Ralegh published or allowed to be published with his signature or initials during his lifetime: the poem "in commendation of the Steele Glasse" (1576), the two sonnets in praise of *The Faerie Queene* (1590), the praise of the translation of Lucan's *Pharsalia* by Sir Arthur Gorges (1614), and "Conceipt begotten by the eyes," published in Francis Davison, *A Poetical Rhapsody* (1602). It should be noted that four of the five are commenda-

tory poems. In 1602, Ralegh presumably made the publisher of *England's Helicon* paste cancel-slips over his initials which had been subscribed to two poems (cf. *Poems*, pp. 102–03).

3   *Poems*, p. xxiv.

4   Thomas Fuller, *The History of the Worthies of England* (London, 1662), p. 261.

5   For Ralegh's poem ("Fortune hathe taken away my love"), see Walter Oakeshott, *The Queen and the Poet* (London, 1960), Plate VIII, and p. 154. In *The Arte of English Poesie* (1580), Puttenham had used the third stanza as an example of *"Anaphora*, or the Figure of Report," but the entire poem was not known until Oakeshott found the copy in "Phillipps MS. 3602." Subsequently, another manuscript copy (Archbishop Marsh's Library, Dublin, "MS Z. 3. 5. 21." fol. 30^v) was discovered by L. G. Black (*T.L.S.* [May 23, 1968], p. 535).

For the Queen's reply ("Ah silly pugge wert thou so sore afraid"), see L. G. Black, ibid. See also "Ladies comfortable and pleasant answer," a broadside ballad of a somewhat later date which removes the personal references and, among other things, changes "silly pugge" to "silly soul" (in Oakeshott, app. 2, pp. 218–19).

6   Oakeshott, p. 5.

7   In *The Eloquent "I"* (Madison, 1968), Joan Webber has distinguished between the "Conservative Anglican" and "Radical Puritan" sensibilities: "The Anglican turns himself into art, while the Puritan turns art into life, using art for the benefit of life" (p. 9). Ralegh, embracing both positions, seems to precede the split in consciousness represented here.

8   Cecil Papers 144/238a–247b; in *Poems*, pp. 24–44. On the basis of "a backward flourish on the intitial 1" (*Poems*, p. 122), Miss Latham reads "11 th" and "12" for "21 th" (one-and-twentieth) and "22", but her reading is not generally accepted. See the reproduction of the title and opening lines of the poem in Philip Edwards, *Sir Walter Ralegh*, facing page 96.

Following Philip Edwards, I have quoted *Ocean to Cynthia* without the spaces between the stanzas provided by Miss Latham. These spaces are absent from Ralegh's manuscript and tend to interrupt the troubled flow of the original. Due to the length of the 21st Book, I have included line numbers with the quotations.

The two "Books" are preceded in the Hatfield House MS. by two other poems in Ralegh's hand: "If Synthia be a Queene, a princes, and supreame," an enigmatic piece of 7 lines, and the sonnet "My boddy in the walls captived."

9 Spenser's compliments may account for Gabriel Harvey's reference to Ralegh in notes made at the end of his copy of Speght's *Chaucer:* "His [Sir Edward Dyer's] Amaryllis, & Sir Walter Raleigh's Cynthia, how fine and sweet inventions?" (*Poems,* p. lx). Ralegh's poetry is also praised in Puttenham's *Arte of English Poesie* and Meres's *Palladis Tamia.*

10 All citations of Spenser are to *The Works of Edmund Spenser: A Variorum Edition,* ed. Edwin Greenlaw, *et al.* (Baltimore, 1932–57).

11 This is the generally accepted date; cf. *Poems,* pp. xxxv, xlv; Philip Edwards, 99–101; Lefranc, 101–09. For dissenting opinions, see A. M. Buchan, "Ralegh's *Cynthia*—Facts or Legend," *M.L.Q.* 1, no. 4 (1940) : 461–74, and Katherine Duncan-Jones (above, chap. 2, n. 4).

12 Cf. Lefranc, who speaks of the titles as a "trompe-l'oeil" (131–32).

13 *Poems,* p. xli.

14 "Now we have present made . . . ," in Oakeshott, 205–06; also Plate V. Oakeshott found another manuscript of the poem, a version in five voices, and Lefranc recently uncovered still another manuscript copy in the Cecil Papers at Hatfield House (app. E, 602–03).

15 Lefranc, p. 111. Cf. also Philip Edwards, pp. 99 ff., and Oakeshott, pp. 140 ff.

16 There is debate on which poems in *The Phoenix Nest* are by Ralegh. Cf. *Poems,* pp. xlv–li and 157–62; also Hyder E. Rollins, ed., *The Phoenix Nest* (Cambridge, Mass., 1931); Helen Estabrook Sandison, ed., *The Poems of Sir Arthur Gorges* (Oxford, 1953); Lefranc, pp. 94–98 and 120–23.

17 Lefranc, p. 120.

18 Ibid. Also app. F, 604–13.

19 Ibid., p. 112.

20 *The Book of the Courtier,* p. 70.

21 Cf. also the possible echo in *The History of the World:* "Hee shall finde nothing remaining, but those sorrowes, which grow up after our fast-springing youth; over-take it, when it is at a

stand; and over-top it utterly, when it begins to wither" (Pref.,
sig. D1ᵛ).

22 Lefranc, p. 80, n. 22.

23 C. S. Lewis, *English Literature in the Sixteenth Century* (C ‹-
ford, 1954), p. 519. Lewis hesitates to classify Ralegh's poems as
either "Golden" or "Drab".

24 *Poems*, pp. 120–21. Cf. Percy, *Reliques*, 3 vols. (London, 1765),
2 : 84.

25 Erwin Panofsky, *Studies in Iconology* (New York, Torchbook
edition, 1962), p. 112. Chap. 4 ("Blind Cupid") and chap. 5
("The Neoplatonic Movement in Florence and North Italy")
are both relevant.

26 *The Book of the Courtier*, p. 354.

27 Cf. *Letters*, pp. 19, 21, 34, 37, 40, 45, 46.

28 A reproduction of this portrait is included as the frontispiece
in Lefranc.

29 It was long believed that Ralegh had married Elizabeth
Throckmorton only in the summer of 1592, after she had become pregnant. But evidence has recently been brought to light
which suggests that Ralegh had been secretly married for some
time—perhaps as long as four years! Cf. Lefranc, "La date du
mariage de Sir Walter Ralegh, un document inédit," *Etudes
Anglaises* 9 (1956) : 193–211. This finding has been disputed by
Oakeshott, p. 45. If the secret marriage really were of four
years' duration, Ralegh would be revealed as an even greater
actor than I have argued him to be.

30 A. L. Rowse, *Ralegh and the Throckmortons* (London, 1962),
p. 162; Lefranc, pp. 137–38, n. 10.

31 MS Ashmole 1729, fol. 177; in Helen Estabrook Sandison, "Arthur Gorges: Spenser's Alcyon," *PMLA*, 43 (1928) : 657–58.

The letter bears the date 26 July 1592, inscribed by Cecil's
secretary. Lefranc has questioned the accuracy of this date in
"La date du mariage de Sir Walter Ralegh," pp. 207–10.

Gorges probably alludes specifically to the 23rd canto of
Ariosto's poem, in which Orlando sees a token of the love of
Angelica and Medoro and grows mad with grief and rage.

32 Lefranc has cited and analyzed most of the passages dealing
with Ralegh's treatment of "l'affaire Throckmorton," pp. 137 ff.

33 Though there may be a deliberate ambiguity here—not between Ralegh's love for the queen and his love for Elizabeth

Throckmorton, but between his love for the queen and the love which the queen once felt for him. Cf. Donald Davie, "A Reading of *The Ocean's Love to Cynthia*," in *Elizabethan Poetry*, Stratford-upon-Avon studies no. 2 (London, 1960), pp. 71–89; also Lefranc, pp. 135, n. 7; 139, n. 14.

34 To Robert Cecil, July 1592, and Lord Admiral Howard, August [?] 1592.

35 Cf. Oakeshott, pp. 174–75; Lefranc, p. 106.

36 The opposition of pastoral and anti-pastoral worlds is a theme that concerned Ralegh before *Ocean to Cynthia* and in a context quite apart from his relationship with the queen. In "The Nimphs reply to the Sheepheard" *(Poems,* pp. 16–17), Ralegh's famous reply to Marlowe's "The passionate Sheepheard to his love," the shepherd's amorous images of delight are answered with a melancholy vision of Time the Destroyer. But there is none of the anguish which is felt in *Ocean to Cynthia*, no sense of personal involvement in the process of aging and decay. Moreover, the "Nimphs reply" is carefully matched in form and style to the "Passionate Sheepheard," while the poet of *Ocean to Cynthia* insists that with the destruction of the pastoral world, the necessary conditions for the old, flowing verses are also lost.

37 C. S. Lewis, *English Literature in the Sixteenth Century*, p. 520.

38 Philip Edwards attempts to separate what is finished from what is unfinished by analysing the various ink marks in the manuscript—lines, dots, inverted commas—as "tokens of dissatisfaction, or reminders to revise" (p. 102). According to Edwards, broken syntax, images "which do not obey the rules of decorum and logical aptness that Ralegh normally adheres to so excellently," and passages of "strident" emotion were all due for revision and correction, and so "we must clearly make reservations in our criticism, bearing in mind that we have before us poetry being created, and not a finally completed work of art" (pp. 105–06). But poetry-in-process was precisely Ralegh's aim in *Ocean to Cynthia*, and the poem's incompleteness is one of his most powerful themes.

39 "Ocean" probably had its origin in the queen's nickname for Ralegh—"Water" (probably a pun on the Devonshire pronunciation of "Walter" as well as a reflection of Ralegh's interest in

the sea). I see no evidence that "Cynthia" refers, as E. C. Wilson would have us believe, to "the mature maritime spirit of Elizabethan England" (*England's Eliza* [Cambridge, Mass., 1939], p. 279).

40   Lefranc (pp. 509 ff.) has painstakingly sorted out some of these patterns, but there emerges from his discussion a still greater sense of the ambiguity of the imagery.

41   Philip Edwards, p. 80.

42   William Empson, *Seven Types of Ambiguity* (New York, 1931), p. 48.

43   Sir Philip Sidney, *Poems,* ed. W. A. Ringler (Oxford, 1965), p. 112.

44   Lefranc, pp. 504–05.

45   The word "mind" is used more than a score of times in *Ocean to Cynthia,* along with "fancy," "thoughts," "conceit," "affections," "memory," "heart," "spirit," "soul," "fantasy," "invention," "dreams," and "imagination."

46   Ralegh was hastily sent to Dartmouth to stop the sailors from carrying off all the spoils and robbing the queen of her profits.

47   Oakeshott, pp. 205–06 and Plate 5. Cf. Lefranc, pp. 602–03. I have used Oakeshott's transcription, although there appear to be slight discrepancies between it and the autograph version reproduced in Plate 5.

48   Lefranc, pp. 125–26. The lyric is dated 1602 in another copy (Hatfield House MS.) It is just possible that the endorsement is incorrect and that the lyric dates from before *Ocean to Cynthia,* but this is highly unlikely.

49   Even the search for the golden kingdom which took Ralegh to Guiana in 1595 may be glanced at in "She as the valley of Perue/Whose summer ever lastethe."

CHAPTER 4

1   See, for example, David B. Quinn, *Ralegh and the British Empire* (London, 1947); A. L. Rowse, *The Expansion of Elizabethan England* (London, 1955); James A. Williamson, *The Age of Drake* (London, 1938); J.W. Shirley, "Sir Walter Raleigh's Guiana Finances," *H.L.Q.,* 13 (1949–1950) : 55–69. See also the introductions to the editions of Ralegh's *Discoverie of Guiana* by Sir Robert H. Schomburgk (London, 1848 [Hakluyt Society, 1st series, III]), and V. T. Harlow (London, 1928).

2 A full transcript is reprinted in *Willobie His Avisa,* ed. G. B. Harrison (New York, 1926), app. 3. The testimony is evaluated by Ernest A. Strathmann, *Sir Walter Ralegh: A Study in Elizabethan Skepticism* (New York, 1951), esp. pp. 46–52, 139–46, and by Lefranc, 379–93. Citations are to Harrison's text, although I have adopted Strathmann's corrections of a few misreadings.

3 Ironside's testimony appears to be accurate and reliable. Moreover, one of the members of the investigating commission, Sir Ralph Horsey, had been present at the dinner party during which the discussion took place.

4 Cf. Ralegh's letters from Ireland in 1581, bitterly criticizing his superior's conduct of the war (*Letters,* pp. 11–18). In 1576, George Gascoigne's satire *The Steele Glas* was published with a commendatory poem by "Walter Rawely of the middle Temple" (*Poems,* p. 3). Ralegh's poem includes the prophetic lines "For whoso reapes renowne above the rest,/With heapes of hate shall surely be opprest."

5 E. G. R. Taylor, "Hariot's Instructions for Raleigh's Voyage to Guiana, 1595," *Journal of the Institute of Navigation,* 5 (October, 1952) : 345.

6 Cf. Walter I. Trattner, "God and Expansion in Elizabethan England: John Dee, 1527–1583," *Journal of the History of Ideas,* 25 (1964): "English science in the sixteenth century was, on the whole, practical and experimental. Most leading scholars were not interested in abstract theory, except in so far as it was necessary for determining fundamental principles. . . . A few, on the other hand, were infused with the older medieval attitude and sought knowledge for its revelation of the truths of God. For Dee, however, the two traditions did not conflict; rather, they were in harmony and indeed complemented each other" . (p. 34). See likewise, Frances A. Yates, *Giordano Bruno and the Hermetic Tradition* (London, 1964).

7 There is still some mystery surrounding this recall. Ralegh seems to have deliberately staged the scene, for he knew about the orders to relinquish command to Frobisher three months before he set sail. It is possible that because Frobisher (unlike Ralegh) was extremely unpopular among the sailors, the queen and Ralegh agreed to put off the transfer of commands until the fleet was already out to sea. Or alternately, Ralegh may

simply have staged the whole business himself, to enhance his
reputation and stifle rumors of his impending disfavor.

8   A. L. Rowse, *Ralegh and the Throckmortons* (London, 1962),
    pp. 181–82. Rowse even suggests that Ralegh himself dictated
    his wife's letter to Cecil begging that "for my sake you will
    rather draw sur watar towardes the est then heulp hyme for-
    ward toward the soonsett, if ani respecke to me or love to him
    be not forgotten" (*Letters*, p. 397).

9   I have used V. T. Harlow's edition (London, 1928) throughout.

10 As I am primarily concerned with the nature of Ralegh's per-
    sonal vision and his expression of it within the convention of
    the travel book, I have not discussed the actual details of the
    expedition, for which see especially Quinn and Harlow.

11 Cf. J. H. Parry, *The Age of Reconnaissance* (New York, Mentor
    edition, 1963), pp. 232 ff.

12 Cf., for example, Spenser, "The Shepheardes Calender," i,
    37–40; xii, 103–08.

13 Cf. likewise: "These *Tivitivas* are a verie goodlie people and
    verie valiant, and have the most manlie speech and most delib-
    erate that ever I heard of what nation soever" (p. 38).

    A subsequent pamphlet on the Guiana enterprise, thought to
    have been written for Ralegh by Thomas Hariot, leans heavily
    on religious arguments: "By this meanes infinite nombers of
    soules may be brought from theyr idolatry, bloody sacrifices, ig-
    noraunce, and incivility to the worshipping of the true God
    aright to civill conversation . . . besids that presently it will
    stopp the mouthes of the Romish Catholickes, who vaunt of
    theyr great adventures for the propogacion of the gospell. . . ."
    (*Discoverie*, app. C, p. 138).

    Passages such as these only emphasize Ralegh's avoidance of
    them in the *Discoverie*.

14 Ovid, *Metamorphoses*, trans. Frank J. Miller (London, Loeb
    edition, 1916), I : 100–01.

15 Ralegh wrote his own lively account of the Cadiz action in *Let-
    ters*, pp. 146–56.

16 *Correspondence of King James VI of Scotland with Sir Robert
    Cecil and Others in England*, ed. John Bruce (London, Cam-
    den Society, 1861), pp. 18–19.

17 Edward Edwards, 1 : 375.

18 Agnes M. C. Latham, "Sir Walter Ralegh's Farewell Letter to

his Wife in 1603: A Question of Authenticity," *Essays and Studies by Members of the English Association,* 25 (Oxford, 1939) : 44.

19   Ibid., p. 45.

20   Ibid., pp. 40–41. Cf. Miss Latham's closing remarks: "I should like finally to point out, in defense of those who have found the letter affecting, that it is not in every way false. Ralegh was indeed in pressing peril, and I think there is genuine emotion in it as well as feigned. How could there not be? That is what makes it so hard to interpret. It is neither entirely sincere nor entirely pretence. We are dealing, after all, with a very grim pretending and one that comes very near to truth" (p. 58).

21   Edward Edwards, 1 : 377.

22   Carleton to Chamberlain, dated Winchester, November 27, 1603, in Cayley, 2 : 11–12.

23   David Jardine, *Criminal Trials* (London, 1832), 1 : 404–07.

24   Cf. Catherine Drinker Bowen, *The Lion and the Throne: The Life and Times of Sir Edward Coke* (Boston, 1956): "To say that from Ralegh's trial dated a change in the laws would be to say too much. Yet from that day there entered it is said the possibility of change—a groping after procedure which might give to the unfriended single prisoner fair chance against the solid power of the state" (pp. 223–24).

25   *The Just Defence of John Lilburn* (1653), in *The Leveller Tracts, 1647–1653,* ed. William Haller (New York, 1944), p. 455; also in Webber, *The Eloquent "I",* pp. 54–55. Webber suggests that Lilburne's trial for treason "represents the climax of all his writing and of his career. No single piece of his work has less claim to be called his art, yet this trial must be considered the keystone of his life and art partly because it is here that the two become absolutely one and the same" (p. 70).

26   For the sentence, see Bowen, p. 217; for Ralegh's reply, see Jardine, p. 452.

27   *Letters,* p. 277; cf. also *Letters,* p. 281: "I do therefore, on the knees of my hart, beseich your Majesty to take councell from your own sweet and mercifull disposition, and to remember that I have loved your Majesty now twenty yeares, for which your Majestie hath yett geven me no reward. . . . Save me, therfore, most mercifull Prince, that I may owe your Majesty my life itt sealf" (November [?], 1603).

28   *Poems,* pp. 49–51. For attributions to Ralegh, pp. 140–43.
29   Philip Edwards, pp. 93–96; Lefranc, pp. 84–85.
30   Rosemond Tuve, *Elizabethan and Metaphysical Imagery* (Chicago, 1957), p. 300, n. 29.
31   *Paradise Lost,* III, 362–63; *The Pilgrim's Progress,* ed. Louis L. Martz (New York, 1949), p. 159. All quotations from Milton are from *Complete Poems and Major Prose,* ed. Merritt Y. Hughes (New York, 1957).

CHAPTER 5

1   F. J. Levy, *Tudor Historical Thought* (San Marino, 1967), p. 294.
2   Christopher Hill, *Intellectual Origins of the English Revolution* (Oxford, 1965), p. 192.
3   Lily B. Campbell, *Shakespeare's "Histories," Mirrors of Elizabethan Policy* (San Marino, 1947), p. 79.
4   Ralegh did not begin to write the *History* until winter, 1608–09, almost six years after his imprisonment had begun (Lefranc, app. J, 638–42). Lefranc attempts to date the composition of the various parts of the *History* with what seems to me an impossible degree of precision: e.g., "En principe, 9,74 mois s'étaient écoulés depuis le jour où la première page avait pris forme, et ce passage aurait donc été écrit vers le 22 janvier 1609–10" (p. 640).
5   *H.W.,* Pref., sig. E4^v. According to Francis Osborne, Henry declared that "No King but my Father would keep such a bird in a Cage" (*Memoires,* pp. 141–42).
6   Cf. Lefranc, pp. 320–29.
7   For publishing history, see John Racin, Jr., "The Early Editions of Sir Walter Ralegh's *The History of the World,*" *Studies in Bibliography (Virginia),* 17 (1964) : 199–209.
8   Lefranc, p. 326.
9   R. G. Collingwood, *The Idea of History* (Oxford, 1946), p. 247.
10   Ralegh misses almost entirely the poetic, mythic qualities of Genesis and fills his retelling of the first days of Creation with technical terms appropriate to the alchemical experiments he was at that time conducting in his small laboratory in the Tower: "operative Spirit," "resolved," "operative Virtue," "refraction," "evaporation," etc. Likewise, he rejects the allegorical interpretation of Paradise and sets out to discover its precise lo-

cation, as he had set out years before to discover the fabulous
city of El Dorado (ı, iii, 2, p. 34; ı, iii, 3, p. 38; ı, iii, 5, p. 40).
And his extensive knowledge of shipbuilding is brought to bear
on the discussion of the size and construction of Noah's Ark (ı,
vii, 8–9, pp. 109–13).

11 For example, Xenophon: ııı, x, 5, pp. 116 ff.; Archimedes: v, iii,
15, pp. 516 ff.

12 Cf. C. A. Patrides, *The Phoenix and the Ladder: The Rise and
Decline of the Christian View of History* (Berkeley, 1964), pp.
43 ff.; Levy, *Tudor Historical Thought*, pp. 9–32, 288–90; John
Taylor, *The "Universal Chronicle" of Ranulf Higden* (Oxford,
1966), pp. 147–48; R. L. P. Milburn, *Early Christian Interpretations of History* (London, 1954), pp. 74–95. John Racin, "An
Analysis of Sir Walter Ralegh's *The History of the World*,"
(diss., Ohio State University, 1961), pp. 89–159.

Racin's fine study is concerned throughout with the purpose
of historiography in the *History*. Though my methods and
goals are quite different from his, certain of my conclusions are
similar. Cf. especially, in Racin, pp. 158 and 198–200.

13 ı, i, 15, pp. 19–22; ııı, i, 9, p. 17; ııı, v, 8, p. 57; etc. (cf. Lefranc, app. G, p. 631).

14 ıv, ii, 3, pp. 175–76.

15 v, vi, 8, p. 755.

16 E.g. Pref., sig. C3^v; Lefranc, pp. 449–50.

17 ı, v, 5, pp. 76–78; v, i, 4, pt. 1, pp. 323–24.

18 Pref., sig. C3^r–D1^v; ııı, i, 11, p. 21.

19 Pref., sig. D2^r; ı, ix, 1, p. 180.

20 ı, ix, 1, p. 180.

21 This distinction is implicit in all providential history, of
course, and was invoked in almost all the historical writing of
the period. Cf., for example, Giovanni Botero, *A Treatise, concerning the Causes of the Magnificencie and Greatness of
Cities,* trans. Robert Preston (London, 1606), p. 91: "Why do
some cities grow and others stagnate? Some . . . say it is,
bycause God the governor of all things, doth so dispose, no
man doth doubt of that. But, forasmuch as the infinit wisedome of God, in the administration and the government of
nature, worketh secondary causes: My question is, with what
meanes that eternall providence maketh little, to multiply;
and much, to stand at a stay, and go no further" (Cited in

Levy, p. 249). Ralegh is credited with a translation of part of
Botero's treatise. (*Works* [1829], viii, pp. 541–47).

22 A few of the biblical stories seem to interest Ralegh as much
for their political and psychological dimensions as for their significance as examples of God's justice: e.g., Jehoram, ii, xx, pp.
518–27; Athalia, ii, xxi, pp. 528–41.

23 Cf. Christopher Hill, *Intellectual Origins of the English Revolution*, p. 222.

24 *Paradise Lost*, xi, 808 ff., 890 ff.

25 Cf. Arnold Williams, *The Common Expositor, an account of
the commentaries on Genesis, 1527–1633* (Chapel Hill, N.C.,
1948), pp. 34, 36, 101–02, 140.

26 Cf. also iv, v, 8, p. 264; iv, v, 9, pp. 267–69; v, ii, 6, p. 407;
v, vi, 4, p. 725.
   For Ralegh's borrowings from Machiavelli, see Lefranc, pp.
222–53, 614–32.

27 But cf. v, ii, 2, pt. 4, p. 385: "In *England* we had many bond-
servants, untill the times of our last civile warres: and I thinke
that the Lawes concerning *Villenage* are still in force, of which
the latest are the sharpest. And now, since slaves were made
free, which were of great use and service, there are growne up
a rabble of Rogues, Cutpurses, and other the like Trades;
slaves in Nature, though not in Lawe.
   "But whether this kind of dominion [slavery] be lawfull, or
not; *Aristotle* hath well proved, that it is naturall. And
certainely we finde not such a latitude of difference, in any
creature, as in the nature of man: wherein (to omit the infinite distance in estate, of the elect & reprobate) the wisest ex-
cell the most foolish, by far greater degree, than the most
foolish of men doth surpasse the wisest of beasts. Therfore
when Commiseration hath given way to Reason; we shall find,
that Nature is the ground even of Masterly power, and of servile obedience, which is thereto correspondent."

28 Racin, "Analysis," pp. 151 ff.

29 Otto, Bishop of Freising, *The Two Cities*, trans. Charles C.
Mierow (New York, 1928), p. 184.

30 ii, iv, 1, p. 265: "Here being againe prest with want of water
they murmured the fourth time, and repented them of their
departure from *Ægypt*, where they rather contented themselves
to bee fed and beaten after the manner of beasts, than to suffer

a casuall and sometime necessarie want, and to undergoe the
hazzards and travailes which every manly minde seeketh after,
for the love of God and their owne freedomes." Apart from this
passage, the theme of liberty is not of great importance in the
books treating biblical history.

31 Near the beginning of Book v, Ralegh alludes to the Prince's
death "of which, like an Eclypse of the Sunne, wee shall finde
the effects hereafter" (v, i, 6, p. 351).

32 Lefranc, p. 333.

Chapter 6

1 Jean Calvin, *Institutes of the Christian Religion,* trans. F. L.
Battles, ed. J. T. McNeill (Philadelphia, 1960), 1 : 294 (ii, iii,
5).

2 Frances A. Yates, *Giordano Bruno and the Hermetic Tradition*
(Chicago, 1964), p. 155.

3 *The Original Writings & Correspondence of the Two Richard
Hakluyts,* ed. E. G. R. Taylor (London [Hakluyt Society, ser. 2,
vol. 77] 1935), 2 : 366–67. The translation of the Latin dedication is by F. C. Francis.

4 Cf. Walter Oakeshott, "Sir Walter Ralegh's Library," *The Library,* 23 (London, The Bibliographical Society, 1968), pp.
285–327, especially entries nos. 90, 95, 110, 143, 160c, 162, 183.

5 From a summary of a pamphlet (1592) by the Jesuit Robert
Parsons, quoted in Strathmann, p. 25.

6 Cf. Anthony Esler, *The Aspiring Mind of the Elizabethan
Younger Generation* (Durham, N.C., 1966), esp. pp. 170–81.

7 Dated "Paris the 30th of December 1586," *Original Writings &
Correspondence,* ed. Taylor, p. 355. I have modernized "w^{ch}"
and "wth".

8 Cf. Lefranc, pp. 439–40 and app. P, 678–82. Lefranc argues
that Hermeticism was an important, if partially hidden, element of Ralegh's thought.

9 Alchemy: *H.W.,* v, iii, 15, pp. 516–17; Magic: *H.W.,* i, xi, pp.
199–213. Ralegh is careful to distinguish "naturall *Magicke*"
from necromancy and other evil arts: "the Art of *Magicke* is of
the wisedome of nature; other artes which undergoe that title
were invented by the falshood, subtletie, and envie of the De-
vill" (i, xi, 2, p. 204). Lawful magic "containeth the whole Phi-

losophie of nature: not the brablings of the *Aristotelians,* but that which bringeth to light the inmost vertues, and draweth them out of natures hidden bosome to human use" (I, xi, 2, p. 202). For Ralegh, the boundaries between science, magic, and medicine were unclear.

10 I am indebted to Harlow, *Ralegh's Last Voyage,* throughout this chapter. See also Quinn, 240–71; Agnes M. C. Latham, "Sir Walter Ralegh's Gold Mine: New Light on the Last Guiana Voyage," *Essays and Studies,* new series 4 (1951) : 94–111.

11 As it had, for example, in *H.W.,* I, i, 15, p. 21: "making them beleeve that all their vices are vertues."

12 Letter to Cecil, 1611, in Harlow, p. 111.

13 Letter to King James, 1611, in Harlow, p. 108. See also Ralegh's letters to Queen Anne in Harlow, pp. 106–07 (in *Letters,* pp. 333–35).

14 Harlow (pp. 16–17) argues that Cecil (who died in 1612) was not actually opposed to the Guiana scheme or even to a war with Spain, but merely advised circumspection and caution. However, Cecil's plan of a preliminary voyage without Ralegh's presence suggests that, if he did not object to the Guiana scheme itself, Cecil did not favor Ralegh's release from the Tower under any conditions.

15 Harlow, pp. 23 ff.

16 D. Harris Willson, *King James VI and I* (New York, 1956), pp. 262 ff., 362 ff. G. P. V. Akrigg, *Jacobean Pageant* (Cambridge, Mass., 1962), p. 329.

17 Actually, the warnings did not arrive until too late.

18 "A declaration of the *Demeanour and Carriage of Sir Walter Ralegh,* Knight," in Harlow, p. 341. See chap. 1, n. 6.

19 Harlow, pp. 39–41. Harlow offers alternative interpretations: James may have known about and countenanced Ralegh's negotiations with the French. If Ralegh could obtain French troops, then the actual fighting with the Spanish could be the responsibility of another sovereign, and James would have an excuse, however thin. On the other hand, James may have believed that a carefully handled expedition could avoid any overt hostility against the Spanish, and that the Orinoco was a sufficiently valuable strategic position to risk the anger of Spain.

20 Harlow, p. 46.

21 "Declaration," in Harlow, p. 336.

22 Cf. Louis Martz, *The Paradise Within* (New Haven, 1964).
23 Cf. Letter of Samuel Jones to the Privy Council, in Harlow, p. 237. Ralegh was forced by mutineers to land in Ireland and was, by his own account, afraid for his life during the whole return voyage.
24 Letter of 29 June 1617, in *Lismore Papers*, 2nd ser., ed. A. B. Grosart (London, 1887), 2 : 85.
25 In any event, as David Quinn notes, "The commanders of the shore party insisted that Ralegh must stay to cover their retreat, as they would not trust any of the others to do so" (*Ralegh and the British Empire* [London, 1947], pp. 256–57).
26 "Declaration," in Harlow, p. 344. The "Declaration" is, of course, royal propaganda, but it is by no means a completely distorted account of the affair.
27 It did not exist, that is, in the fantastic form given to it by Ralegh's imagination. Ralegh's mine has been "identified" as the Caratal Gold-field; see C. Le Neve Foster, "The Caratal Gold-field," *Proceedings of the Geological Society*, in *The Quarterly Journal of the Geological Society*, 25 (London, 1869) : 336–43.
28 "*Sir Walter Raghleys Large Appologie* for the ill successe of his enterprise to Guiana," in Harlow, pp. 328–29. See *Letters*, pp. 356–58, 361.

Appendix

1 Lefranc, pp. 86–87.
2 Ibid. "Il est à peine nécessaire de préciser que, toute sa vie durant, Ralegh n'eut que mépris pour les puritains et leur doctrine" (pp. 87–88).
3 For these, see *Poems*, pp. 128–38. Lefranc grants that "une tradition manuscrite ancienne et relativement large attribue ce poème à Ralegh" (p. 88). The poem was also attributed in the seventeenth century to Lady Anne Southwell, the Earl of Essex, Joshua Sylvester, the Third Earl of Pembroke (William Herbert), and Dr. Latworth.
    The attacks and replies are for the most part, quite crude:

> . . . If Rawhead this denye
> Tell him that hee doth lye.
>
> . . . .
> Go, Eccho of the minde,

a careles troth protest;
make answere that rude *Rawly*
no stomack can digest.

[*Poems*, p. 135; Lefranc, p. 89]

4   Lefranc, app. N, pp. 665–75.
5   "MS. Rawlinson Poetry 212" (in the Bodleian Library). See also,
    "MS. Rawlinson Poetry 172" ("Dr. Latworthe lye to all es-
    tates"), "MS. Folger 1.28" (in the Folger Library), and "MS.
    Taverham" (described by H. Harvey Wood, "A Seventeenth-
    Century Manuscript of Poems by Donne and Others," *Essays
    and Studies*, 16 [1930] : 179–90).Wood first identified the Dr.
    Latworthe of these manuscripts as Richard Latewar (or Late-
    warr) of St. Johns.
6   Lefranc, pp. 670, 672, 673.
7   *Poems*, pp. 129–30.
8   Lefranc, p. 87.
9   Ibid., p. 86.
10 See, for example, Alvin B. Kernan, *The Cankered Muse* (New
    Haven, 1959), and Louis Lecoq, *La Satire en Angleterre de
    1588 à 1603, Etudes Anglaises* 32 (Paris, 1969).
    Both the Folger and Taverham MSS. describe "The Lie" as
    "Satyra Volans" or "a flying Satyre" (*Poems*, p. 129).
11 A pair of poems attacking and defending "The Lie"—"Courts
    scorne" and "Courts comender" (*Poems*, pp. 137–38)—are a
    perfect example of this kind of controversy: the attack claims
    that the satire is completely negative and slanderous, the de-
    fense argues that the poet only satirizes perversions of values
    and corrupted institutions and that he is really the true friend
    of the court, church, laws, and so forth.
12 Cf. Hiram Haydn, *The Counter-Renaissance* (New York, 1950),
    esp. chap. 2.
13 Lefranc, p. 86.
14 Ibid., p. 86.

Index